Folklore Bibliography
for 1973

INDIANA UNIVERSITY FOLKLORE INSTITUTE
MONOGRAPH SERIES, VOL. 28

Bloomington, 1975

Merle E. Simmons

Folklore Bibliography
for 1973

Published for the Folklore Institute

by the Research Center for Language and Semiotic Studies

Indiana University, Bloomington

INDIANA UNIVERSITY PUBLICATIONS

FOLKLORE INSTITUTE MONOGRAPH SERIES

Editor: Richard M. Dorson

VOLUME 28

The Indiana University Folklore Series was founded in 1939
for the publication of occasional papers and monographs.

ISBN 87750-189-0

Library of Congress Catalog Card Number 75-18190

Orders from the United States and Canada should be placed with Humanities Press,
Atlantic Highlands, N. J. 07716. Orders from all other countries should be sent to the
Research Center for Language and Semiotic Studies, 516 East Sixth Street, Indiana
University, Bloomington, Indiana 47401 U.S.A.

CONTENTS

FOLKLORE BIBLIOGRAPHY FOR 1973

The publication of this bibliography for 1973 represents a new venture. For nine years I have been preparing similar bibliographies for *Southern Folklore Quarterly*, and the present book is, in reality, a continuation of that effort, which was in its turn an extension of the annual compilations for *SFQ* that Ralph Steel Boggs and Américo Paredes had published over a time span of almost three decades. Users of this new bibliography will find that it differs little from the ones that I prepared for 1964-1972 inclusive, particularly those of most recent years, except that it is almost one-hundred percent annotated and the annotations now tend to be longer and somewhat more detailed than were those that I normally wrote for the bibliographies done during the 1960's.

Readers long familiar with the *SFQ* bibliographies will be aware that the present compilation contains perhaps fifty percent more entries than most of the bibliographies that were published by Boggs and Paredes in the late 1950's and early 1960's. This is so in spite of the fact that I have had to narrow the geographical scope of the work during the past five or six years. Instead of attempting to cover the entire world, all recent bibliographies, this one included, have focused only upon the American continent, Spain, Portugal, and other areas in the world where Spanish or Portuguese is spoken. This kind of limitation I regretted, of course, and I was particularly reluctant to abandon coverage of French, Italian, and Romanian folklore because these linguistic and cultural areas were particularly attractive to a Professor of Spanish with a personal interest in the Romance languages. Yet, as the bibliography mushroomed during the first years after I took it over, it clearly became necessary to limit its length in some judicious manner. I could not reasonably expect the editors of *SFQ* to allow the bibliography to occupy an increasingly disproportionate amount of space in their fine journal—and I should like to state here that I appreciate the cooperation I received from a succession of editors who let the size of the bibliography increase as far as the realities of their budgets permitted—but the inevitable reduction in geographical coverage was, nevertheless, a source of no little anguish. I don't know now whether it will be possible in the future to resume coverage of some or all of the areas that I personally should like to include once again, but this is at least a hope. I hasten to stress, however, that the present bibliography is still restricted to the countries of the two Americas, Spain and Portugal, and other areas of the Luso-Hispanic world. In practical terms this means that I have listed all works known to me about the folklore of the parts of the world just mentioned, no matter where published, all books or articles on folklore or related fields written by authors who are natives or residents of these areas, and all publications on folklore of any kind issued by publishing houses or printers in the same geographical regions.

These observations about coverage and related problems lead me to remark further that the dramatic rise in numbers of entries noted above derived from two circumstances that call for comment. The first of these is the notable increase in quantity of folklore research published the world over during the last decade or so. Surely there are ever more scholars at work, particularly in the United States where major folklore programs at universities like Indiana, Pennsylvania, Texas, and U.C.L.A. stand as impressive testimony to increasing interest in the serious study of folklore as an academic discipline. This is a most important aspect of the total picture. For the ever growing size of my bibliographies, however, I also claim some personal credit since I have sought, year after year, to expand and improve my efforts. From the first I have striven to approach completeness, believing, as I do, that an annual bibliographical survey of the type that I try to provide should be as complete as possible for whatever geographical area it professes to cover, and that this kind of coverage is to be preferred over more superficial and selective treatment of a wider area.

I realize, of course, that some users of my bibliography may not agree with me on this point, particularly in view of the fact that many of the publications I am obliged to list under the kind of coverage just described are obviously of mediocre quality, and in some cases even this description overstates their worth. All competent folklorists are aware that our discipline probably suffers more than most from an overabundance of undistinguished or bad books and articles, many of them written by well-meaning people whose enthusiasm and zeal simply are not matched by their professional training or intellectual rigor. A bibliographer probably has more reason to be aware of this problem than anybody else.

At this point, however, I submit that professional snobbishness on the part of "trained" folklorists must be restrained; at least it should be held in check by those of us who prepare general bibliographies. Like it or not, works by amateurs and unsophisticated collectors of folklore, even some of the poorest publications, not infrequently contain material of genuine interest and value to the trained scholar who has sufficient perception to separate the wheat from the chaff and use it to advantage. As I noted in an introduction to an earlier bibliography, among the innumerable truths that the genius of Miguel de Cervantes bequeathed to the world were the words that he placed in the mouth of Don Quijote's friend, Sansón Carrasco, who declared that "No hay libro tan malo que no tenga algo bueno," or, "There is no book so bad that it doesn't contain something good." Though this proposition may be debatable in absolute terms, to it I humbly adhere, at least when I compile my annual bibliographies; and for this reason I hereby warn my reader that the compilation he now has in his hands is an annotated but not a critical bibliography. Its goal is to provide serious folklorists a substantially complete and comprehensive guide to all work done in their discipline, whether scholarly or unscholarly.

Even in preparing a bibliography that aspires to be comprehensive rather than narrowly selective, the lot of a compiler is fraught with difficulties, many of which stem from the perennial problem of defining what is and what is not folklore. Without here reviewing the polemics about definitions that have caused so much spilling of ink among many competent folklorists with differing views on this question, suffice it to say that I have customarily used quite deliberately the broadest of criteria in deciding whether a given item should or should not be listed. Briefly stated, my general procedure has been to include any borderline item that I thought a serious folklorist might find of value in his work.

I must point out also that other similar problems that revolve around the propriety of including or rejecting certain entries sometimes have their origins in the various scholarly traditions or methodological approaches that tend to characterize different countries or cultural areas. A perceptive reader may wonder, for example, why I list here numerous items about folk speech and dialectology from some countries and not from others. The answer is simply that subjects that one country studies as folklore another often assigns to some other discipline or methodological approach. In Spain, for example, the phenomena just mentioned are favorite topics for study by folklorists (let it be remembered that Spain's leading folklore journal is entitled *Revista de Dialectología y Tradiciones Populares*); or, put another way, many Spanish scholars who deal with folk speech and dialects treat them as important aspects of traditional or regional life, and this orientation produces results that clearly fall in the area of folklore studies. In countries like the United States, on the other hand, most dialectal and similar linguistic studies are increasingly left to professional linguists whose highly sophisticated techniques of linguistic analysis only rarely shed much light on the cultural matters that are of interest to folklorists. Exceptions there are, of course, in both Spain and the United

States, but I mention this as only one representative example of problems that inevitably complicate the bibliographer's task. Actually each individual book or article is a separate problem in itself and criteria for admitting or rejecting a given item must be based on whether it contains material that because of its subject matter, its methodological approach, or its conclusions might be of value to folklorists. In formulating innumerable decisions that the bibliographer must make, his only recourse is to exercise in each instance his best subjective judgment based on as much knowledge, common sense, and humillity as he can muster and then beg the indulgence of those readers who feel that his judgment has been faulty.

The organization of this bibliography is according to genres and continues the pattern and the identifying letters (e.g., B for folktales, C for song and dance, etc.) that Ralph Steele Boggs adopted over thirty years ago. I confess that I have sometimes considered changing this format, particularly after observing Manuel Dannemann's recent success in organizing an excellent bibliography of Chilean folklore by grouping entries according to a "functional classification" rather than by genre. It is certainly true that Danneman's effort merits praise and perhaps emulation, but for the present I have elected to continue organizing my own more ample bibliography along traditional lines simply because the genre approach seems to have worked pretty well in practice. I suspect also that most folklorists still consider themselves to be primarily ballad scholars, students of material folklore, riddle specialists, etc. (i.e., that as scholars they tend to orient their research toward some particular genre or genres of folklore), so the traditional generic divisions are probably still useful. The continuing existence of thriving specialized journals such as *Fabula* for folktale research and *Proverbium* for papers on proverbs and popular sayings suggests that the genre approach remains alive and well however much many good folklorists are also interested in functional, structural, or other innovative approaches to their research.

Last among the major problems that I should like to treat here is that of balancing the need to keep as up-to-date as possible against the great desirability of personally examining as many books and articles as I can in order to describe their contents accurately and to provide dependable bibliographical data based on first-hand information. This is not overly difficult in the case of journal articles. Unless periodicals are behind in their publication schedules, as many are, and unless librarians have been too zealous in removing recently completed volumes of journals and reviews from their shelves and sending them to the bindery, a bibliographer working as I do in a first-class research library like that of Indiana University can personally examine almost all of the most important journals within a reasonable lapse of time after their publication. Keeping current with books, however, is a much more diffucult task because these are not always acquired by libraries promptly upon publication, and new books must normally be bound and catalogued before the bibliographer can get his hands on them. This sometimes results in substantial delays.

All of this I mention by way of explaining why I have adopted what I call a "three-year rule," meaning that the bibliography for any given year routinely includes items published during a time span of about three years. For example, this bibliography for 1973 also contains some publications that appeared in 1971 and 1972. Occasionally I include publications dated even earlier than 1971 if they seem unusually important to me, though I usually assume that if I have missed a publication for a period of three years there is a lessened need to include it at all. If such a work is truly important, it will in all probability find its way into the bibliographies of subsequently published books and articles and thus finally come to the attention of interested scholars. If it is of minor importance, then it probably does not need to be included at such a late date, even though I probably would have listed it had I been able to provide reliable data about it while it was still fresh. Delays such as I am describing are usually attibutable, of course, to the fact that I seldom list items that I cannot annotate from personal examination or by drawing upon reliable reviews. Even in the latter case I include works I have not seen only if I have great confidence in the reviewer or other source from which I have gleaned my information because I know from long experience that this kind of dependence upon second-hand data is at best fraught with multiple possibilities for error. Whenever I think there is a good chance that I myself will be able ultimately to consult a given item within a reasonable length of time, I generally defer listing it for the time being rather than run the risk of providing faulty information. This explains why I list in this 1973 bibliography a substantial number of books published in 1971 or 1972. The titles of many of these were known to me a year or two ago, but I waited to list some of them until I could actually examine them.

A few explanations of some minor details are also in order at this point. Volume numbers of journals are given in this bibliography in large Roman numerals while issues within a volume are indicated by Arabic numbers. Only in two cases do I use abbreviations for the names of cities: "N. Y." stands for New York and "B. A." for Buenos Aires. Not really an abbreviation but rather a usage that is in accordance with normal practice is my consistent use of "México" to signify México, D. F. (i.e., Mexico City). I call the reader's attention also to the list of abbreviations that I employ to identify frequently cited journals or books. Books identified in this manner are usually collections containing numerous contributions by different authors. I should state also that throughout the bibliography I normally ignore second or subsequent editions of books unless at least twenty-five years have elapsed since the last previous edition. However, if a new edition has been *significantly* revised and I conclude that it should be called to the attention of scholars for that reason, I occasionally waive this rule.

No work of the kind that I am publishing here is ever the product of one person alone. While I personally have done the lion's share of compiling and putting this bibliography together, my research assistant, Miss Patricia Haseltine, an excellent student of folklore in our doctoral program at Indiana University, has also labored diligently in running down bibliographical items and writing descriptions of their contents. If users of the present work find merit in it, much credit must go to Miss Haseltine. I should like to express publicly my own thanks to her. Also my collaborators in a very real sense are the friends scattered all over the world who from time to time have sent me copies of their own or other people's books and articles or have passed along important and often elusive bibliographical information from their respective countries. I must refrain from mentioning these individuals by name because they are legion, but I want them all to know that I appreciate their aid and assistance and I earnestly ask not only them but other users of my bibliography as well to continue to supply me with data. Future compilations will, I hope, be better than this one because friends, both old and new, have helped to make it so.

I am well aware, of course, that errors will be found in this bibliography. I try to hold them to a minimum, but I know that some inevitably creep in despite my best efforts to eliminate them. For these and for all other deficiencies that users detect in this work I beg their kind indulgence. The blame for all of them is mine and mine alone.

Merle E. Simmons

Indiana University
Bloomington, Indiana

ABBREVIATIONS

AA – American Anthropologist. American Anthropological Association. Menasha, Wisconsin.

AFFword – AFF Word. Publication of Arizona Friends of Folklore. Flagstaff, Arizona.

African Folklore – African Folklore, comp. by Richard M. Dorson. Bloomington, Indiana: Indiana University Press, 1972. vii, 587 pp.

AI – América Indígena. Instituto Indigenista Interamericano. México, D. F.

Américas – Américas [English edition]. Organization of American States. Washington, D. C.

EL – La Estafeta Literaria. Madrid.

Ethnology – Ethnology: An International Journal of Cultural and Social Anthropology. University of Pittsburgh. Pittsburgh, Pennsylvania.

Ethnomusicology – The Society for Ethomusicology. Wesleyan University Press. Middletown, Connecticut.

FAUFA – Folklore Annual of the University Folklore Association. Center for Intercultural Studies in Folklore and Oral History. University of Texas. Austin, Texas.

FForum – The Folklore Forum: A Communication for Students of Folklore. Graduate Students of the Folklore Institute, Indiana University. Bloomington, Indiana.

HandH – Hunters and Healers: Folklore Types and Topics, ed. by Wilson M. Hudson. Austin, Texas: Encino Press, 1971. (*Texas Folklore Society Publications, No. XXXV.*)

Hispania – The American Association of Teachers of Spanish and Portuguese. Appleton, Wisconsin.

IF – Indiana Folklore. The Hoosier Folklore Society. Edited at Bloomington, Indiana, and published by the Indiana University Research Center for the Language Sciences, Bloomington, Indiana.

JAF – Journal of American Folklore. American Folklore Society. University of Texas Press. Austin, Texas.

JEMFQ – John Edwards Memorial Foundation Quarterly. Folklore and Mythology Center. University of California. Los Angeles, California.

JFI – Journal of the Folklore Institute. Edited at Indiana University. Bloomington, Indiana, and published by Mouton & Company. The Hague, Netherlands.

JFSGW – Journal of the Folklore Society of Greater Washington. Washington, D. C.

JOFS – Journal of the Ohio Folklore Society. The Ohio Folklore Society. Ohio State University. Columbus, Ohio.

JPC – Journal of Popular Culture. Bowling Green State University. Bowling Green, Ohio.

KFQ – Keystone Folklore Quarterly. The Pennsylvania Folklore Society. Williamsport, Pennsylvania.

KFR – Kentucky Folklore Record. Kentucky Folklore Society. Western Kentucky State College. Bowling Green, Kentucky.

Masterkey – *The Masterkey*. The Southwest Museum. Los Angeles, California.

MLFS – *Medieval Literature and Folklore Studies: Essays in Honor of Francis Lee Utley*, ed. by Jerome Mandel and Bruce A. Rosenberg. New Brunswick, N. J.: Rutgers University Press, 1970. viii, 408 pp. illus.

MSF – *Mid-South Folklore*. Arkansas State University. State University, Arkansas.

Names – *Names; Journal of the American Name Society*. Potsdam, N. Y.

NCFJ – *North Carolina Folklore Journal*. The North Carolina Folklore Society. North Carolina State University. Raleigh, North Carolina.

NSC – *Names in South Carolina*. Columbia, South Carolina.

NYFQ – *New York Folklore Quarterly*. New York Folklore Society. Cooperstown, N. Y.

1971 YIFMC – *1971 Yearbook of the International Folk Music Council*, ed. by Charles Haywood. Manufactured in Canada: UNESCO, 1972, 203 pp.

1972 YIFMC – *1972 Yearbook of the International Folk Music Council*, ed. by Charles Haywood. Manufactured in Canada: UNESCO, 1973. 200 pp.

ORTF – *Observations and Reflections on Texas Folklore*, ed. by Francis Edward Abernethy. Austin. Texas: The Encino Press, 1972. viii, 151 pp. (*Publications of the Texas Folklore Society, No. XXXVII.*)

PIHS(I) – *Publicaciones del Instituto de Etnografía y Folklore* «Hoyos Sainz», Vol. I. Santander, España: Diputación Provincial de Santander, 1970. Vols. II and III were published in 1971 and 1972 respectively and are identified as *PIHS(II)* and *PIHS(III)*.

Proverbium – Helsinki, Finland.

RCF – *Revista Colombiana de Folclor*. Organo del Instituto Colombiano de Antropología. Bogotá, Colombia.

RDTP – *Revista de Dialectología y Tradiciones Populares*. Consejo Superior de Investigaciones Científicas, Departamento de Dialectología y Tradiciones Populares. Madrid.

REP – *Revista de Etnografía*. Museu de Etnografia e Historia. Porto, Portugal.

RMC – *Revista Musical Chilena*. Facultad de Ciencias y Artes Musicales. Universidad de Chile. Santiago de Chile.

SOH – *Selections from the Fifth and Sixth National Colloquia on Oral History*, ed. by Peter D. Olch and Forrest Pogue. N. Y.: The Oral History Association, 1972. vi, 110 pp.

SFQ – *Southern Folklore Quarterly*. University of Florida. Gainesville, Florida.

TFSB – *Tennessee Folklore Society Bulletin*. Tennessee Folklore Society. Middle Tennessee State University. Murfreesboro, Tennessee.

Thesaurus – *Thesaurus: Boletín del Instituto Caro y Cuervo*. Bogotá, Colombia.

WF – *Western Folklore*. California Folklore Society. University of California Press. Berkeley and Los Angeles, California.

A   GENERAL FOLKLORE

Scholars, Research Materials, and Methods

1. *Abstracts of Folklore Studies*, ed. by Richard E. Buehler and others. Austin, Texas: American Folklore Society.

A continuing serial publication that appears four times per year and contains excellent abstracts of articles on folklore and related subjects that have appeared in journals or reviews. Vol. XI:1 (Spring, 1973), contains Abstracts 1-308, pp. 1-52; No. 2 (Summer, 1973), contains Abstracts 309-556, pp. 1-47; No. 3 (Fall, 1973), contains Abstracts 557-808, pp. 1-51.

2. ADLER, Thomas. "Communications: The American Folklife Center, A Personal Examination and Appraisal of the Idea." *FForum*, VI:4 (October, 1973), 242-245.

Appraises a bill currently before the U. S. Congress to establish an American Folklife Center, enumerates the proposed functions of the center and ramifications for folklorists, and advocates sending letters of support for the bill to Congressmen.

3. ARDISSONE, Elena, and SALVADOR, Nélida. *Bibliografía argentina de artes y letras; compilaciones especiales: Bibliografía de la revista Nosotros 1907-1943*. B.A.: Fondo Nacional de Las Artes, 1972. 700 pp.

The section of Folklore (pp. 182-189) contains 90 items appearing in the magazine *Nosotros* between the years 1908 and 1943. Some are briefly annotated.

4. BASCOM, William. "Folklore and the Africanist." *JAF*, LXXXVI: 341 (July-September, 1973), 253-259.

Defends himself and other Africanists against charges made by Richard M. Dorson in the introduction to *African Folklore* published in 1972 (New York: Garden City).

5. BASCOM, William. "Folklore, Verbal Art, and Culture." *JAF*, LXXXVI:342 (October-December, 1973), 374-381.

Seeks to clear up some misunderstandings concerning definitions of the three terms indicated that the author has suggested on various occasions.

6. BASCOM, William R. "In Memoriam: Richard Alan Waterman (1914-1971)." In 1972 *YIFMC*. Pp. 146-151.

Renders tribute to the recently deceased ethnomusicologist, traces his career and notes his contributions to scholarship, and gives a selected bibliography of his most important publications.

7. BENARÓS, León. "Cosquín: cita para el folklore de las Américas." *Boletín Interamericano de Música* (Washington, D. C.), No. 83 (Noviembre, 1971-Febrero, 1972), 34-38.

Reports on the Festival Nacional de Folklore held annually in Cosquín, Argentina, and also on the courses, lectures, and publications of the Ateneo Folklórico of Cosquín.

1

8. *Bibliografía argentina de artes y letras, 49/50 (Enero-Junio, 1971)*.
B.A.: Fondo Nacional de las Artes, 1972. 134 pp.

The section of Folklore (pp. 33-35) contains 21 items published between 1961 and 1971. Some are briefly annotated.

9. BRIGGS, Katharine M. "The Necessity of Scepticism." *JFI*, IX:1 (June, 1972), 5-9.

Surveys and criticizes modern trends in the study of folklore.

10. BUNCH, John B. "The Legal Considerations of Privacy, Property, Copyright, and Unfair Practises in the Publication of Folklore Material." *FForum*, VI:4 (October, 1973), 211-216.

Dicusses the rights and laws of privacy, copyright, property, and fair practice as they relate to the informant, the field collector, the scholar, and the archivist. Advises obtaining written releases for folklore material.

11. CARDOZO, Luis, and others, comps. *Bibliografía de la literatura indígena venezolana*. Mérida, Venezuela: Centro de Investigaciones Literarias, Universidad de los Andes, 1970. 122 pp. memeographed.

Produced by Professor Cardozo and his students in the Seminario de Literatura Indígena Venezolana, this very useful bibliography of indigenous literature contains numerous entries of interest to folklorists, (e.g., sections on riddles, songs, tales, legends, conjurations, myths, proverbs, etc.). The first part of the work treats these subjects by genres and the second part is a listing by authors. Includes an index.

12. CARO BAROJA, Julio. "Cosas humanas y tiempo de ellas." *RDTP*, XXIX (1973):1-2, pp. 49-59.

A statement of historical theory applied primarily to historical and cultural problems. Calls for greater attention to the passage of time in studying such phenomena and rejects mechanistic interpretations of cultural and ethnographic matters where time is considered to be of little importance.

13. CARO BAROJA, Julio. "Don Luis de Hoyos Sainz (1868-1951)." In *PIHS (III)*, 7-18.

Tribute to the Spanish anthropologist and folklorist.

14. CARO BAROJA, Julio. "Mundos circundantes y contornos histórico-culturales." *RDTP*, XXIX (1973):1-2, pp. 23-47.

A statement of anthropological and ethnological theory which questions much recent methodology on the grounds that it is too mechanical and that it ignores extremely important historico-cultural factors. The author uses Spanish examples to support his criticism. Of interest to folklorists and any other students of culture.

15. CASHION, Gerald. "A Conversation with S. A. Babalola." *FForum, Bibliographic and Special Series, No. 11: Studies in Yoruba Folklore* (1973), 63-69.

An interview with S. A. Babalola, Professor of Oral Literature at the University of Lagos in Nigeria, concerning the study of folklore in Nigeria, Babalola's interest in Yoruba tortoise tales, and folklore theory in general.

16. CASTERLINE, Gail Farr. "Sources and Literature for Western American History: A List of Dissertations." *Western Historical Quarterly* (Logan, Utah), IV:3 (July, 1973), 307-326.

Lists Ph.D. dissertations. Includes a section on "Literature, Folklore, Journalism" which contains some works specifically on folklore. Some dissertations in other sections on "Indians," "Ethnic Groups," etc. may also be of interest to folklorists.

17. CHAMBERS, Keith S. "The Indefatigable Elsie Crews Parsons—Folklorist." *WF*, XXXII:3 (July, 1973), 180-198.

Traces the career of Parsons as a folklorist focusing mostly on her work as a collector of folktales in many parts of the world. Appraises the strengths and weaknesses of her research and publications and also notes the support she gave through her own activities and through financial help to the American Folklore Society and many individual scholars.

18. CONKLIN, Harold C. *Folk Classification: A Topically Arranged Bibliography of Contemporary and Background References Through 1971.* New Haven, Connecticut: Yale University, 1972. 501 pp.

An unannotated bibliography of more than five thousand items dealing with cultural, biological, and physical folk classifications. Discusses the theory and methodology of studying classification systems. Includes studies published all over the world through 1971.

19. CUNNINGHAM, Keith. "Fakelore vs. Folklore—Again." *FForum*, VI:1 (January, 1973), 44-45.

Notes the recent appearance on newspaper editorial pages of arguments against Richard Dorson's concept of "fakelore" and questions the meaning of the popular press's attempt to revive the controversy.

20. DANTAS, Paulo. "Região centro-oeste: uma dinámica para o folclore do abandono (conferência)." *Boletim Bibliográfico, Biblioteca Municipal Mário de Andrade* (São Paulo), XXX (Abril-Junho, 1972), 85-100.

A rambling but fairly stimulating lecture given at a Simpósio sobre Folclore e Turismo Cultural. Discourses on the author's dynamic conception of folklore and calls for more attention to the folklore of Brazil's western regions (i.e., the state of Goiás and surrounding areas). Criticizes interest in folklore that stems solely from concern for tourism.

21. DE CARO, F. A. "The Chadwicks and Lord Raglan: A Retrospective Analysis." *FForum*, VI:2 (April, 1973), 75-86.

Reviews *The Growth of Literature* (Cambridge, 1932-1940) by Hector and Nora Chadwick with focus on its claim for the historical validity of tradition in opposition to the myth-ritual theory of Lord Raglan.

22. DELANCEY, Virginia, and DELANCEY, Mark. *A Bibliography of Cameroun Folklore.* Waltham, Mass.: African Studies Association, 1972. iii, 69 pp.

An annotated bibliography of five hundred items dealing with folk narratives, folk music, and oral history of Cameroun (Africa).

23. DONATO, Hernâni. *Dicionário das mitologias americanas (incluindo as contribuições míticas africanas).* São Paulo, Brasil: Editôra Cultrix, 1973. 275 pp.

A most useful dictionary of terms having to do with innumerable subjects related to mythology, folklore of many types (e.g., dances, beliefs, rites, etc.), investigators, etc. It covers all of the Americas with particular stress on Amerindian and Afro-American terms. Definitions are often lengthy and detailed. Includes a copious bibliography.

24. DORSON, Richard M., moderator. "The Academic Future of Folklore." *JAF Supplement* (May, 1972), 104-125.

Presents eight papers concerned with study and career opportunities in folklore in the U.S. as delivered at a plenary session of the American

Folklore Society, November, 1971. Participants include Richard Dorson, Ronald Baker, Robert Byington, George Carey, Robert A. Georges, Thomas A. Green, Ellen J. Stekert, and Robert T. Teske.

25. DORSON, Richard M. "In Memoriam: Edwin C. Kirkland, 1902-1972." *SFQ*, XXXVII:2 (June, 1973), 123-125.

Discusses the career and contributions to American and Asian folklore scholarship of Edwin C. Kirkland, former editor of the *Southern Folklore Quarterly*.

26. DORSON, Richard M. "Is Folklore a Discipline?" *Folklore* (London), LXXXIV: Autumn, 1973, pp. 177-205.

An excellent essay which treats the history of scholarly investigation of folklore throughout Europe and the U.S., its present status in North American and English universities (with particular attention to the author's personal experience as director of the Folklore Institute at Indiana University), and the strengths and weaknesses of folklore as a discipline with a respectable and respected intellectual base.

27. DORSON, Richard M. "The Lesson of 'Foxfire.'" *NCFJ*, XXI:4 (November, 1973), 157-159.

Notes that the Ford Foundation has supported Eliot Wigginton, author of *The Foxfire Book*, and the Institutional Development and Economic Affairs Service (IDEAS) in order to promote amateur study of folklore without guidance from professional folklorists. Dorson holds that unless corrected such undiscriminating study of local cultures will lead into the sands of fakelore.

28. DORSON, Richard M. "The Oral Historian and the Folklorist." In *SOH*. Pp. 40-49.

Discusses the differences in concepts held and methods used by folklorists and oral historians. Urges the expansion of oral history to include oral folk history, not merely elitist history.

29. DRAKE, Richard B. "A Strategy for Regional Studies: A Rationale for a New Journal." *Appalachian Notes* (Lexington, Kentucky), I:1 (First Quarter, 1973), 1-7.

In stating reasons for launching a new journal, *Appalachian Notes*, the editor provides a historical survey of journals about Appalachia published from 1895 to the present. It is a useful summary for anyone interested in the area, including folklorists, since many of the journals deal with folklore either systematically or sporadically.

30. ELLIS, Richard N. "The Duke Indian Oral History Collection at the University of New Mexico." *New Mexico Historical Review*, XLVIII:3 (July, 1973), 259-263.

Describes the collection of taped interviews with Indian informants that has been assembled by the Duke Project at the University of New Mexico. Some of them contain tribal legends and animal tales as well as other folklore.

31. *Ethnographic Fieldwork: A Mirror for Self and Culture.* Special issue of *Anthropological Quarterly* (Washington, D.C.), XLVI:1 (January, 1973), 1-58.

An entire special issue of the *Anthropological Quarterly* which contains six papers by different scholars on problems related to ethnographic fieldwork. Many of the subjects treated, methodological procedures described, and problems faced are similar to those of folklorists working in the field. I have not listed the papers separately in this bibliography.

32. "Expresiones folklóricas." Separata de *Los quince años del Fondo Nacional de las Artes*. B.A.: Fondo Nacional de las Artes, 1973. [10 pp.]

An interesting and informative summary of the financial and other support provided by the Comité de Expresiones Folklóricas and the Instituto de Folklore under the direction of Augusto Raúl Cortazar for folklore-related activities in Argentina (e.g., loans to individuals and institutions, publications, fellowships, cycles of lectures, promotion of handcrafts, etc.).

33. FLANAGAN, John T. "Folklore." In *American Literary Scholarship: An Annual, 1971*, ed. by J. Albert Robbins. Durham, North Carolina: Duke University Press, 1973. Pp. 342-368.

Briefly reviews selected books, articles, and bibliographies on folklore published in 1971.

34. "Folklore." *AA*, LXXV:4 (August, 1973), 1044-1058.

The folklore section of a Reviews Issue of *AA*. Contains some high quality reviews of twelve recent books on folklore.

35. "Folklore in the News." *WF*, XXXII:3 (July, 1973), 199-204.

A listing of newspaper articles that have to do with subjects of interest to folklorists. Items are divided according to subject matter and are not annotated.

36. FONTANA, Bernard L. "Savage Anthropologists and Unvanishing Indians of American Southwest." *Indian Historian* (San Francisco), VI:1 (Winter, 1973), 5-8, 32.

Challenges most of the work done by anthropologists and ethnographers as having concentrated almost wholly on aspects of Southwestern Indian life regarded by investigators to be aboriginal or peculiarly Indian (i.e., "savage"). Argues that rapid assimilation that nevertheless preserves certain traditional modes of perception is the true picture. Of interest to students of Indian folklore.

37. FORTÚN, Julia Elena. *Actual problemática del folklore en Latino América*. La Paz: Ministerio de Salud Pública, Sección de Imprenta y Publicaciones, n.d. no pagination [14 pp.].

Presented at the Third Interamerican Conference on Ethnomusicology and the Twenty-First Conference of the International Folk-Music Council (IFMC), this paper treats the place of folklore in Latin American culture and problems related thereto, with special emphasis on Bolivia. Proposes some courses of action.

38. FORTÚN, Julia Elena. "Encuesta folklórica dirigida al magisterio nacional." *AI*, XXXII:3 (Julio-Septiembre, 1972), 999-1024.

Gives a questionnaire used by the Bolivian Ministry of Education to assist teachers in studying different kinds of materials of interest to folklorists.

39. FRIEDEMANN, Nina S. "La comunicación y el folclor colombiano: un enfoque antropológico." *RCF*, IV:10 (1966-1969), 115-123.

Discourses upon certain aspects of folklore as a means of intercultural communication between groups both inside and outside a given culture. Uses some dances as examples. Includes a brief bibliography.

40. GARCIA, Marcolina Martins, and BREDA, Judite Ivanir, comps. *Divisão regional para o estudo e defesa do folclore no estado de Goiás*. Goiánia, Goiás: Universidade Federal de Goiás, Museu Antropológico,

1972. 99 pp. illus.

A kind of manual or guide to the study of folklore in the state of Goiás (Brazil). It represents an effort on the part of the Museu Antropológico to systematize research in the state by establishing geographical divisions, codes for identifying localities, questionnaires for making investigations, etc. Includes many charts, maps, photographs, bibliography, etc.

41. GARCÍA DE DIEGO, Pilar. "Pliegos de cordel." *RDTP*, XXVII (1971):Cuadernos 3-4, pp. 371-409; XXVIII (1972):Cuadernos 1-2, pp. 157-188; Cuadernos 3-4, pp. 317-360; XXIX (1973):Cuadernos 1-2, pp. 235-275.

A continuing catalogue of chap-books that are housed in the library of the Departamento de Dialectología y Tradiciones Populares of the Instituto «Miguel de Cervantes», which is part of the Consejo Superior de Investigaciones Científicas, Madrid, Spain. Lists and describes the *pliegos* which contain ballads, prose narratives, and other types of folkloric or popular literature.

42. GARCÍA GUINEA, M. A. "Semblanza de Luis de Hoyos Sainz." In *PIHS (II)*, 13-20.

Tribute to the famous pioneer Spanish anthropologist and folklorist with an appreciation of his work. Includes a photograph of Hoyos Sainz.

43. GASTIL, Raymond D. "The Pacific Northwest as a Cultural Region: A Symposium." *Pacific Northwest Quarterly* (Seattle, Washington), LXIV:4 (October, 1973), 147-162.

Not about folklore, but it addresses itself to a question that is of interest to folklorists: i.e., how useful it is to think of Oregon, Washington, and parts of Idaho and Montana as forming a clearly defined cultural region. There are comments on Gastil's paper by Norman Clark, Richard W. Etulain, and Otis A. Pease. Includes charts and a map.

44. GILBERT, Helen. "Folklore Studies, a Curriculum Proposal." *FForum*, VI:3 (July, 1973), 165-167.

Prints a curriculum proposal for an undergraduate program in folklore submitted to the College of St. Benedict in St. Joseph, Minnesota. Describes the study of folklore, relates it to local interests, and outlines a course program.

45. GILLESPIE, Angus K. "Teaching Folklore in the Secondary School: The Institutional Setting." *JOFS*, II:2 (August, 1973), 17-25.

Considers some of the problems inherent in teaching folklore in secondary schools and then explains how the author has organized such a course in a private school. Includes some examples of assignment sheets used and describes other materials and useful books.

46. GLASSIE, Henry. "A Folkloristic Thought on the Promise of Oral History." In *SOH*. Pp. 54-57.

Criticizes the continued neglect by historians and journalists of the oral traditions and history of the common people of all ages.

47. GLASSIE, Henry. "Structure and Function, Folklore and the Artifact." *Semiotica* (Bloomington, Indiana), VII (1973):4, pp. 313-351.

Deals with the concepts of structure and function and their applicability within folkloristics.

48. GÓMEZ VERGARA, Max. *Qué es el folklore*. Tunja, Colombia: Universidad Pedagógica y Tecnológica de Colombia, Ediciones "La Rana y el Aguila," 1971. 61 pp. (*Colección Nueva Universidad, No. 3*.)

A basic little manual which seeks to define what folklore is, tell something of its history as a discipline, distinguish between what is folkloric and what is "popular," etc. Treats the subject on a world-wide basis but with special attention to Colombia and Latin America. Includes a small bibliography.

49. GREGOROVICH, Andrew, comp. *Canadian Ethnic Groups Bibliography: A Selected Bibliography of Ethno-Cultural Groups in Canada and in the Province of Ontario.* Toronto: Ontario Dept. of the Provincial Secretary and Citizenship, 1972. xvi, 208 pp.

A basic bibliographical guide for the study of Canadian ethnic groups. Folklore is not treated as such, but students of Canadian ethnic folklore would undoubtedly find some of the bibliography valuable. Part I deals with general works and Part II with individual ethnic groups.

50. HALPERT, Herbert. "The Beginnings of the *Hoosier Folklore Bulletin.*" *FForum, Bibliographic and Special Series, No. 10* (1973), i-vi.

Discusses his early association with and contributions to the *Hoosier Folklore Bulletin*, his training and career as a folklorist, and the nature of his work. This precedes the "Index to *Hoosier Folklore Bulletin* (1942-1945) and *Hoosier Folklore* (1946-1950)" listed separately in this bibliography under the name of I. Sheldon Posen (see item No. 75 below).

51. HAYWOOD, Charles. "Ralph Vaughan Williams and Maud Karpeles." In *1972 YIFMC.* Pp. 4-8.

On the occasion of the 25th anniversary of the International Folk Music Council, the editor of its *1972 Yearbook* renders homage to its first president, Ralph Vaughan Williams, and to Maud Karpeles. Includes photographs of both.

52. HICKERSON, Joseph, ROSENBERG, Neil V., and GILLIS, Frank J. "Current Bibliography and Discography." *Ethnomusicology*, XVII:1 (January, 1973), 96-131; 2 (May, 1973), 280-317; 3 (September, 1973), 507-543.

An excellent unannotated bibliography of several hundred items listed alphabetically within sections under the following major subheadings: General, Africa, Americas, Asia and Oceania, Europe, Dance, Republications and Dissertations.

53. HOFFMAN, Alice M. "Oral History in the United States." *Journal of Library History* (Tallahassee, Florida), VII:3 (July, 1972), 277-285.

An informative short discussion of the state of oral history studies in the U.S. and the work of the Oral History Association. Deals briefly with some goals, techniques, and problems.

54. HOWARD, Helen Addison. "Literary Translators and Interpreters of Indian Songs." *Journal of the West* (Los Angeles), XII:2 (April, 1973), 212-228.

A biographical-bibliographical profile of seven outstanding women who have translated Indian songs and interpreted Indian life and rituals. They are Alice C. Fletcher, Frances Densmore, Mary Hunter Austin, Natalie Curtis (Burlin), Alice Corbin (Henderson), Eda Lou Walton, and Ruth Murray Underhill.

55. HYMES, Dell. "An Ethnographic Perspective." *New Literary History, A Journal of Theory and Interpretation* (Charlottesville, Virginia), V:1 (Autumn, 1973), 187-201.

At the end of a special issue with many contributors' ideas on "What is literature?," the author offers some commentary on the other papers as an ethnographer views them. Some of his thoughts revolve around the place of oral literature and language itself in the ethnographic picture, and some of this discussion touches on the concerns of folklorists.

56. "In Memoriam: Archer Taylor, 1890-1973." *FForum*, VI:4 (October, 1973). [no pagination]

Robert J. Adams, Richard M. Dorson, Wayland D. Hand, and Felix J. Oinas write about their association with Archer Taylor.

57. IRELAND, Florence. *The Northeast Archives of Folklore and Oral History: A Brief Description and a Catalog of Its Holdings.* Orono, Maine: The University Press, 1973. 86 pp. (*Northeast Folklore, Vol. XIII.*)

A catalogue of the Archives at the University of Maine. Included are student research papers, field-collected materials, tape recordings, etc. The author describes the Archives in an introduction and explains how the catalogue is to be used.

58. IVEY, William. "The Folklorist as Oral Historian." In *SOH.* Pp. 58-62.

Compares the views held by the folk community and the historians about the history of Calumet, Michigan. Bases the comparison on recent fieldwork there.

59. JONES, Loyal. "The Foxfire Phenomenon." *Appalachian Notes* (Lexington, Kentucky), I:1 (First Quarter, 1973), 9-13.

Ponders the immense success of *The Foxfire Book* published in 1972 by high school students at Rabun Gap, Georgia, and speculates on why a book on folklife and folklore appealed to such a large reading audience.

60. KELLOGG, Robert. "Oral Literature." *New Literary History, A Journal of Theory and Interpretation* (Charlottesville, Virginia), V:1 (Autumn, 1973), 55-66.

A literary theorist ponders some basic questions having to do with the nature of oral and written literature and interrelationships between the two.

61. KETNER, Kenneth Laine. "In Defense of Nagel." *JAF*, LXXXVI: 339 (January-March, 1973), 57-59.

Criticizes the inaccurate quotation and use of Ernest Nagel's *The Structure of Science* by Dan Ben-Amos in his review of Bertel Nathhorst's monograph on structuralism. Ben Amos replies to this criticism on pp. 59-60.

62. KNOBLOCH, Fred F. "In Memoriam: Arthur Kyle Davis, Jr., 1897-1972." *SFQ*, XXXVII:2 (June, 1973), 127-129.

Discusses the life and contributions to folklore of Arthur Kyle Davis, folklore scholar and collector.

63. LAFÓN, Ciro René. *Nociones de introducción a la antropología.* B.A.: Editorial Glauco, 1972. 362 pp.

An introduction to anthropological sciences that includes folklore as one area of study within social anthropology.

64. MADDEN, David. "The Necessity for an Aesthetics of Popular Culture." *JPC*, VII:1 (Summer, 1973), 1-13.

The author calls for greater attention to developing a theory of aesthetics for popular art in order to posit some positive concepts for studying it. Surveys some of the statements that others have made on the subject (e.g., Santayana, Tolstoy, Croce, *et al.*) and makes some suggestions and observations of his own.

65. MARANDA, Elli Köngäs, and MARANDA, Pierre. *Structural Models in Folklore and Transformational Essays.* The Hague: Mouton, 1971. 145 pp. (*Approaches to Semiotics, Vol. X.*)

Examines the structure and provides models for Schwänke, Sagen, riddles, myths, proverbs, etc. drawing upon Lévi-Strauss' formula for the study of myth structure. Maps transformations in two Eskimo narratives and a Finnish riddle metaphor. Contains a bibliography and charts.

66. MERRIAM, Alan P. "Richard Alan Waterman, 1914-1971." *Ethnomusicology*, XVII:1 (January, 1973), 72-94.

Surveys the life and works of the recently deceased anthropologist whose research included many books and articles on African and Afro-American folk music with much attention to Latin America. Includes a bibliography.

67. "Mid-South Folklore: Policies and Goals." *MSF*, I:1 (Spring, 1973), 3-4.

A statement of the goals of the newly established journal, *Mid-South Folklore*, as "a scholarly, regional folklore periodical" dealing with the folk culture of the south central United States (Arkansas, Kentucky, Louisiana, Mississippi, Missouri, Oklahoma, Tennessee, and Texas). Presumably written by editor William M. Clements.

68. MILES, Elton R. "Paisanos at Alpine." In *ORTF*. Pp. 73-77.

Describes the scholarly and social activities at the meetings of the "Paisanos" or "fellow countrymen" of Texas which include members of the Texas Folklore Society and their families. Focuses upon a memorable meeting at Sul Ross State University in 1968. Contains photographs.

69. MONTELL, William Lynwood. "The Oral Historian as Folklorist." In *SOH*. Pp. 50-53.

Discusses the collecting of history in folk communities and urges that this type of material be used to complement written historical literature.

70. "News of Ohio Folklore and Folklorists." *JOFS*, II:2 (August, 1973), 56-60.

Provides information about courses on folklore given in high schools and colleges in the Ohio area, notices of various folk festivals, etc.

71. NICHOLAISEN, W. F. H. "Folklore and Geography: Towards an Atlas of American Folk Culture." *NYFQ*, XXIX:1 (March, 1973), 3-20.

Discusses some problems and procedures that bear upon the successful mapping of folk cultural phenomena. Points to the need for an *American Folklore Atlas* and reports on efforts to create one which were initiated at a meeting of the American Folklore Society in 1971. Includes notes.

72. OINAS, Felix. "Folklore and Politics in the Soviet Union." *Slavic Review* (N.Y.), XXXII (1973):1, pp. 45-58.

Discusses the changes in direction of Soviet folklore research as a result of constant changes in Soviet politics. The crucial periods are the beginnings of the 1930's, 1946-1947 ("Zhdanovshchina"), and after 1956 (de-Stalinization).

73. OLCH, Peter D., and POGUE, Forrest C., eds. *Selections from the Fifth and Sixth National Colloquia on Oral History.* N.Y.: The Oral History Association, 1972. vi, 110 pp.

Presents a selection of papers delivered at the Fifth and Sixth National Colloquia on Oral History held at Pacific Grove, California, in 1970 and

Bloomington, Indiana, in 1971. The papers written by folklorists (Richard Dorson, William Lynwood Montell, Henry Glassie, and William Ivey) are listed separately in this bibliography. Eight other papers that are primarily of interest to oral historians are not listed here.

74. PEPPARD. Murray B. *Paths Through the Forest: A Biography of the Brothers Grimm*. N.Y.: Holt, Rinehart and Winston, 1971. xvi, 266 pp.

Traces the lives of Jacob and Wilhelm Grimm and reviews the scholarly studies and the tale collections of both. Evaluates somewhat their contributions to philology, mythology, and folklore studies. Contains a bibliography and one photograph.

75. POSEN, I. Sheldon, TAFT, Michael, and TALLMAN, Richard S., comps. *Index to Hoosier Folklore Bulletin (1942-1945) and Hoosier Folklore (1946-1950)*. Bloomington, Indiana: Folklore Forum Society, 1973. ix, 83 pp. (*FForum Bibliographic and Special Series, No. 10*.)

Provides indexes according to subjects, authors, and titles, song titles, song first lines, children's rhymes' first lines, tale-types and motifs for the *Hoosier Folklore Bulletin* and *Hoosier Folklore*. Emphasizes the regional aspect of the journals and indexes the material pertaining in any way to certain states. There is an introduction by Herbert Halpert (see item No. 50 above.).

76. RANDOLPH, Vance. *Ozark Folklore: A Bibliography*. Blooming-ton, Indiana: Research Center for the Language Series, 1972, 572 pp. (*Folklore Institute Monograph Series, 24*.)

Lists hundreds of items in alphabetical order under such headings as Songs and Ballads, Folk Speech, Place Names, Stories and Anecdotes, Games and Riddles, Superstitions, Folk Arts and Crafts, Plays, etc. Most listings are annotated. Includes an index.

77. REUSCH, Kathy. "Folklore for Children: Study Units for Fifth or Sixth Grades." *JOFS*, II:2 (August, 1973), 32-42.

The author explains how she has tried to introduce folklore into sixth-grade classes and offers some representative daily lesson plans. She deals mostly with tales, legends, myths, and songs.

78. ROACH, Bruce B. "Abuse and Disabuse: Structural Folklore and the College Classroom." *JOFS*, II:2 (August, 1973), 4-15.

Explains methods of teaching folklore to college students which the author has devised through the use of structural analysis of tales and folk music. Gives examples and discusses some of the theoretical concepts underlying his approach.

79. RODRIGUES, José C. Sousa. "Introdução bibliográfica comen-tada à antropologia." *Vozes* (Petranópolis, Brasil), LXVII:2 (Março, 1973), 5-14.

A bibliographical essay which surveys books readily accessible in Portuguese about anthropology (i.e., ten sections about various aspects of anthropology). Though not about folklore per se, some of the books listed and described undoubtedly contain information of value to folklorists.

80. ROY, Carmen. *Canadian Centre for Folk Culture Studies—Annual Review, 1972*. Ottawa: National Museum of Man, 1973. 21 pp. (*Canadian Centre for Folk Culture Studies, Paper VI*.)

Lists and describes the exhibitions, collections, research, and publica-tions of the Canadian Centre for Folk Culture Studies.

81. ROY, Carmen, ed. *Présentation du Centre Canadien d'Études sur*

la Culture Traditionelle/An Introduction to the Canadian Centre for Folk Culture Studies. Ottawa: National Museum, National Museums of Canada, March, 1973. 88 pp. (*Mercury Series, Canadian Centre for Folk Culture Studies Paper No. 7.*)

Traces the history of the Centre and describes its activities in the areas of research, publications, archiving, organization of photograph and slide collections, etc. Includes a tabulation of "Multicultural Studies and Resources at the Canadian Centre for Folk Culture Series." The volume is divided into two separate parts: pp. 1-46 is a French version of the work; pp. 47-88 is an English version of the same text.

82. SHILS, Edward. "Tradition." *Comparative Studies in Society and History* (N.Y.–London), XIII (1971):2, pp. 122-159.

Discusses such questions as the structure, form, and functions of traditions. Has occasion to treat matters of interest to folklorists (e.g., the temporal character of belief systems, the properties of traditional beliefs, the processes involved in the transmission of traditional norms and beliefs, etc.).

83. SIMMONS, Merle E., comp. "Folklore Bibliography for 1972." *SFQ*, XXXVII:3 (September, 1973), 153-313.

1189 annotated items classified by subject matter. Includes an index of authors. The work covers the two Americas, Spain, and Portugal.

84. STAHL, Sandra K., ed. "Folklore Archives: Ethics and the Law." *FForum*, VI:4 (October, 1973), 197-210.

Prints an edited transcription of a panel discussion held in Washington, D.C. at the American Folklore Society Meeting, November 11, 1971, which concerned the way archives deal ethically and legally with the materials they possess. Participants were Ellen J. Stekert, Alan Jabbour, Frank J. Gillis, Edward D. Ives, D. K. Wilgus, and Bruce R. Buckley.

85. USOIGWE, G. N. "Recording the Oral History of Africa: Reflections from Field Experiences in Bunyoro." *African Studies Review* (East Lansing, Michigan), XVI:2 (September, 1973), 183-201.

A discussion of collecting techniques that may be of interest to folklorists. Includes examples of questionnaires and a bibliography.

86. VARAS REYES, Víctor. *La investigación folklórica.* Potosí, Bolivia: Editorial de la Universidad Boliviana "Mayo Tomás Frías," 1973. 44 pp.

Offers general notions about folklore designed for use in a course for tourist guides who work in the city of Potosí.

87. WAX, Rosalie H. *Doing Fieldwork: Warnings and Advice.* Chicago and London: University of Chicago Press, 1971. x, 395 pp.

An informative "how I did it" book on fieldwork by an anthropologist who has worked in Japanese American relocation centers in World War II and in two American Indian communities. Of value to folklorists.

88. WELCH, d'Alté A. *A Bibliography of American Children's Books Printed Prior to 1821.* Worcester, Mass.: American Antiquarian Society and Barre Publishers, 1972. lxvi, 516 pp.

Lists almost 1500 titles of "primarily . . . narrative books written in English, designed for children under fifteen years of age." A scholarly piece of work that contains a great deal of information of interest to folklorists.

89. WILGUS, D. K. "'The Text Is the Thing.'" *JAF*, LXXXVI:341

(July-September, 1973), 241-252.

The Presidential Address delivered at the 1972 American Folklore Society meeting at Austin Texas. Wilgus argues the continued importance of studying the folklore text and its history and demonstrates by discussing several versions of "The Little Grave in Georgia," a song recorded in America on phonograph records and found in several Irish versions.

90. WILHELM, Gene. "A Tribute to Dr. Fred B. Kniffen." *Pioneer America* (Falls Church, Virginia), III:2 (July, 1971), 1-7.

A *Festschrift* in honor of Kniffen, a professor at Louisiana State University and a leader in the study of settlement geography and material folk culture in the United States. Gives a brief bibliography of some of Kniffen's works.

91. WILSON, Edward M. "Antonio Rodríguez-Moñino (1910-1970)." *Romance Philology* (Los Angeles and Berkeley), XXV:3 (February, 1972), 298-310.

An extended tribute to the recently deceased Spanish scholar whose monumental works, primarily in the fields of editions and bibliography, were of great importance to literary, particularly ballad, scholarship in Spain. Contains much information about Rodríguez-Moñino and his work.

92. YEN, Alsace. "On Vladimir Propp and Albert B. Lord: Their Theoretical Differences." *JAF*, LXXXVI:340 (April-June, 1973), 161-166.

Criticizes the translation of Propp's "sjužét" into "theme" rather than "plot." Capsulizes and distinguishes the essential theses of Propp and Lord and compares their respective methodological emphases.

Related Subjects, Miscellaneous Texts, and Studies

93. ABADÍA M., Guillermo. *Compendio general de folklore colombiano*. Bogotá: Imprenta Nacional, 1970. 300 pp. (*Revista Colombiana de Folklor, Suplemento No. 1.*)

An excellent manual for the study of Colombian folklore which starts with basic concepts and moves in a logical and well organized manner to treat practically every aspect of the subject in 23 chapters (here called *tesis*). Includes photographs, drawings, maps, and charts, but lacks bibliographical aids for further study.

94. ABBOTT, Katharine M. *Old Paths and Legends of the New England Border: Connecticut, Deerfield, Berkshire*. Detroit: Singing Tree Press, 1969. xiv, 408 pp. illus.

A reissue of the 1907 edition (N.Y. and London: G. P. Putnam's Sons). Describes spots of legendary or historical interest in Connecticut and Western Massachusetts with an emphasis upon colonial settlement of the area. Contains numerous illustrations.

95. ABBOTT, Katharine M. *Old Paths and Legends of New England: Saunterings over Historic Roads with Glimpses of Picturesque Fields and Old Homesteads in Massachusetts, Rhode Island, and New Hampshire*. Detroit: Singing Tree Press, 1969. xvii, 484 pp. illus.

A reissue of the 1903 edition (N.Y. and London: G. P. Putnam's Sons). Sketches the history and legends of New England towns with information derived from written sources. Contains many illustrations.

96. ABERNETHY, Francis Edward, ed. *Observations and Reflections*

on Texas Folklore. Austin: The Encino Press, 1972. viii, 151 pp. illus. (*Publications of the Texas Folklore Society, No. XXXVII.*)

Presents a collection of reminiscences of Texas folklorists and studies of folklore and life in Texas. Also contains a brief historical sketch of the Texas Folklore Society. Includes selections written by Mody C. Boatright, Ronnie C. Tyler, William A. Owens, C. L. Sonnichsen, Patrick B. Mullen, Joyce Gibson Roach, Elton R. Miles, Sarah Greene, J. Mason Brewer, Bill C. Malone, Bill Brett, R. Henderson Shuffler, and Francis Edward Abernethy. These contributions are listed separately in this bibliography.

97. ALTMAN, Sig. *The Comic Image of the Jew: Explorations of a Pop Culture Phenomenon.* Rutherford, New Jersey: Fairleigh Dickinson University Press, 1971. 234 pp.

Analyzes the image of the Jew as a comic figure in American film, theater, television, and books. Contains an appendix listing N.Y. plays with Jewish characters from 1964-1970. Includes bibliography.

98. ALVARADO PINTO, Carlos Román. *Prosas vernáculas.* Guatemala: Tip. Nacional, 1967. 75 pp. illus.

Non-scholarly literary sketches about Guatemalan life and customs, some of which are folkloric in character (e.g., traditional dress, dances, ceremonies, superstitions, etc.).

99. ÁLVAREZ BLÁZQUEZ, Xosé M.ª *O libro do porco.* Vigo: Edicións Castrelos, 1972. 65 pp.

A collection of Galician pig lore that contains 218 proverbs and sayings, 92 songs, some tales, riddles, games, prayers, etc. that have to do with pigs.

100. ANDERSON, Eugene Newton. *Essays on South China's Boat People.* Taipei: Orient Cultural Service, 1972. 146 pp. (*Asian Folklore and Social Life Monographs, Vol. XXIX.*)

Reprints three previously published articles on the origins, the beliefs in sacred fish, and the folksongs of the socially distinct group of people living on boats in southern China. Also prints two new studies on the belief structure and the fish nomenclature and taxonomy of the boat people of Hong Kong. Includes charts.

101. ANDERSON, Frank J. "Medieval Beasties." *Natural History* (N.Y.), LXXXII:1 (January, 1973), 58-63.

A non-scholarly but entertaining treatment of some mythical or legendary animals that were part of folklore, particularly during the medieval period and through the 16th century.

102. ANTÚNEZ, Francisco. *Los alacranes en el folklore de Durango.* Segunda edición. Aguascalientes, México: Impreso por el autor, 1972. xiv, 138 pp.

Most of the book is about the history of scorpions in Durango (Mexico), effects of their venom, serums, etc. But the author does mix in some genuine folklore (e.g., words of songs or *corridos* about scorpions, some tales and anecdotes, a few proverbs and sayings, etc.), though without indicating sources in most cases. Includes a bibliography, indexes, and a few illustrations.

103. ARCINIEGAS, Germán. "Our First Anthropologist." *Américas*, XXIII:11-12 (November-December, 1971), 2-10.

A non-scholarly popularized article with some interesting information about the Catalan Ramón Ponç (also known as Pane, Pané, and Pan) who accompanied Columbus on his second voyage and wrote down some ethnographic data about customs, origin myths, shamanism, magic practices, cures, etc. of the Indians of Hispaniola. Includes illustrations.

104. ARMAS LARA, Marcial. *El folklore guatemalteco en la tradición y leyenda a través de los siglos*. Guatemala: Tipografía Nacional, 1970. 200 pp. illus.

Treats certain aspects of Guatemalan history, traditions, and folklore (e.g., fiestas, religious processions, Day of the Dead customs, Moors and Christians dance-dramas, Christmas *posadas*, Holy Week customs, several literarily retold legends and tales, etc.). The book has little unity, but it contains some useful information and good photographs.

105. ARNER, Robert D. "John Smith, the 'Starving Time,' and the Genesis of Southern Humor: Variations of a Theme." *Louisiana Studies* (Natchitoches, Louisiana), XXI:1 (Spring, 1973), 383-390.

Notes the existence of cannibalism as a theme for shocking humor in the South from the time of John Smith in Virginia through various literary and other manifestations (e.g., tall tales) down at least to the end of the 19th century.

106. ARNOLD, Charles A. *Folklore, Manners, and Customs of the Mexicans of San Antonio, Texas*. San Francisco: R and E Research Associates, 1971. 45 pp.

Publication of a 1928 thesis (The University of Texas). Describes the life patterns, dances, celebrations, superstitions, and customs of Mexicans in San Antonio. Also retells six local legends.

107. ARPAD, Joseph J., and LINCOLN, Kenneth R. *Buffalo Bill's Wild West*. Palmer Lake, Colorado: Filter Press, 1971. 38 pp. illus.

Presents the script of Buffalo Bill's widely performed show, *Wild West*, prefaced by a sketch of Cody's life and the show's history. Includes a discussion of the show's influence on the popular image of the cowboy and the Indian.

108. ASHCOM, B. B. "The 'Cruell, Craftie Crocodile.'" In *Homenaje a William L. Fichter*. Madrid: Castalia, 1971. Pp. 33-46.

Deals with crocodile lore in the medieval period. Examines the etymology of the word, the role of the crocodile in bestiaries, tales and fables, references to "crocodile tears" in Spanish and English literature, etc.

109. AUBERT, Alvin. "Black American Poetry, Its Language and the Folk Tradition." *Black Academy Review* (Buffalo, N.Y.), II(1971):1-2, pp. 71-80.

Discusses the characteristics of black poetry in cultural and historical terms. Relates it to blues songs, gospel songs, folk sermons, etc. and shows how contemporary black artists are drawing upon Afro-American folk sources.

110. AVERILL, Patricia, and BERRY, Benjamin. "Media Review: Black Radio." *JOFS*, II:1 (April, 1973), 38-40.

Surveys radio stations in Ohio that cater to black audiences and notes aspects of their programming, personalities, commercials, etc. that are of interest to investigators of black folklore.

111. BABCOCK, Wilfred. "Jim Parker: Train Robber and Murderer." *AFFword*, I:2 (July, 1971), 1-7.

Relates in literary fashion the story of an Arizona cowboy-bad-man who was tracked down and hanged for his crimes.

112. BALL, Larry D. "Black Jack Ketchum: The Birth of a Folk Hero." *MSF*, I:1 (Spring, 1973), 19-25.

Traces the rise of an outlaw folk hero, Thomas E. "Black Jack" Ketchum, who led a band through the Southwest between 1896 and 1899 and was executed in Clayton, New Mexico, in 1901. Gives biographical information and stories about Ketchum's life and death. Includes notes.

113. BANTA, Martha. *Henry James and the Occult: The Great Extension*. Bloomington: Indiana University Press, 1972. 273 pp.

A scholarly study of Henry James' literary use of such supernatural elements as ghosts, vampires, self-hauntedness, etc. Includes copious notes and bibliography.

114. BARNES, Al. *Vinegar Pie and Other Tales of the Grand Traverse Region*. Detroit: Harlo, 1971. xx, 184 pp.

Regional history of people and places in the Traverse City area of northern Michigan as written by a newspaperman. Folklorists will find a chapter on "Vinegar Pie" and other foods and some tales about lost ships, colorful local people, etc. Includes photographs and an index.

115. BARNES, Daniel R. "'Physical Fact' and Folklore: Hawthorne's *Egotism, or the Bosom Serpent*." *American Literature* (Durham, North Carolina), XLIII:1 (March, 1971), 117-121.

Offers evidence that the theme of a serpent within a human stomach used by Hawthorne was known in early 19th-century oral tradition.

116. BARTON, Sandra L. "*Log of a Cowboy* and *In Cold Blood*." *AFFword*, I:2 (July, 1971), 1-6.

Notes similarities in the conception of Truman Capote's *In Cold Blood* and Andy Adams' *The Log of a Cowboy* and seeks to analyze why this genre of literature—a novel that relies on actual occurences—has been so successful and so widely popular.

117. BATTLE, Martha Y. "Hermes and Odysseus: The Evolution of a Myth." *Southern Humanities Review* (Auburn, Alabama), VII:2 (Spring, 1973), 201-209.

Seeks to show that the personality of Homer's Odysseus corresponds in every particular to the traditional conception of the God Hermes in Greek mythology and hence is not drawn from history.

118. BERLIN, Brent, BREEDLOVE, Dennis E., and RAVEN, Peter H. "General Principles of Classification and Nomenclature in Folk Biology." *AA*, LXXV:1 (February, 1973), 214-242.

Seeks to show that there are a number of strikingly regular structural principles of folk biological classification which are quite general in different cultures. Draws upon Tzeltal, Hanunóo, Karam, Cantonese, Navajo, Guaraní, and other taxonomies for examples. Includes numerous charts and a bibliography.

119. BIGGAR, George C. "Mountain Music Plus." *Old Time Music* (London), No. 3 (Winter, 1971-1972), 16-18.

Reprints a 1935 article about the music, dances, arts, and crafts that made up the National Folk Festival in Chattanooga, Tennessee.

120. BIRD, Donald Allport, and DOW, James R. "Benjamin Kuhn: Life and Narratives of a Hoosier Farmer." *IF*, V:2 (1972), 143-263.

Studies the life and folklore of an Indiana informant whose repertoire of tales, anecdotes, and other folklore has been gathered by three different investigators. Attempts an in-depth analysis of the informant's relationship to his material. Gives many narrative texts, motif numbers, photographs, commentary, and conclusions.

121. BLOK, Anton. "The Peasant and the Brigand: Social Banditry Reconsidered." *Comparative Studies in Society and History* (N.Y.-London), XIV:4 (September, 1972), 494-503.

Takes issue with Eric J. Hobsbawm's theories about brigandage and the expression of popular protest as contained in his *Primitive Rebels* (1959) and *Bandits* (1969). Holds that social protest is expressed in myths and legends about bandits but that Hobsbawm describes these without penetrating them. Hobsbawm offers a reply on pp. 503-505.

122. BLUESTEIN, Gene. *The Voice of the Folk: Folklore and American Literary Theory*. N.p.: University of Massachusetts Press, 1972. 170 pp.

Studies and comments upon the relationship between American literature and folklore. Contains chapters on such things as "Folklore and Ideology," "The Emerson-Whitman Tradition," "Folklore and the American Character," "The Sources of American Folksong," "The Poetry of Rock-Folk Tradition and the Individual Talent," etc.

123. BOATRIGHT, Mody C. "Why I Cursed God." In *ORTF*. Pp. 17-19.

Recalls a childhood religious experience.

124. BONILLA, Luis. "Simbolismo de la tortuga." *EL*, No. 519 (1 julio, 1973), 7-8; "Simbolismo del caballo." No. 522 (15 agosto, 1973), 4-8; "Mitología del laberinto." No. 524 (15 septiembre, 1973), 8-11; "Mito y realidad del cambio." No. 525 (1 octubre, 1973), 14-16; "El prestigio del cuerno." No. 528 (15 noviembre, 1973), 11-14.

A series of popularized essays on various aspects of myths, legends, rituals, etc. They contain a fair amount of basic information from all over the world. Includes many photographs.

125. BOSEN, Barbara. "Danish Stories from Ephraim, Utah." *AFFword*, II:3 (October, 1972), 24-34.

The author reminisces about life in the Danish Mormon town of Ephraim, Utah. She includes many tales, anecdotes, and jokes of the community, but also deals with customs, beliefs, cures, etc.

126. BRANDON-SWEENEY, Beverly. "Kinesics and Its Interpretation." *FAUFA*, Nos. 4-5 (1972-1973), 23-51.

Reports on results obtained in a study of kinesics based upon the gestures and movements used in story-telling sessions. By varying the gestures the reseacher develops some tentative hypotheses that suggest the need for further investigation. Includes bibliography.

127. BRANN, Dolly. "I Can Remember: An Interview with Mr. and Mrs. L. D. Brann." *NYFQ*, XXVIII:4 (March, 1973), 244-256

A high school student interviews her parents, both Kentuckians, in search of folklore. Their replies include words without music of some songs, some tale texts, reminiscences about customs, description of pork curing methods, etc.

128. *Brasil, histórias, costumes e lendas*. São Paulo: Editora Três, Ltda., n.d. 326 pp.

Surveys by geographical areas numerous aspects of Brazilian culture. Treats such folkloric subjects as dances, Carnival customs, legends, fiestas, music and musical instruments, popular theatre, songs and poetry, material folklore, etc. Intended as a fairly comprehensive but superficial overview, the work contains expository texts by Alceu Maynard Araújo and numerous handsome drawings in color by José Lanzellotti.

129. BRITT, Kent. "Pennsylvania's Old-Time Dutch Treat." *National Geographic* (Washington, D.C.), CXLIII:4 (April, 1973), 564-578.

Photographs with commentaries about the 23rd annual Kutztown, Pennsylvania, Folk Festival. Excellent color photos are by H. Edward Kim.

130. BROWN, Irving. *Gypsy Fires in America: A Narrative of Life among the Romanies of the United States and Canada*. Port Washington, N.Y./London: Kennikat Press, 1972. viii, 244 pp. illus.

Reissue of the 1924 edition (N.Y.: Harper and Brothers). Describes life among some gypsies in the U.S., some of them of Spanish background. Touches on certain aspects of folklore or folklife (e.g., songs, music, fortune telling, dancing, customs, etc.). Includes many photographs.

131. BROWNE, Ray B., FISHWICK, Marshall, and MARSDEN, Michael T. *Heroes of Popular Culture*. Bowling Green, Ohio: Bowling Green University Popular Press, 1972. 190 pp. illus.

Contains fifteen chapters by as many authors on various aspects of the hero in U.S. popular culture. Marshall Fishwick provides a prologue and Ray B. Browne an epilogue. None of these contributions has been listed separately in this bibliography.

132. BROWNE, Ray B., ed. *Popular Culture and the Expanding Consciousness*. N.Y., London, Sydney, Toronto: John Wiley and Son, 1973. 200 pp.

Contains sixteen articles by fifteen different writers plus an introduction. Practically all are reprinted from other books or journals, mainly the *Journal of Popular Culture*, so they are not listed separately in this bibliography. Some, however, deal with the concerns of folklorists, particularly with matters having to do with the relationship between popular culture and folklore.

133. BYRD, James W. "'Tin Lizzie' Lore and Other Folk Material." *TFSB*, XXXIX:4 (December, 1973), 135-137.

Points out various kinds of West Texas folklore (i.e., folk idioms, anecdotes, beliefs, stories, Christmas customs, etc.) that are found in Leo Somerville's *Charge of the Model T's* (San Antonio: The Naylor Co., 1972).

134. CALDERÓN ESCALADA, José. *Campoo, panorama histórico y etnográfico de un Valle*. Santander, España: Instituto de Etnografía y Folklore «Hoyos Sainz», Diputación Provincial de Santander, 1971. 235 pp. illus.

The focus of the work is primarily historical as it treats the past of the Campoo region of Santander. However, the sections that deal with ethnography touch on customs, woodcrafts, costumes, and certain aspects of popular speech.

135. CARLOCK, Mary Sue. "The Frontier Preacher as a Character Type in Methodist Autobiographies.'" In *HandH*. Pp. 19-33.

Examines the autobiographies of mid-19th-century Methodist circuit riders and draws a generalized sketch of their public image.

136. CARLSON, Vada F. "The Flood and the Lady Doc." *AFFword*,

II:3 (October, 1972), 1-2.

Relates the story of how a pioneer woman gave medical treatment to victims of a flash flood that occurred in Navajo County, Arizona, in 1880.

137. CARR, Jess. *The Second Oldest Profession: An Informal History of Moonshining in America*. Englewood Cliffs, N.J.: Prentice-Hall, Inc., 1972. xvi, 250 pp. illus.

Treats the history and the various methods of moonshining in the U.S. using some information gained from direct interviewing of moonshiners, ex-moonshiners, judges, and agents. Also discusses distilling methods used throughout the world since ancient times. Contains a glossary of moonshining terms, a bibliography, and numerous photographs and illustrations.

138. CARVALHO-NETO, Paulo de. *El folklore de las luchas sociales, un ensayo de folklore y marxismo*. México: Siglo XXI Editores, 1973. 217 pp. (*Colección Mínima, 64*.)

Studies the folklore of Latin American social conflict as seen mostly in songs, folktales, sayings, etc. Deals with the struggle of blacks and Indians against oppression, the folklore of hunger, the folklore of poverty, etc. interpreted in the light of Marxist ideas.

139. CASCUDO, Luiz da Câmara. *Ensaios de etnografia brasileira (pesquisas na cultura popular do Brasil)*. Rio de Janeiro: Ministério da Educação e Cultura, Instituto Nacional do Livro, 1971. 194 pp.

A miscellany of 28 articles of varying length, many of them about folklore (e.g., traditional verses and songs, games, popular speech, folklore of the sea, etc.). They have undoubtedly been printed elsewhere, but no bibliographical data are given.

140. CASCUDO, Luís da Câmara. *Seleta de . . . .* Organização, estudos e nota do professor Américo de Oliveira Costa. Rio de Janeiro: Livraria José Olympio Editôra, 1972. xii, 197 pp. illus.

An anthology of selections from the works of the distinguished Brazilian folklorist with an introductory "Perfil de Luís da Câmara Cascudo" by Oliveira Costa. Most of the selections have to do with various aspects of folklore.

141. CASH, Joseph H., and HOOVER, Herbert T., eds. *To Be an Indian: An Oral History*. N.Y.: Holt, Rinehart, and Winston, Inc., 1971. xii, 239 pp. illus.

Oral history texts of Indians representing many tribes of the western part of the U.S. Interviews are grouped into four sections, the first of these, "Things that Guide the People" containing myths and moral tales, memories of old customs, accounts of the Sun Dance and certain rituals, etc. Includes many photographs, a map, and indexes.

142. CASTAÑÓN, Luciano. "Apuntes folklóricos sobre la vaca en Asturias." *RDTP*, XXVIII (1972): Cuadernos 3-4, pp. 291-315.

Offers a miscellany of different kinds of Asturian folklore about cows. Includes such things as riddles, songs (words without music), illnesses and their cures, superstitions, items of speech used in talking to cows, proverbs, etc.

143. CHICK, Dick. "The Lost Bowie Mine: The Errant Past and Elusive Present of a Misplaced Hole in the Ground." *American West* (Palo Alto, California), IX:6 (November, 1972), 42-47.

Surveys history and legend surrounding the lost silver mine known to Spaniards of 18th-century Texas as the Los Almagres mine. The author tells of his partially successful efforts to locate the mine, known since the 19th century as the Lost Bowie Mine.

144. CIRRE, M. Manzanares de. "El otro mundo en la literatura aljamiado-morisca." *Hispanic Review* (Philadelphia), XLI:4 (Autumn, 1973), 599-608.

Treats some themes related to death and the afterlife as they appear in certain old literary texts written in Spanish using Arabic characters. Some of this could be very illuminating to folklorists interested in Hispano-Arabic culture, though the author does not actually deal with folkloric aspects of her subject.

145. CLAIRMONTE, Glenn. "William Allen White and the Little People." *Fate: True Stories of the Strange and the Unknown* (Highland Park, Illinois), XXV (1972):12, pp. 105-106.

Calls attention to a passage in White's *Autobiography* (1944) where the Kansas newspaperman reported once having seen tiny people three to four inches in height dancing and humming.

146. CLAYTON, Lawrence. "Hamlin Garland's Negative Use of Folk Elements." *FForum*, VI:2 (April, 1973), 107-108.

Shows how Garland used negatively certain folkloric elements such as motifs, character types, games, songs, and folk speech in order to denounce the "agrarian myth" and the urban appreciation of pastoral life.

147. CLINE, Ruth H. "Heart and Eyes." *Romance Philology* (Berkeley and Los Angeles), XXV:3 (February, 1972), 263-297.

A scholarly study of 12th-century literature, mostly French texts, that incorporates motifs having to do with the strife between the heart and the eye. Traces the motifs to ancient literature, including Arabic sources such as the *Arabian Nights*. Some of the material treated is popular or folkloric.

148. COFFIN, Tristram. "Folk Logic and the Bard." In *MLFS*. Pp. 331-342.

Holds that narrative inconsistencies and lack of character motivation in Act I of *Macbeth* are a result of Shakespeare's adherence to a "folk-logic." Presents the text of an American Indian tale to illustrate this logic.

149. COFFIN, Tristram Potter and COHEN, Hennig, eds. *Folklore from the Working Folk of America*. Garden City, N.Y.: Anchor Press, 1973. xxxviii, 464 pp.

Presents an anthology of American folklore and folklife taken from various books and journals. Includes folktales, anecdotes, songs, verses, riddles, folk speech, and information about superstitions, customs, rituals, dances, and festivals. Includes informant data, motif numbers, ballad numbers, etc. Deals with such heroes as Johnny Appleseed, Casey Jones, and Joe Hill. Music is provided for some songs.

150. COLL TOMÁS, Baltasar. *Folklore de Lluchmajor: rondalles, feines, costums, festes*. Lluchmajor: Imprenta Moderna, 1971. 124 pp. illus.

An anthology of basic articles on various aspects of Balearic folklore reprinted from many different sources. Most appeared thirty or forty years ago, though some are more recent.

151. COLLEY, Ann. "Don L. Lee's *But He Was Cool or: He Even*

Stopped for Green Lights, an Example of the New Black Aesthetic."
Concerning Poetry (Bellingham, Washington), IV (1971):2, pp. 20-27.

Seeks to show among other things that Lee's free verse rhythm is based
upon black musical patterns and the sermons of black preachers.

152. COLLINGS, Peter. "The Huichol Indians: A Look at a Present-
Day Drug Culture." *Masterkey*, XLVII:4 (October-December, 1973),
124-133.

The first installment of a survey article on the Huichol Indians who live
in the states of Nayarit and Jalisco (Mexico). Among other things it treats
some folkloric subjects such as beliefs, shamanism, the use of peyote,
myths, etc.

153. COOPER, Horton. *North Carolina Mountain Folklore and
Miscellany*. Murfreesboro, N.C.: Johnson Publishing Co., 1972. 168 pp.
illus.

Discusses North Carolina mountain people's social customs, seasonal
activities, folk medicine, food preparation, children's games and stories,
and legends of Civil War or post-Civil War occurrences. Presents some
tongue-twisters, riddles, children's rhymes, magic formulas, examples of
folk speech, songs and ballads, superstitions, etc. The author is native to
the area and draws largely upon his own knowledge of its folklore.
Contains illustrations.

154. CORTELYOU, Geoffrey, and GREENE, Kathleen. "Pop Owen."
NYFQ, XXVIII:4 (March, 1973), 293-304.

A brief biography and character sketch of Pop Owen, an owner of a
gasoline station in Burnt Hills, N.Y., who paints scenery, farms, houses,
etc. Gives photographs of some of his paintings and of Owen himself.

155. COTHRAN, Kay L. "Magazine Travel Accounts of Piney Woods
Folklife." *TFSB*, XXXIX:3 (September, 1973), 80-86.

Reviews 19th-century travel accounts which tell of encounters with
southern backwoods "crackers." Criticizes the biases of the writers but
finds some valuable information concerning material culture in their
accounts.

156. CRAIGIE, William A. *Scandinavian Folk-lore: Illustrations of the
Traditional Beliefs of the Northern Peoples*. Detroit: Singing Tree Press,
1970. xx, 454 pp.

Reissue of a book published in 1896 (London: Alexander Gardner).
Contains translations of Icelandic, Faeröese, Danish, Norwegian, and
Swedish stories about gods, trolls and giants, berg-folk and dwarves, elves
or huldu-folk, nisses or brownies, water-beings, monsters, ghosts and
wraiths, wizards and witches, and churches, treasures and plagues. Provides
linguistic and explanatory notes.

157. CROWE, Richard. "Missouri Monster." *Fate: True Stories of the
Strange and the Unknown* (Highland Park, Illinois), XXV (1972):12, pp.
58-66.

Relates events in the town of Louisiana, Missouri, where monster
sightings and foul smells along with strange lights in the sky at night gave
cause for much alarm in July of 1972.

158. CUNNINGHAM, Keith. "Arizona Postcards." *AFFword*, II:4
(January, 1973), 1-2.

The editor of *AFFword* initiates what he expects to be a continuing
series of reproductions of old postcards. The first five cards reproduced
here are photographs of Arizona Indians.

159. CUNNINGHAM, Keith. "Notes and Queries: The Volunteer Organist." *AFFword*, II:3 (October, 1972), 38-39.

Cunningham as editor of *AFFword* appeals to folklorists to collect folk poetry of the kind that made up "recitations" of years past. He gives the text of one example, "The Volunteer Organist."

160. CURTIS. Edward S. *In a Sacred Manner We Live: Photographs of the North American Indian*. Barre, Massachusetts: Barre Publishers, 1972. 149 pp.

A selection of over one hundred photographs of life among various western Indian tribes and among Eskimos as photographed by Curtis during the late 19th and early 20th centuries. Many are of interest to ethnographers and some to folklorists. An introduction, commentary, and bibliographical notes are provided by Don D. Fowler.

161. CUTTING, Edith E. *Lore of an Adirondack County*. Ithaca, N.Y.: Cornell University Press, 1972. 86 pp.

Reissue of the 1944 edition (Ithaca, N.Y.: Cornell University Press). Sketches the folklore of Essex County in New York State. Includes treatment of lumber camp life, anecdotes and tall tales, stories of hidden treasure, weather lore, folk medicine, proverbial sayings, games, legends, ballads, and songs (no music). The author herself, her family, and neighbors were informants.

162. DAMIÁN, Juan. *Salmos criollos*. N.p. [Uruguay] : Centro Nacional de Medios de Comunicación Social, 1972. no pagination [70 pp. mimeographed].

An adaptation of a work done earlier for Argentina by a Benedictine monk, H. Mamerto Menapace. This new work by a Jesuit provides versions of 41 biblical psalms translated into popular Uruguayan speech and using verse forms that could be set to music and sung. Not true folklore but an interesting attempt to use folk speech to adapt religious materials for use by country people in Uruguay.

163. DAVIS, Hubert J. *Christmas in the Mountains: Southwest Virginia Christmas Customs and Their Origins*. Murfreesboro, North Carolina: Johnson Publishing Co., 1972. 144 pp. illus.

A nostalgic recounting of holiday rhymes, games, dances, decorations, superstitions, and legends. Traces much of the lore to its European origins.

164. DEW, Walton N. *A Dyshe of Norfolke Dumplings*. Norwood, Pa.: Norwood Editions, 1973. 112 pp. illus.

Reissue of the 1898 edition (London: Jarrold and Sons). Sketches in a humorous manner the folklore of Norfolk County, England, the author's home. Includes customs, beliefs, dialect, epitaphs, nicknames, proverbs, weather lore, some songs, etc.

165. DÍAZ DE STERN, María. *Mi pucha cibaeña*. Santo Domingo, República Dominicana, 1973. 81 pp. illus.

Some literary poems written in the rural dialect used in the area north of the city of Santiago de los Caballeros, R. D. Interspersed are some *coplas* that sound as though they are genuine folklore, though this is not made clear. Includes photographs.

166. DOBIE, J. Frank. "Observations and Reflections of a Deer Hunter." In *ORTF*. Pp. 3-15.

Recalls deer hunting experiences in Texas. Discusses common hunting knowledge.

167. DORNAS FILHO, João. *Archegas de etnografia e folclore*. Belo

Horizonte, Brasil: Imprensa/Publicações, 1972. 267 pp.

A miscellany of chapters on various aspects of Brazilian folklore as interpreted by the author, whose limited knowledge of folkloristics is obvious. Treats such subjects as folklore theory (the author's own), legends, songs, festivals, games, traditional religious practices, etc.

168. DORSON, Richard M., comp. *African Folklore*. Bloomington, Indiana: Indiana University Press, 1972. vii, 587 pp.

Presents papers delivered at the African Folklore Conference held at Indiana University in 1970 and a selection of previously unpublished narrative texts from Sudan (collected by Sayyid Hurreiz), Liberia (Bai T. Moore and Jangaba Johnson), Ghana (Mona Fikry-Atallah), Mali (Charles Bird), Cameroun (Philip Noss), Gabon (James W. Fernández), and South Africa (Harold Scheub). Gives notes identifying Thompson motif and Aarne-Thompson type numbers. An introductory essay by Dorson discusses the relationship of folklore to oral literature, anthropology, and oral history in African studies and evaluates major contributions from scholars in these fields from a folkloristic point of view. Supports the study of African folklore as an end in itself. The conference papers are listed separately in this bibliography.

169. DORSON, Richard M. *Folklore: Selected Essays*. Bloomington: Indiana University Press, 1972. 311 pp.

Presents a selection of the author's own essays on folklore techniques, narrative style, oral traditional history, urban folklore, etc. published between 1959 and 1971. An introduction discusses the nature of folklore study in the U.S.

170. DOWLING, Eugenia B. "The Heroes of the Men Who Made America". *The Delta Kappa Gamma Bulletin* (Austin, Texas), XXXVIII:2 (Winter, 1972), 34-40.

Treats heroes such as Davey Crockett, Mike Fink, John Henry, Paul Bunyan, *et al.* as the creations of fable-minded frontiersman. Claims that Paul Bunyan can be traced back to before 1840.

171. DRESSER, Norine. "Telephone Pranks." *NYFQ*, XXIX:2 (June, 1973), 121-130.

Discusses teen-age prank telephone calls which the author considers a form of folklore. Based upon information gathered from over four hundred junior and senior high school students in the Los Angeles area. Gives many examples.

172. DUDLEY, Edward, and NOVAK, Maximilian E., eds. *The Wild Man Within: An Image in Western Thought from the Renaissance to Romanticism*. Pittsburgh: University of Pittsburgh Press, 1973. xi, 333 pp. illus.

Eleven chapters by eleven different authors on various aspects of the wild-man myth in European and American philosophical and literary tradition from ancient times to the present. I have not listed these contributions separately in this bibliography, but there is some folklore, at least literary folklore, in them.

173. DUNDES, Alan, comp. *Mother Wit from the Laughing Barrel: Readings in the Interpretation of Afro-American Folklore*. Englewood Cliffs, N.J.: Prentice-Hall, 1973. xiv, 673 pp.

An anthology of writings on American Negro folklore that appeared in various publications by black and white folklorists, anthropologists, writers, sociologists, etc. The selections deal with attitudes toward folklore, the origins of Afro-American folklore, folk speech, word plays such as "the dozens," customs and beliefs, folksongs, and folk narratives.

174. DURÁN-SANPERE, Agustí. *Grabados populares españoles.* Barcelona: Editorial Gustavo Gili, 1971. 222 pp. illus.

Studies through commentary and 237 illustrations in both color and black and white the history of popular illustrations in Spain from the 15th century to the present. Touches on practically every kind of printed illustration including chap-books of ballads and other popular literature, calendars of fiestas, illustrations of regional dress, etc. Includes bibliography.

175. ELIADE, Mircea. *Zalmoxis the Vanishing God: Comparative Studies in the Religions and Folklore of Dacia and Eastern Europe.* Chicago: University of Chicago Press, 1972. x, 260 pp.

A translation to English of *De Zalmoxis à Gengis-Khan* (Paris, 1970). Studies the history of the Dacians, their god Zalmoxis, the Mandragora cult, etc. Focusing on Geto-Dacian religion and folklore, discusses comparatively various subjects found widely dispersed in the world (e.g., the Dragos legend, the "cosmogenic dive,", the ballad of the clairvoyant lamb, etc.).

176. ELLIS, M. LeRoy. "La culture acadienne dans le sud-est du Texas." *Revue de Louisiane/Louisiana Review* (Lafayette, Louisiana), II:1 (Été-Summer, 1973), 99-101.

Reports briefly on some research done by students in a class on French culture given by the author at Lamar University. They studied French influences, including some folklore (e.g., song, festivals, voodoo, cuisine, etc.) in southeastern Texas.

177. ENTERLINE, James Robert. *Viking America: The Norse Crossings and Their Legacy.* Garden City, N.Y.: Doubleday and Co., 1972. xix, 217 pp.

Still another book on the Vikings in America. Draws heavily upon the *sagas* as oral tradition. Also touches on possible European influences on Indian culture (including folklore). Includes notes and bibliography.

178. ERDOES, Richard. "My Travels with Medicine Man John Lame Deer." *Smithsonian* (Washington, D.C.), IV:2 (May, 1973), 30-37.

Reminisces about travels around the U.S. with John Lame Deer in order to publicize their collaborative book, *Lame Deer—Seeker of Visions* (see item No. 233 of this bibliography). Not much real folklore here, but there are some excellent color photographs about certain rituals.

179. ESCOBAR, Juan Carlos. *Tradiciones argentinas.* Córdoba, Argentina: Gabe, S. R. L., 1972. 88 pp. illus.

Offers nineteen literary sketches (i.e., *tradiciones* somewhat in the style of the famous Peruvian *tradiciones* of Ricardo Palma) based on historical events and legends of the Cordoba region of Argentina. They draw not only upon legends but also upon popular songs, sayings, etc.

180. EVANS, George Ewart. *Tools of Their Trades: An Oral History of Men at Work c. 1900.* N.Y.: Taplinger Publishing Co., 1971.

An absorbing study of various crafts and callings (e.g., wheelwright, saddler, gardener, farm worker, etc.) that draws upon oral tradition as set down in interviews, many of them transcribed verbatim. There is a great deal of folklore here. Also contains chapters on dialect, place names, and numerous aspects of folklife. Includes appendices, bibliography, an index, and drawings.

181. FEINBERG, Leonard, ed. *Asian Laughter: An Anthology of Oriental Satire and Humor.* N.Y.-Tokyo: John Weatherhill, Inc., 1971. xix, 576 pp.

A large anthology of jokes, folktales, anecdotes, poetry, drama, essays, short stories, and proverbs divided into sections for China, Japan, India, and Ceylon and dating from the 5th century B.C. to the present. Sources of folklore are seldom indicated, but there is a bibliography and an index.

182. FELDMAN, Burton, and RICHARDSON, Robert D., eds. *The Rise of Modern Mythology, 1680-1860* Bloomington/London: Indiana University Press, 1972. xxvii, 564 pp. illus.

A large anthology of statements about myths, studies of myths, and interpretations of myths taken from about eighty different authors who wrote between 1680 and 1860. Some are literary men, some are philosophers, and some are folklorists. The editors provide an introduction, extensive commentaries, a lengthy bibliography, and an index.

183. FERRIS, William R., Jr. "Folklore and the African Novelist: Achebe and Tutuola." *JAF*, LXXXVI:339 (January-March 1973), 25-36.

Reviews the work of African novelists, focusing upon language problems and the shifts from traditional to modern society and from communal to individual life styles. Discusses the use of traditional lore in the works of the Nigerian writers Amos Tutuola and Chinua Achebe.

184. FETTERMAN, John. "On the Road with an Old-Time Circus." *National Geographic* (Washington, D.C.), CXLI:3 (March, 1972), 410-434.

Describes life in a tent-show travelling circus, the Hoxie Brothers Gigantic 3-Ring Circus, and tells something about its people. Includes good color photographs. Peripheral to folklore, but of interest to students of traditional entertainment and popular culture.

185. FIGUEIREDO, Napoleão, and SILVA, Anaíza Vergolino e. *Festas de santo e encantados.* Belém, Brasil: Academia Paraense de Letras, 1972. 37 pp. illus.

Describes in anthropological terms the Alto Cairari region in the state of Pará (Brasil) and then treats briefly on the basis of fieldwork such things as festivals, myths and legends, cures and curers, the day of the dead, etc. Includes bibliography and photographs.

186. FIKRY-ATALLAH, Mona. "Wala Oral History and Wa's Social Realities." In *African Folklore*. Pp. 237-253.

Studies the social structure of the Wala townspeople of Northern Ghana through oral history accounts which reveal social conflict between landowners, princes, and Muslims.

187. FLURY, Lázaro. *Poesía folklórica: grados de su proyección.* Santa Fe, Argentina: Librería y Editorial Colmegna, S. A., 1972. 25 pp.

Deals with transference into written poetry of folk meters, rhymes, language, musical accent, etc. and provides *copla* and *décima* examples of pure, semi-pure, and free "projection." Also discusses the exceptional case of Guaraní poetry in which such distinctions cannot be drawn so clearly.

188. FOLEY, Augusta Espantoso de. *Occult Arts and Doctrine in the Theater of Juan Ruiz de Alarcón.* Genève: Librairie Droz, 1972. 108 pp.

Studies Alarcón's literary use of magic arts (necromancy, pacts with the Devil, divination, omens, etc.) in six of his Spanish plays of the 17th century.

189. "Folklore de Camagüey: mitos, cuentos, pregones, refranes, apodos, leyendas, cuartetas, décimas y tipos populares." *Signos* (Santa

Clara, Cuba), III:2 (Enero-Abril, 1972), 15-67.

A miscellany of tale texts, jokes, proverbs, nicknames, street-vendors' cries, myths and legends, and popular poetry from Camagüey (Cuba). Some of the texts are real folklore, others are not. Informant information is sparse.

190. FOWLER, Don D., and FOWLER, Catherine S., eds. *Anthropology of the Numa: John Wesley Powell's Manuscripts on the Numic Peoples of Western North America, 1868-1880.* Washington, D.C.: Smithsonian Institution Press, 1971. xiv, 307 pp.

Contains ethnographic, linguistic, and mythological data about the Numic peoples of the Great Basin area of the West. Some information about ceremonies, curing practices, myth texts, etc. may be of possible interest to folklorists.

191. FRANCO FERNÁNDEZ, Roberto. *El folklore de Jalisco.* Guadalajara, México: Ediciones Kerigma, 1972. 211 pp.

A catch-all of chapters on customs, festivals, music, dances, etc. found in various parts of the state of Jalisco. Some deal with aboriginal groups, others with Hispanic or Mexican folklore. The approach is unscholarly, though there is a short bibliography.

192. GALANES, Adriana Lewis de. "Popularismo estilizado: una travesura cervantina." *MLN* (Baltimore, Maryland), LXXXVIII:2 (March, 1973), 337-346.

Points to a lyric interlude in Cervantes' play *Pedro de Urdemalas* where the author utilizes elements from popular tradition associated with St. John's Eve in order to deal in a unique way with some basic problems of Nature and Art, Reason and Fantasy, etc.

193. GENTRY, Raymond R. *Letters to Bob.* Alliance, Nebraska: Iron Man Industries, 1973. 226 pp. illus.

Said to contain information about some subjects of possible interest to folklorists interested in cowboy life on the central plains around the turn of the century (e.g., "letters" on "The Sod House," "Branding Times," etc.).

194. GINGERICH, Orland. *The Amish of Canada.* Waterloo, Ontario: Conrad Press, 1972. 244 pp. illus.

Essays a comprehensive view of various Amish groups in Canada. The treatment of religious beliefs and practices and a few other subjects contains some material of interest to students of folk life. Includes many photographs, bibliography, and an index.

195. GLASER, Lynn, ed. *Indians or Jews? An Introduction by Lynn Glaser to a Reprint of Manasseh ben Israel's The Hope of Israel.* Gilroy, California: Roy V. Boswell, 1973. xii, 74; iv, 86 pp.

Part I, an introduction by Glaser, deals with the question of Jewish ancestry of the American Indians, who according to some theories and legends are descendants of the lost tribes of Israel. Part II is a facsimile reprint of a 17th-century English translation of Rabbi Manasseh's work in Latin on the subject, *Spes Israelis*, published in Amsterdam in 1650.

196. GORMAN, Carl N. "Navajo Vision of Earth and Man." *Indian Historian* (San Francisco), VI:1 (Winter, 1973), 19-22.

A Navajo artist-professor surveys some basic Navajo beliefs and practices. Touches on religion, origin myths, ceremonies, prayers, stories, etc.

197. GOWER, Herschel. "The Vision of Jeannie Robertson (As Told

by Herself)." *TFSB*, XXXIX:4 (December, 1973), 129-130.

Presents a transcription of Scottish folksinger Jeannie Robertson's telling of a vision she experienced while near death.

198. GRANDA, Germán de. "Algunas notas sobre la población negra en las Islas Canarias (siglos XVI-XVIII) y su interés antropológico y lingüístico." *RDTP*, XXVIII (1972): Cuadernos 3-4, pp. 213-228.

Notes a lack of studies of the Negro in the Canary Islands and discusses the Negro's influence there and his cultural importance in such things as popular speech and other folklore. The bibliography is extremely useful, particularly a survey of works on *other* groups (i.e., Moorish, Portuguese, etc.) who have influenced culture in the Canaries.

199. GREENE, Sarah. "From Amnesia to Illegitimacy: The Soap Opera As Contemporary Folklore." In *ORTF*. Pp. 79-90.

Discusses the importance of daily TV soap operas to many Americans and presents the results of interviewing in Upshur County, Texas, to discover viewers' reasons for watching such shows.

200. GRIDLEY, Lou Ella E. "Few Are Left to Know." N.p.: Chenango County Historical Society by Chenango Union Printing, 1970. 66 pp. illus. (*Folklore of Chenango County, Vol. II.*)

Continues the work listed as item No. 201 below. Treats place names, children's lore (songs, riddles, games, etc.) poems and songs (no music), epitaphs, etc.

201. GRIDLEY, Lou Ella E. *"Way Back of Sundown."* N.p.: Chenango County Historical Society by Chenango Union Printing, 1969. 56 pp. illus. (*Folklore of Chenango County, Vol. I*)

Tells something of the history of Chenango County, N.Y., and then has chapters on trickster tales, tall tales, the supernatural, folk sciences, weather lore, and folk vocabulary. Notes contain data on informants.

202. GRIMBLE, Arthur, and GRIMBLE, Rosemary, ed. and illus. *Migrations, Myth and Magic from the Gilbert Islands.* London and Boston: Routledge and Kegan Paul, 1972. 316 pp. illus.

The daughter arranges and publishes an account based on the field notes and other documents of her father who spent 22 years in the Gilbert Islands. Deals mostly with various kinds of folklore (e.g., beliefs, magic, ceremonies, songs, legends, tales, customs, cures, material culture, etc.). Includes drawings and maps.

203. GRONOW, Pekka. "A Preliminary Check-List of Foreign-Language 78's." *JEMFQ*, IX:Part 1 (Spring, 1973), No. 29, 24-31.

Discusses the attention North American recording companies gave to the production of foreign language records for immigrant sub-cultures since 1901. Presents a check-list of these recordings and illustrations.

204. *Guía turística del carnaval de Oruro, Bolivia, año 1971.* Oruro, Bolivia: H. Alcaldía Municipal, 1971. 122 pp. illus.

A guide to the Carnival celebration in Oruro, Bolivia. Contains basic information and a few sections by various authors on certain folkloric aspects of the celebration. In Spanish with English translation of all sections.

205. GUNDA, Béla. "Sex and Semiotics." *JAF*, LXXXVI:340 (April-June, 1973), 143-151.

Explains the use of signs in the form of objects and human gestures to indicate a willingness or unwillingness for sexual intercourse or marriage in Hungarian peasant communities. Establishes models for this behavior.

206. HAIGHT, Canniff. *Country Life in Canada Fifty Years Ago: Personal Recollections and Reminiscences of a Sexagenarian.* Belleville, Ont.: Mika Silk Screening, 1971. xi, 310 pp. illus.

Reissue of the 1885 edition (Toronto: Hunter, Rose and Co.). Describes aspects of pioneer life in Ontario, during the 1830's. Includes work, home building, politics, education, business, superstitions, marriage customs, etc.

207. HAMMOND, Peter B. *An Introduction to Cultural and Social Anthropology.* N.Y.: Macmillan Company; London: Collier-Macmillan Ltd., 1971. xiv, 456 pp. illus.

A comprehensive introduction to cultural and social anthropology in textbook form. Several sections contain material on anthropological approaches to various aspects of folklore: e.g., myths, rituals, magic, witchcraft, cures, oral traditions, music, dance, festivals, language, ethno-linguistics, material culture, etc.

208. HARRISON, Molly. *The Kitchen in History.* N.Y.: Charles Scribner's Sons, 1972. 142 pp. illus.

Deals with cooking and kitchens all over the world from prehistoric times to the present. Treats the subject chronologically as an aspect of social history, but there is a fair amount of folklore (e.g., recipes, home cures, traditional customs and practices, objects of material culture, etc.). Includes many photographs and drawings, selected bibliography and an index.

209. HARTWIG, Gerald W. "Oral Traditions Concerning the Early Iron Age in Northwestern Tanzania." *African Historical Studies* (Boston, Mass.), IV (1971):I, pp. 93-114.

Treats the role of two semi-professional "historians" among the Kerebe people and notes that some of the traditions that are orally preserved by one of the informants may be a thousand years old. Shows that some of them are historically verifiable from other sources.

210. HAWKINS, Beverly. "Folklore of a Black Family." *JOFS*, II:I (April, 1973), 2-19.

A paper for a college class in folklore. It contains various kinds of folklore (e.g., tales, jokes, superstitions, proverbs, children's rhymes, etc.) collected from members of a *single* family. Stress is placed upon differences between informants of different ages and sex.

211. HEARN, Lafcadio. *Shadowings.* Rutland, Vermont, and Tokyo: Charles E. Tuttle Co., 1971. 268 pp. illus.

Reissue of the 1900 edition (Boston: Little, Brown, and Co.). Offers literary versions of some Japanese tales and other chapters on such things as crickets, Japanese female names, old Japanese songs, etc. Contains considerable folklore in literary guise.

212. HENDRICKS, George D. "Classical and Literary Motifs in TV and Movie Westerns." In *HandH.* Pp. 127-131.

Notes the use of folk motifs in TV Westerns such as *Lawman, Maverick,* and *Paladin* and also in the movie *High Noon.*

213. HILL, Errol. *The Trinidad Carnival: Mandate for a National Theatre.* Austin and London: University of Texas Press, 1972. 139 pp. illus.

Among many broad subjects treated in connection with Carnival celebrations there are important linguistic, cultural, ethnomusicological, and historical data of value to folklorists with differing interests.

214. HODGSON, Bryan, and BARTLETT, Linda, photographer. "Mountain Voices, Mountain Days". *National Geographic* (Washington, D.C.), CXLII:1 (July, 1972), 118-146.

An interesting popularized view of life in Appalachia. Touches on certain aspects of folk life and such folk oriented institutions as the Appalachian South Folklife Center, the Big Creek Sewing Cooperative, which produces traditional quilts, etc. Includes good color photographs.

215. HOFFMAN, Jim. "Merry-Go-Round Man." *Lithopinion* (N.Y.), VIII:3, Issue 31 (Fall, 1973), 62-71.

Relates an interview with a man who worked for many years on the carousel at Savin Rock Amusement Park in West Haven, Connecticut. He reminisces about amusement-park customs, running the merry-go-round, repairs on the carousel and its organ, etc. Some good photographs by Jade Hobson enhance this evocation of popular entertainment.

216. HOLLIDAY, Carl. *The Wit and Humor of Colonial Days (1607-1800).* Detroit: Grand River Books, 1972. 320 pp.

Reissue of the 1912 edition (Philadelphia: J.B. Lippincott Co.). Reviews popular satirical ballads, witty anecdotes, and the humorous writings of Americans such as Nathaniel Ward, William Byrd, and Benjamin Franklin as found in proceedings of historical societies, magazines, and books from the first settlement to the 19th century. Includes a bibliography.

217. HOYOS SANCHO, Nieves de. *El folklore en el camino de Santiago.* Madrid: Imprenta Aguirre, 1969. 20 pp. illus. (*Publicaciones de la Real Sociedad Geográfica, Serie B, Número 494.*)

Deals with *one* of the roads to Santiago followed by medieval pilgrims (the one from Roncesvalles through Burgos, Sahagún, León, etc.) and discusses legends and other folklore about places along the route. Includes a map and some photographs.

218. HUDSON, Wilson M., ed. *Hunters and Healers: Folklore Types and Topics.* Austin: Encino Press, 1971. ix, 171 pp. (*Texas Folklore Society Publications, Number XXXV.*)

A series of articles on various aspects of the folklore of Texas, California, Arkansas, Mexico, and Thailand written by the following authors: Frances Edward Abernethy, John Q. Anderson, Mary Sue Carlock, E. Paul Durrenburger, George D. Hendricks, W. H. Hutchinson, Norman L. McNeil, Elton Miles, Patrick B. Mullen, Hermes Nye, Carroll Y. Rich, E. J. Rissman, Joyce Gibson Roach, Henry Schmidt, and Jimmy M. Skaggs. These articles are listed separately in this bibliography.

219. HUTCHINSON, W. H. "Cabeza de Vaca was a Piker." In *HandH.* Pp. 109-111.

Discusses a possible 1879 hoax perpetrated by two men in California who found a parchment written in Spanish. The text gave evidence that deserters from Hernando de Soto's expedition had reached California in 1542.

220. "Image of Haiti." *Américas*, XXIV:3 (March, 1972); "Image of Colombia." Nos. 6-7 (June-July, 1972); "Image of Ecuador." No. 9 (September, 1972); "Image of Guatemala." Nos. 11-12 (November-December, 1972); "Image of El Salvador." XXV:2 (February, 1973); "Image of Costa Rica." Nos. 8-9 (August-September, 1973); "Image of Bolivia." No. 10 (October, 1973).

For some years *Américas* has been publishing occasional 24-page supplements about each of the countries that belong to the Organization of American States. Each supplement gives general historical, cultural, social, and economic information about the country under discussion, and there is always a brief section on "Music and Folklore." Of possible value only to completely uninformed readers, these sections might be of interest to students of primary or secondary schools.

221. IRELAND, Tom. "Catholic World View and 'The Baltimore Catechism.'" *FAUFA*, Nos. 4-5 (1972-1973), 101-134.

Hypothesizes that the Baltimore Catechism of 1885 and its subsequent revisions, which were for many years the basis of Roman Catholic religious instruction in the U.S., reflect certain important aspects of a Catholic world view (and indeed of the world view of Western Civilization in general). Includes bibliography.

222. IRIBARREN CHARLIN, Jorge. *Folklore hurtado*. Santiago de Chile: Museo de la Serena, 1972. 90 pp.

Sketches the folklore of the Valle del Río Hurtado, Provincia de Coquimbo (Chile). Describes such things as housing, folk medicine, artisanry, and foods, gives examples of popular expressions and proverbs, discusses the spiritual and magical worlds, and offers some songs and narratives. Information from both recent and older collections provides the source material. Contains a map.

223. JACOBS, Melville. "Areal Spread of Indian Oral Genre Features in the Northwest States." *JFI*, IX:1 (June, 1972), 10-17.

Distinguishes contrastive classes of stylistic features in the oral literature genres of Indians in Oregon, Washington, and Idaho.

224. JOHNSON, Robbie Davis. "Folklore and Women: A Social Interactional Analysis of the Folklore of a Texas Madam." *JAF*, LXXXVI:341 (July-September, 1973), 211-224.

Discusses the function of the folklore used by a madam in a whorehouse in a Texas town. Presents transcriptions of several of the jokes and conversations analyzed.

225. JORGENSEN, Joseph. *The Sun Dance Religion: Power for the Powerless*. Chicago: University of Chicago Press, 1972. xii, 360 pp. illus.

A historical study that deals with the redemptive religious movement as practiced after about 1890 to the present by the Ute and Shoshone Indians of Wyoming, Idaho, Utah, and Colorado. Treats the ritual and ideology of the Sun Dance in the context of the culture, politics, and economics of reservation life.

226. KEITH, Herbert F. *Man of the Woods*. Syracuse, N.Y.: Syracuse University Press, 1972. xi, 164 pp. illus.

An Adirondack woodsman and guide discusses living, logging, hunting, hiking, and the people he has known in or near the town of Wanakena, N.Y. Contains a map and photographs.

227. KEMPKES, Wolfgang. *International Bibliography of Comics Literature*. N.Y.: R. R. Bowker, 1971. 224 pp. illus.

Lists without annotation 3831 items (mostly newspaper and magazine articles) dealing with sociological, psychological, pedagogical, and structural aspects of comic strips. Covers materials written in Europe, the U.S., and South America before 1969. Reviews the history of comics from 1896 to 1970 in a brief introduction.

228. KENT, George E. "Langston Hughes and Afro-American Folk and Cultural Tradition." In *Langston Hughes, Black Genius: A Critical*

Evaluation, ed. by Therman B. O'Daniel. N.Y.: William Morrow and Co., 1971. Pp. 183-210.

Points out certain qualities of folklore and folk traditions that are reflected in Hughes' poetry, novels, and plays. Most concern human values and ways of meeting life.

229. KILLION, Ronald G., and WALLER, Charles T. *A Treasury of Georgia Folklore*. Atlanta: Cherokee Pub. Co., 1972. 267 pp. illus.

Presents a selection of folklore materials collected by WPA Federal Writer's Project interviewers in Georgia from 1936 to 1940. Includes folk tales, folk medicine, superstitions and beliefs, folk wisdom, customs, children's lore, and folk songs. Music is presented for a few of the song texts.

230. KORTEPETER, C. Max. *Modern Near East: Literature and Society*. N.Y.: Center for Near Eastern Studies, N.Y. University, 1971. 83 pp.

Presents papers offered at the 2nd Near Eastern Round Table Conference held at New York University. Some of the papers touch on traditional forms of poetry and other literature. They have not been listed separately in this bibliography.

231. KROUP, Ben Adam. "A Folk 'Digital' Computer." *FForum*, VI:1 (January, 1973), 45-48.

Describes in terms of modern arithmetic the traditional way peasants of southeastern Europe used the fingers of the hand to make mathematical calculations.

232. LAIR, John. "High Jinks on White Top." *Old Time Music* (London), No. 2 (Autumn, 1971), 16-17.

Reprint of an article published in *Stand By* (September 14, 1935) about the White Top (Virginia) Folk Festival and the people who took part in it (John Lomax, George Pullen Jackson, fiddlers, dancers, *et al.*)

233. LAME DEER, John (Fire), and ERDOES, Richard. *Lame Deer, Seeker of Visions: The Life of A Sioux Medicine Man*. N.Y.: Simon and Schuster, 1972. 288 pp. illus.

An autobiography written with the collaboration of Erdoes. Lame Deer, a medicine man of the Minneconjou Sioux, describes Sioux life, beliefs, and traditions in the 20th century. Touches on such things as religion, the Sun Dance, the Ghost Dance, the *yuwipi* ceremony, etc.

234. LANDRETH, Helen. *Dear Dark Head, An Intimate Story of Ireland*. N.Y.: Kraus Reprint Co., 1972. xiii, 385 pp.

Reissue of the 1936 edition (N.Y.-London: Whittlesey House, McGraw-Hill Book Co.). The early part of this historico-literary account of Ireland's past makes extensive use of old legendary sources that the author rewrites here in literary style.

235. LAZAR, Moshe, ed. *The Sephardic Tradition: Ladino and Spanish-Jewish Literature*. N.Y.: W.W. Norton and Co., 1972. 222 pp.

An anthology of texts translated into English and preceded by an introduction which treats the history of Sephardic Jews and their language, culture, and folklore. Texts given are ballads (i.e., *romances*), the *Poema de Yoçef*, some legends, some Ladino sayings and proverbs, and a play, *Contra la verdad no hay fuerza*. Includes an index.

236. LEADABRAND, Russ. *Exploring California Folklore: The San Joaquin Valley, the Mountains, the Coast, and the Desert*. Los Angeles: Ward Ritchie Press, 1972. 112 pp. illus.

A very personal literary evocation of California sights, past history, and present circumstances. Although the author calls this folklore, and there is an occasional retold yarn or historical account, genuine folklore is actually quite scarce.

237. LESTER, Joan. "The American Indian: A Museum's Eye View." *Indian Historian* (San Francisco), V:2 (Summer, 1972), 25-31.

An interesting discussion of the ways in which American Indian cultures were exhibited in 19th-century anthropological museums. Asks the question of whether the museums helped create stereotypes of Indian culture.

238. LIMA, Herman. *Roteiro da Bahia*. Segunda edição aumentada. Salvador, Bahia, Brasil: Imprensa Oficial da Bahia, 1969. 128 pp. illus.

In literary style the author evokes his memories of life in Bahia. Describes many things of interest to folklorists (e.g., traditional foods, festivals, customs, epigrams, popular verses, etc.) but the approach is purely subjective and impressionistic.

239. LINDFORS, Bernth. "Critical Approaches to Folklore in African Literature." In *African Folklore*. Pp. 223-234.

Evaluates impressionistic, interpretive, and anthropological criticism of African literature by non-African critics. Urges that Africans themselves criticize their own literary art.

240. LLOMPART, Gabriel. "Otra nota sobre el molino místico." *RDTP*, XXIX (1973):1-2, pp. 163-168.

The author adds some information to an earlier study of an old theme found in a Catalan ballad: i.e., the mystic mill to which sinners bring their sins in sacks. Includes a reproduction of a 16th-century Italian print that illustrates the theme.

241. LOONEY, Ralph, and DALE, Bruce, photographer. "The Navajos." *National Geographic* (Washington, D.C.), CXLII:6 (December, 1972), 740-781.

A general and popularized report on the present state of the Navajos of Arizona. Among other things the article touches on many folkloric subjects (e.g., traditional customs, dress, crafts, rituals, healers, legends, etc.).

242. LYNCH, Kevin. *What Time Is This Place?* Cambridge, Massachusetts, and London, England: M.I.T. Press, 1972. viii, 277 pp.

A curious kind of long essay-book which deals with time and change as evidenced particularly in the physical world. But customs and traditions occasionally receive attention as time and culture are examined. There is little folklore here, but folklorists will find much to ponder.

243. MACDOUGALL, Diane Newell. "Sourdough Thermometer." *The Beaver* (Winnipeg, Canada), Outfit CCCIV:1 (Summer, 1973), 48-49.

Tells how during the Klondike gold rush in the early 1890's, thermometers, according to Yukon folklore, were improvised from various ingredients that were available to sourdoughs, including such things as Perry Davis Painkiller, St. Jacob's Oil (a liniment), etc. Includes a photograph.

244. MCDOWELL, Bart. *The American Cowboy in Life and Legend*. Washington, D.C.: National Geographic Society, 1972. 211 pp. illus.

The author evokes cowboy life from Montana to central Mexico and from the 19th century to the present in literary style. William Albert Allard provides innumerable superb photographs. In both text and photographs folklorists, particularly students of folklife, will find much that is of interest.

245. MCGARRY, Thomas, MARUSKA, Kim, and BRUNETTI, Michael. "A Day With Lawrence Older." *NYFQ*, XXVIII:4 (March, 1973), 263-270.

Three high school students collaborate in publishing an interview with Lawrence Older, a singer of folksongs. Here, however, he reminisces about lumbering and glassmaking in the region of Middle Grove, N.Y.

246. MCGHEE, Nancy B. "Langston Hughes: Poet in the Folk Manner." In *Langston Hughes, Black Genius: A Critical Evaluation*, ed. by Therman B. O'Daniel. N.Y.: William Morrow and Co., 1971. Pp. 39-64.

Points out elements in Hughes' poetry that have their roots in black folk poetry and song, folk speech, jazz and blues, etc.

247. MCHUGH, Vincent, ed. *Caleb Catlum's America; The Enlivening Wonders of His Adventures, Voyages, Discoveries, Loves, Hoaxes, Bombast and Rigmaroles in All Parts of America, from His Birth in 1798 almost to the Present Year, Told by Himself; Together with a Surprising Account of His Family from Eric the Red Catlum's Discovery of America to Their Vanishment in the Country of the Great Cave, Including the Tale of the Man Sawed Up for Firewood, the Rape of the Temperate Zone, and a Thousand Tricks of Lovemaking*. Ann Arbor: Gryphon Books, 1971. 340 pp. illus.

Reissue of the 1936 edition (N.Y. and Harrisburg, Pa.: Stackpole Sons.) Contains tall tales written by McHugh, who created Caleb Catlum, "folk hero" and tall-tale teller, to narrate the book.

248. MCNEIL, W. K. "The Eastern Kentucky Mountaineer: An External and Internal View of History." *MSF*, I:2 (Summer, 1973), 35-53.

Surveys writings about eastern Kentucky mountaineers and finds them generally unrewarding, particularly those written before about 1920. Tells something of the history of the region and then looks at "internal" evidence, mainly folksongs and folk narratives, that give insight into the mountaineers' way of life and their psychology. Includes copious notes.

249. MADARIAGA, Benito. "El teatro costumbrista inédito de Hermilio Alcalde del Río." In *PIHS(III)*, 19-58.

Gives something of the biography of Alcalde del Río and prints the complete text of a hitherto unpublished play, *La romería de San Juan*, which like Alcalde del Río's well known literary sketches, *Escenas cantabras*, contains considerable folk speech and other kinds of folklore. Of interest to folklorists also is a general bibliographical resumé of books and articles about the customs, folklore, popular speech, etc. of Santander.

250. MAILLET, Antonine. *Rabelais et les traditions populaires en Acadie*. Québec: Les Presses de l'Université Laval, 1971. x, 201 pp. (*Les Archives de Folklore, 13*.)

Studies the ties between Rabelais and oral folk tradition in the Acadie region of Canada. Deals with folktales, legends, rites, customs, beliefs, superstitions, magic, amusements, vocabulary, proverbs, etc.

251. MAILS, Thomas E. *The Mystic Warriors of the Plains*. Garden City, N.Y.: Doubleday and Co., 1972. xvii, 618 pp. illus.

Presents a comprehensive view of the culture of the Plains Indians during their golden age, 1750-1875. There are several chapters on religion (practices, beliefs, visions, and personal medicine, etc.) and considerable attention to arts and crafts.

252. MANDEL, Jerome, and ROSENBERG, Bruce A., eds. *Medieval Literature and Folklore Studies: Essays in Honor of Francis Lee Utley*. New Brunswick, New Jersey: Rutgers University Press, 1970. viii, 408 pp. illus.

A collection of essays by literary scholars and folklorists. Those having to do primarily with folklore are listed separately in this bibliography. See items by Tristram Coffin, Richard M. Dorson, Wayland D. Hand, Jaromír Jech, Seán Ó Súilleabháin, W. Edson Richmond, Bruce A. Rosenberg, Dag Strömback, Archer Taylor, Stith Thompson, and D. K. Wilgus.

253. MARANDA, Pierre. *Introduction to Anthropology: A Self-Guide*. Englewood Cliffs, New Jersey: Prentice-Hall, 1972. xiv, 287 pp.

A textbook kind of how-to-do guide for students in anthropology on how to function as a researcher, set up projects, gather materials, interpret findings, etc. Occasionally includes attention to some concerns of folklorists such as rites, language, mythology, beliefs, customs, folktales, etc.

254. MARSDEN, Catharine. "Holly Legends." *Américas*, XXIII:11-12 (November-December, 1971), 11-16.

A superficial discussion of some folklore having to do with holly (e.g., legends about it, beliefs, its use in making yerba mate tea in South America, etc.). Includes photographs.

255. MARSHALL, Howard W. "The Heroic Urge in Kansas: The Creation of Johnny Kaw." *AFFword*, I:3 (October, 1971), 11-21.

The author tells what he has been able to ascertain about a "fakelore" hero, Johnny Kaw, who was created as a kind of Kansas Paul Bunyan in 1955 by a retired professor of horticulture and local historian, George Filinger. Gives texts of a song and some prose about Johnny Kaw. Includes notes.

256. MARSHALL, Howard W. "Howdy Folks! Welcome to Renfro Valley! Modern Folklore in the Kentucky Mountains." *Journal of Country Music* (Nashville, Tenn.), II:3 (September, 1971), 1-14.

Reports on a country music radio show, The Renfro Valley Barn Dance, broadcast live each Saturday night from Renfro Valley, Kentucky, and listened to throughout the Southern Mountain region and elsewhere. Gives its history and interprets the reasons for its "old time" appeal.

257. MARSHBURN, Joseph H. *Murder and Witchcraft in England, 1550-1640, as Recounted in Pamphlets, Ballads, Broadsides and Plays*. Norman, Oklahoma: University of Oklahoma Press, 1971. xxvii, 287 pp. illus.

In 47 separate sections, each dedicated to a particular incident treated in broadsides, pamphlets, ballads, or plays, the author surveys some of the most notable cases of murder or witchcraft that inspired such types of popular literature. Includes illustrations, bibliography, a section of auxiliary entries, and an index.

258. MARTÍ, Samuel. *Mudrā: manos simbólicas en Asia y América*. México: Litexa, 1971. 163 pp. illus.

Studies analogous symbolic representations of the human hand in Asian (primarily Indian) and Mayan cultures. Reviews the trans-Pacific diffusion theories. Contains many photographs and drawings.

259. MARTINSON, Henry R. "Homesteading Episodes." *North Dakota History* (Bismarck, North Dakota), XL:2 (Spring, 1973), 20-33.

A nostalgic and superficial look at homesteading in North Dakota. It does contain, however, interesting bits of information about sod houses, dances, foods, tools, songs, and many other aspects of folk life.

260. MEALING, Mark. "Doukhobor Society and Folklore: Introduction." *JFSGW*, IV:1 (Spring, 1973), 6-12.

Traces the history of the Doukhobors, a Russian sectarian religious group who migrated to western Canada in 1899. This is the first of a projected series of articles on Doukhobor folklore and folklife.

261. MEIGS, John, ed. *The Cowboy in American Prints*. Chicago: Swallow Press, Sage Books, 1972. 184 pp. illus.

Etchings, lithographs, drypoints, and woodcuts of cowboys as drawn by some 45 artists from 1852 to the present day. The editor provides an introduction on the creation of the cowboy as a romanticized folk hero.

262. METTLER, J. P. "The Pioneers of the White Mountains." *AFFword*, I:4 (January, 1972), 1-9.

Tells about the life of a pioneer family in Arizona in the late 1800's and early 1900's. Describes some aspects of folk life (e.g., making and dyeing wool cloth, soap making, community dances, Christmas celebrations, etc.).

263. MICHAUD, Sabrina, and MICHAUD, Roland. "Bold Horsemen of the Steppes." *National Geographic* (Washington D.C.), CXLIV:5 (November, 1973), 634-669.

Describes many ethnographic features of life among the Turkomans of Afghanistan. Some are of possible interest to folklorists (e.g., marriage customs, food, weaving, games on horseback, etc.). Notable for excellent color photographs.

264. MILES, Elton. "Old Fort Leaton: A Saga of the Big Bend." In *HandH*. Pp. 83-102.

Sketches the history and legend of the feud between the families of Ben Leaton and John Burgess, rival traders on the Rio Grand River in the 1850's.

265. MILLWARD, Celia, and TICHI, Cecelia. "Whatever Happened to Hiawatha?" *Genre* (Plattsburgh, N.Y.), VI:3 (September, 1973), 313-332.

A literary analysis of Longfellow's attempt to write a kind of folk epic in *Hiawatha*. Shows the poem's inadequacies as an epic-heroic poem, and in doing so treats certain folkloric elements (e.g., legendary material, the conventions of traditional epic-heroic poems) found in it.

266. MONTAÑA DE SILVA CELIS, Lilia. *Mitos, leyendas, tradiciones y folclor del lago de Tota*. Tunja, Colombia: Universidad Pedogógica y Tecnológica de Colombia, Ediciones "La Rana y el Águila," 1970. 451 pp. illus.

In the first part of the book the author re-creates literarily and with great use of her imaginative powers some pre-conquest Indian legends from the Lake Tota region of Colombia. No sources are indicated. Part II, "Folclor," contains (pp. 237-451) a large collection of *copla* texts, though again no sources are given. There is also a description of a religious fiesta along with music of some dances. The volume ends with a vocabulary and bibliography.

267. MONTEIRO, Lois A. "Nursing-Lore." *NYFQ*, XXIX:2 (June, 1973), 97-110.

A collection of various kinds of nursing lore (i.e., beliefs, anecdotes, euphemisms, and the like) having to do with such subjects as death, obstetrics, terrible mistakes, etc.

268. MONTOYA B., José de Jesús, and MOEDANO N., Gabriel.
"Esbozo analítico de la estructura socioeconómica y el folklore de
Xochitlán, Sierra Norte de Puebla." *Anales del Instituto Nacional de
Antropología e Historia* (México), No. 2, 7ª época (1969 [i.e., 1971]),
257-299.

A broad ethnographic study which among many other things contains
data on subjects of interest to folklorists such as folk cures, magic, fiestas,
traditional prayers, etc. A separate section specifically on folklore contains
words in Náhuatl with Spanish translations of some songs, descriptions of
some dances, beliefs, etc.

269. MULLEN, Patrick B. "Myth and Folklore in the Ordways." In
HandH. Pp. 133-145.

Examines the regionalisms and the function of folklore in William
Humphrey's *The Ordways*, a novel about a family in northeast Texas.

270. MULLIN, Robert N., and WELCH, Charles E., Jr. "Billy the Kid:
The Making of a Hero." *WF*, XXXII:2 (April, 1973), 104-111.

Shows that nationwide publicity and books following his death
enhanced the popularity of Billy the Kid over other desperados of the
Southwest such as Dave Rudabaugh whose deeds were even more
notorious than those of Billy the Kid.

272. NEWBERY, Sara Josefina. "Los pilagá: su religión y sus mitos
XXVIII:4 (March, 1973), 286-292.

A high school student reports on her own grandmother's reminiscences
about her early life in Poland and subsequent life in the Schenectady,
N.Y., area. Touches on some folkloric subjects (e.g., Easter customs in
Poland).

272. NEWBERRY, Sara Josefina. "Los pilagá: su religión y sus mitos
de origen." *AI*, XXXIII:3 (Julio-Septiembre, 1973), 757-768.

Treats religious beliefs and origin myths of a small group of Indians
(about 1,350 people) who live in the province of Formosa (Argentina).
Includes some field-collected texts.

273. NICHOLSON, John. *Folk Lore of East Yorkshire*. Norwood, Pa.:
Norwood Editions, 1973. xii, 168 pp. illus.

Reissue of the 1890 edition (London: Simpkin, Marshall, Hamilton,
Kent, and Co.). Describes customs, beliefs, superstitions, games, charms,
rhymes, etc. and narrates local legends and stories about local heroes of
East Yorkshire, England.

274. NORTHROP, Stuart A. "Turquoise." *El Palacio* (Santa Fe, New
Mexico), LXXIX:1 (June, 1973), 3-22.

As part of a special issue of *El Palacio* on turquoise, a geologist
discusses its history in the world and particularly in America, production
statistics, uses of the stone, etc. Deals in passing with folklore about
turquoise, though the information given is second-hand. Includes photographs and bibliography. Other articles in the same issue provide additional
data but they contain little folklore, so I do not list them here.

275. NOTHDURFT, Lillian. *Folklore and Early Customs of Southeast
Missouri*. N.Y.: Exposition Press, 1972. 77 pp.

Recalls certain aspects of life in southeastern Missouri many years ago
(e.g., folk characters such as the circuit rider, the water witch, the fortune
teller, etc., community get-togethers, entertainment, and the like) and
gives some folklore (e.g., tall tales, singing games, picturesque speech,

proverbs, superstitions, cures, weather signs, etc.). No informant data are given.

276. NYE, Hermes. "Barbara Ellen and the Lincoln Continental: Or, The Commercial Folk Festival." In *HandH*. Pp. 113-125.

Describes the Ozark Folk Festival held in Eureka Springs, Arkansas, in October of 1967. Notes the lack of folklore there, but includes a discussion with Vance Randolph.

277. O'CURRY, Eugene. *On the Manners and Customs of the Ancient Irish*. 3 vols. N.Y.: Lemma Publishing Corporation, 1971.

Reissue of the 1873 edition (London: Williams and Norgate; also Dublin and N.Y.). A huge study of practically all aspects of ancient Irish history and culture as gleaned from old documents. Of interest to folklorists are lengthy sections on such topics as buildings, dress and ornaments, music and musical instruments, Druids and Druidism, food and drink, etc.

278. O'DONNELL, Richard W. "'On the Eighteenth of April, in Seventy-five. . .' Longfellow Didn't Know the Half of It." *Smithsonian* (Washington, D.C.), IV:1 (April, 1973), 72-77.

An amusing article that corrects the many inaccuracies about Paul Revere's ride that are contained in the poem of Henry Wadsworth Longfellow and other traditional accounts of the event. Includes caricature drawings.

279. O'HANLON, John. *Irish Folk Lore: Traditions and Superstitions of the Country; with Humorous Tales*. Norwood, Pa.: Norwood Editions, 1973. x, 312 pp.

Reissue of the 1870 edition (Glasgow: Cameron and Ferguson). Retells many legends and discusses customs, beliefs, ancient festivals, and worship in Ireland.

280. OINAS, Felix. "The Baltic Background of Balto-Finnic Folklore." In *Baltic Literature and Linguistics*, ed. by Arvids Ziedonis and others. Columbus, Ohio: The Ohio State University, 1973. Pp. 109-118. (*Publications of the Association for the Advancement of Baltic Studies, 4.*)

Criticizes the attempts of A. R. Niemi and others to see a strong Baltic influence in Balto-Finnic (Estonia, Ingrian, etc.) folklore. Shows that three Balto-Finnic folksongs attributed to the Balts have a different (mostly Russian) origin.

281. ORTIZ, Adalberto. "La negritud en la cultura latinoamericana: poemas negristas." *Expresiones Culturales del Ecuador* (Quito), No. 1 (Junio, 1972), 10-22.

Discusses the cultural past of Negroes in Latin America, particularly in Ecuador. Treats some aspects of folklore such as masks, drums, the marimba, Negro dances, tales and legends, etc.

282. O'SUILLEABHAIN, Sean "Litríocht Chorca Dhuibhne Agus An Béaloideas" ["The Literature of Corkagreiny and Folklore"]. *Eire* (St. Paul, Minnesota), VI:2 (Summer, 1971), 66-75.

Written in Irish with a summary in English, the article discusses the relationship between literature and the poetry, folktales, and other folklore of the Dingle Peninsula in West Kerry.

283. OWENS, William A. "Return to Pin Hook." In *ORTF*. Pp. 31-34.

Reviews the general history of the people in the author's home town of Pin Hook, Texas.

284. PAREDES CANDIA, Antonio. *Brujerías, tradiciones y leyendas.*

Tomo III. La Paz: Difusión, 1972. 235 pp. illus.

The third volume of item no. 266 of my "Folklore Bibliography for 1971." Offers here additional literary sketches or stories based in some instances on legends of various kinds, tales of witchcraft, etc. Includes drawings.

285. PARISE, Lidia, and GONZÁLEZ, Abel. *"La fin del mundo."* B.A.: Centro Editor de América Latina, 1971. 113 pp. illus.

A curious account of the reaction of the world, and particularly Buenos Aires, to the appearance of Halley's comet in 1910. Treats the fears of disaster, actual suicides, humorous commentaries, etc. occasioned by the event. The approach is not that of a folklorist, but folklorists interested in popular psychology may find the book of interest.

286. PARKMAN, Francis. "Indian Superstitions." *North American Review* (Cedar Falls, Iowa), CCLVIII:4 (Winter, 1973), 3-9.

In a special issue on Indians *The North American Review* reprints this article, which was first published in July, 1866. Interesting historically as an early survey of various Indian beliefs, traditions, tales, etc. by the famous author of *The Oregon Trail*. There are other articles in the same issue that at times touch on Indian folklore in the same manner.

287. PÉREZ DE CASTRO, J. L. "Pesos y medidas populares en Asturias." *RDTP*, XXIX (1973):1-2, pp. 179-233.

Recalls repeated unsuccessful efforts to standardize weights and measures in Asturias from the 17th century to the present, and then through the use of charts surveys the varying measurements actually used in different areas. Concludes with a very useful vocabulary and a bibliography.

288. PERKOWSKI, Jan L. *Vampires, Dwarves, and Witches among the Ontario Kashubs.* Ottawa: Canadian Centre for Folk Culture Studies, July, 1972. 85 pp. illus.

Studies the demonology of the Kashubian people, survivors of the Pomeranian Slavs, who came from Poland in the 1860's. Using proverbs, folktales, beliefs, customs, etc. the author studies function and meaning of vampires, witches, etc. Includes many texts and bibliography.

289. PETERSON, Richard F. "The Grail Legend and Steinbeck's 'The Great Mountains.'" *Steinbeck Quarterly* (Muncie, Indiana), VI:1 (Winter, 1973), 9-15.

Seeks to identify an episode in one of the stories in *The Red Pony* (1937) with the legend of the Holy Grail.

290. PIETROPAOLI, Lydia Q. "The Italians Came Up Watertown Way." *NYFQ*, XXIX:1 (March, 1973), 58-79.

Calls attention to the role Italians have played from the discovery of America to the present in the New York area, particularly in Watertown, a community in upstate New York. Deals with some folklore (e.g., Italian cuisine, customs, games, superstitions, etc.).

291. POGUE, Joseph E. *The Turquoise: A Study of Its History, Mineralogy, Geology, Ethnology, Archaeology, Mythology, Folklore and Technology.* Glorieta, New Mexico: Rio Grande Press, 1972, 206 pp. illus.

A reprinting of the 1915 edition (Washington, D.C.: National Academy of Sciences) with 48 additional unnumbered pages, including publisher's preface and introduction by Rex Arrowsmith, bibliography, and sixteen new color plates. Deals with turquoise in mythology, its use in amulets, superstitions about turquoise, etc.

292. POLLACK, Herman. "On *Jewish Folkways in Germanic Lands.*"
JAF, LXXXVI:341 (July-September, 1973), 293-294.

Defends himself against criticism by Gerald Washaver (*JAF*, LXXXV
[1972], 282-284) claiming his book (*Jewish Folkways in Germanic Lands*)
was intended as a study of the Hebrew concept of *minhagim* and not of
the concept "folkways." Also provides a classification of various types of
minhagim.

293. POLLAK-ELTZ, Angelina. *Vêstigios africanos en la cultura del
pueblo venezolano.* Caracas: Universidad Católica "Andrés Bello," Instituto de Investigaciones Históricas, 1972.

Gives the history of Negroes in Venezuela and then studies their
contribution to folklore in chapters such as the following: "Fiestas
tradicionales," "Instrumentos musicales de procedencia africana," "Creencias animistas y ritos de entierro," "Medicina popular," "Brujería y magia
blanca," "El culto de María Lionza," etc. Includes bibliography and
indexes.

294. PRIEBE, Richard. "Kofi Awoonor's *This Earth, My Brother* as
African Dirge." *FA UFA*, Nos. 4-5 (1972-1973), 78-90.

A literary analysis of Awoonor's novel in English about the colonial
situation of Africa. The author studies the work as a prose poem built on
the structure of a dirge or a lament.

295. QUINTANA, Bertha B., and FLOYD, Lois Gray. *¡Qué Gitano!
Gypsies of Southern Spain.* N.Y.: Holt, Rinehart and Winston, 1972. xviii,
126 pp. illus.

An anthropological report based on extensive fieldwork among Gypsies
of southern Spain. Treats customs, beliefs, attitudes, rituals, and practices
of the Gypsies and devotes an entire chapter to "Deep Song" (i.e., *cante
jondo*). Includes texts of songs without music, a glossary, and bibliography.

296. QUIÑONES, José Dolores. *Folklore de Cuba.* Madrid: Gráficas
UME, 1970. 74 pp.

A disorganized jumble of notes, observations, word-lists, curious facts,
etc. having to do with folklore. Though of scant value, the book does
contain some lists of names of typical Cuban dances, musical instruments,
regional dishes, fruits, etc. and a "mini-diccionario criollo" that might be
of interest to some folklorists.

297. RATIER, Hugo E. *El cabecita negra.* B.A.: Centro Editor de
América Latina, 1971. 117 pp. illus.

Studies cultural and social factors that enter into racial discrimination in
Argentina. Treats mestizos (*cabecita negra* is the Argentine term for
mestizo) as a marginal folk group that adheres to certain traditions.

298. RATIER, Hugo E. *Villeros y villas miseria.* B.A.: Centro Editor
de América Latina, 1971. 113 pp. illus.

An anthropologist studies life in the *villas miseria* of the urban poor in
Argentina who have immigrated from the hinterland. Treats many aspects
of the "folk" culture of these groups.

299. RAY, Grace Ernestine. *Wily Women of the West.* San Antonio,
Texas: Naylor Co., 1972. xviii, 158 pp. illus.

A literary and romanticized treatment of the lives of many notorious
women of the old West (e.g., Belle Starr, Lola Montez, "La Doña Tules,"
Calamity Jane, *et al.*). The narratives treat nothing as folklore and are

heavily documented, but it is obvious that a great deal of folklore enters into the accounts.

300. REDMOND, Eugene B. "The Black American Epic: Its Roots, Its Writers." *Black Scholar* (Sausalito, California), II (1971):5, pp. 15-22.

Examines the literary works of writers such as Countee Cullen, Margaret Walker, James Weldon Johnson, and Langston Hughes and finds the sources of certain aspects of the black epic in folk traditions.

301. RHOADS, Ellen. "Little Orphan Annie and Lévi-Strauss: The Myth and the Method." *JAF*, LXXXVI:342 (October-December, 1973), 345-357.

Using the Lévi-Strauss type of structural analysis, the author examines mythic aspects of some selected episodes of the Orphan Annie comic strip and concludes that the basic contradiction involved is Self-reliance versus Dependency.

302. RIBEIRO, Maria de Lourdes Borges. *Na trilha da independência: história e folclore.* Rio de Janeiro: Ministério da Educação e Cultura, 1972. 216 pp.

Basically a historical reconstruction of the events of 1821 and 1822 which led to Brazil's independence from Portugal, the work occasionally makes reference to folklore about the events or draws upon folkloric sources.

303. RICH, Carroll Y. "The Day They Shot Bonnie and Clyde." In *HandH*. Pp. 35-44.

Recounts the history and legends of 1934 desperados Bonnie Parker and Clyde Barrow. Attempts to distinguish fact from fiction. Includes information gained from interviews.

304. ROACH, Joyce Gibson. "Diesel Smoke and Dangerous Curves: Folklore of the Trucking Industry." In *HandH*. Pp. 45-53.

Surveys the folklore of truck drivers, including vocabulary items, popular songs, and the driving code.

305. ROACH, Joyce Gibson. "Revive Us Again." In *ORTF*. Pp. 65-72.

Discusses and describes revivals in the author's home town in north central Texas.

306. ROBE, Stanley L., ed. *Antología del Saber Popular: A Selection from Various Genres of Mexican Folklore across Borders.* Los Angeles: University of California at Los Angeles, 1971. xviii, 75 pp. (*Aztlán Publications, Chicano Studies Center, Monograph No. 2.*)

A miscellany of different kinds of folklore orally collected by ten contributors among Mexicans and Mexican Americans in Los Angeles, Arizona, south Texas, and elsewhere. There are 114 selections and they include folktales and legends, beliefs, cures, prayers, verses, children's games and lullabies, a *pastorela*, riddles, proverbs, and customs. Stanley L. Robe provides an introduction.

307. ROBERTS, Peter. *The Cambrian Popular Antiquities; or, An Account of Some Traditions, Customs, and Superstitions of Wales, with Observations As To Their Origin, etc., etc.* Norwood, Pa.: Norwood Editions, 1973. viii, 353 pp. illus.

Reissue of the 1815 edition (London). Treats aspects of Welsh life from Druidic Times to the 19th century. Discusses customs, narratives of King Arthur and Merlin, Welsh music, superstitions, astrology, festivals, and games and retells some legends and tales. Examines the possible origins of customs, narratives, and beliefs.

308. ROCCA, Manuel María. "Los chiriguano-chané." *AI*, XXXIII:3 (Julio-Septiembre, 1973), 743-756.

An ethnographic description of two Indian groups who live in the Salta-Jujuy region of Argentina. Touches on certain traditional aspects of their culture (e.g., customs, crafts, beliefs, rituals, festivals, etc.).

309. ROCQUE, Carlos. *Antologia da cultura amazônica. Vol. VI: Antropologia-Folclore*. São Paulo, Brasil: Amazônia Edições Culturais Ltda. (AMADA), 1971. 302 pp.

Contains 48 contributions by as many different authors, 30 of them in a section on anthropology, and 18 in a section on folklore. Those on folklore deal with many subjects such as folktales, beliefs, songs, dances, festivals, ceremonies, traditional drama, etc.

310. RODRÍGUEZ PLATA, Horacio. "Las hormigas 'culonas' en la historia y el folklore." *RCF*, IV:10 (1966-1969), 47-59.

Treats an ant that is eaten in parts of the Department of Santander (Colombia) and is considered a regional delicacy. Gives some of its history, describes various customs related to it, notes beliefs about its curative powers, and offers words without music of some songs.

311. ROTHENBERG, Jerome, ed. *Shaking the Pumpkin: Traditional Poetry of the Indian North Americas*. N.Y.: Doubleday, 1972, xxvi, 475 pp. illus.

Offers selections in translation of various kinds of traditional material that range from myth and song to poetry and "prose." The editor provides commentaries that give ethnographic background, source, translator, etc. for each piece.

312. ROYS, Ralph L. *The Indian Background of Colonial Yucatan*. Norman: University of Oklahoma Press, 1972. xv, 244 pp. illus.

A historico-descriptive view of Indian civilization of Yucatan as the Spaniards found it. Folklorists may find some material of historical interest in chapters on "Physical Appearance and Costume," "Manners and Customs," "Religion," etc. Includes photographs, a glossary, bibliography, and an index.

313. RUSSELL, Tony. "Big Ball in Montreal." *Old Time Music* (London), No. 2 (Autumn, 1971), 4-7.

Reports on the 1971 Festival of American Folklife in Montreal and the country-music artists and blues singers who took part (e.g., Bill Williams, Bill Monroe, the Coon Creek Girls, *et al.*).

314. SÁNCHEZ ROMERO, José. *Folklore español: Castilla (la copla, el baile y el refrán) ensayo*. Madrid: Editorial Prensa Española, 1972. 196 pp.

Surveys Castilian Spanish folklore forms focusing upon the *copla*, the dance, and the proverb and describes the occasions (i.e. fiestas) during which they are performed throughout Spain. Presents the music and words to religious and secular *coplas* and includes a bibliography.

315. SHEPARD, Leslie. *The History of Street Literature*. Detroit, Michigan: Singing Tree Press, 1973. 238 pp. illus.

Studies English chapbooks, pamphlets, broadside ballads, and prose broadsides up to the end of the 19th century. Examines their content, printers and publishers, printing techniques, etc. Reproduces over 130 examples.

316. SHUFFLER, R. Henderson. "San Jacinto, As She Was: Or, What

Really Happened on the Plain of St. Hyacinth on a Hot April Afternoon in 1836." In *ORTF*. Pp. 121-130.

Discusses the significant role played by Emily Morgan, the mulatto mistress of Santa Anna, in the Texan victory at San Jacinto. Indicates that "The Yellow Rose of Texas" may have been written to honor her.

317. SICILIANO, Ernest J. "Don Quijote's Housekeeper—*Algebrista*?" *JAF*, LXXXVI:342 (October-December, 1973), 387-390.

Suggests that a puzzling passage of *Don Quijote* where Quijote's housekeeper avers that she used over six hundred eggs to restore her master to health after one of his adventures may mean that the woman was an *algebrista* (i.e., bone-setter) who used the eggs to make plaster casts.

318. SIEBER, Harry. "Unity of Action in Juan de la Cueva's *Los siete infantes de Lara*." *MLN* (Baltimore, Maryland), LXXXVIII:2 (March, 1973), 215-232.

A literary analysis in terms of its dramatic structure of a 16th-century play based upon a famous historico-legendary episode from Spain's epic-ballad tradition.

319. SILVA, José Calasans Brandão da, BRAGA, Julio Santana, and TOURINHO, Maria Antonieta Campos. *Folclore geo-histórico da Bahia e seu recôncavo*. Rio de Janeiro: Ministério da Educação e Cultura, Campanha de Defesa do Folcore Brasileiro, 1972. 151 pp.

Surveys some folklore of the Bahia region of Brazil, mostly traditions or popular songs about historical, political, or topical subjects. There is a section on superstitions and another of tale texts and some ballads. No informant data are provided.

320. SIMPSON, George Eaton. "Afro-American Religions and Religious Behavior." *Caribbean Studies* (Río Piedras, Puerto Rico), XII:2 (July, 1972), 5-30.

Considers Afro-American religions from three points of view: the cultural, the sociological (structural-functional and political), and the psychological. Deals with some folkloric subjects (e.g., the trickster tradition, dances, ritual objects, folk healing, etc.), but the focus is that of an anthropologist-sociologist.

321. SKAGGS, Jimmy M. "Tales of the Cattle Trail." In *HandH*. Pp. 55-63.

Reviews narrative material found in the written memoirs of some cattlemen and assesses its value to the study of cowboy folklore.

322. SKAGGS, Merrill M. *The Folk of Southern Fiction: A Study in Local Color Traditions*. Athens: University of Georgia Press, 1972. 280 pp.

Studies 19th and 20th-century southern literature in order to see how the plain man was drawn in southern local-color fiction out of a combination of four stereotypes: the mountaineer, the Acadian, the Creole, and the yeoman farmer.

323. SOBOL, Donald J. *The Amazons of Greek Mythology*. South Brunswick and N.Y.: A. S. Barnes and Co., 1972. 174 pp.

Surveys beliefs about Amazons in Greek mythological and historical tradition, their place in literature and art, etc. Includes notes, bibliography, and an index.

324. SONNICHSEN, C.L. "The Folklore of Texas Feuds." In *ORTF*. Pp. 35-47.

Views the clan feuds of Texas as folklore and describes the recurrent patterns of the feuds and the creation of legends about them.

325. SPENCE, Lewis. *Atlantis in America*. Detroit: Singing Tree Press, 1972. 213 pp. illus.

Reissue of the 1925 edition (London: Ernest Benn Limited). Presents archaeological, biological, and geological evidence taken primarily from pre-Colombian American cultures and offered here to show that they all have a common cultural complex whose source must be the Atlantis of myth and legend. Contains photographs.

326. SPERATTI-PIÑERO, Emma Susana. "Los brujos de Valle-Inclán." *Nueva Revista de Filología Hispánica* (México), XXI (1972):1, pp. 40-70.

A scholarly study of Ramón del Valle-Inclán's literary usage of themes having to do with witches, black magic, white magic, etc. in his novels, plays, and short stories. Includes bibliography.

327. SPRATTE, Carol Lynn. "Wyoming County Folklore." *AFFword*, III:1 (April, 1973), 16-39.

A miscellany of various kinds of folklore from Wyoming County, West Virginia. The informant was the author's father and the collection includes yarns and tales, place names, beliefs, words and phrases, cures, recipes, etc.

328. STABLER, Arthur P. *The Legend of Marguerite de Roberval*. N. p: Washington State University Press, 1972. 78 pp. illus.

An absorbing account of the treatment by literary writers and historians of the legend of Marguerite de Roberval, who in the 1540's was marooned on an island in the Gulf of St. Lawrence. Many works are cited and this story is obviously a piece of literary folklore, though the author does not treat it as such nor does he consider possible oral transmission of the tale.

329. STERN, Stephen. "Autograph Memorabilia as an Output of Social Interaction and Communication." *NYFQ*, XXIX:3 (September, 1973), 219-239.

Criticizes the superficiality of existing studies of autograph memorabilia and seeks here to analyze such material not simply in terms of textual features but as an output of social interaction and interpersonal communication. Analyzes texts, comments upon them, and discusses their function. Includes notes.

330. SYMONS, R. D. *Where the Wagon Led: One Man's Memories of the Cowboy Life in the Old West*. Garden City, N.Y.: Doubleday and Co., 1973. xxxii, 343 pp. illus.

Relates the author's experiences as a ranch hand in southwestern Saskatchewan for about fifty years after 1914. Contains considerable cowboy lore of various kinds, sketches by the author, and a glossary.

331. TABOADA CHIVITE, Xesús. *Etnografía galega, cultura espiritual*. Vigo: Editorial Galaxia, 1972. 196 pp.

A basic manual for the general reader that treats broadly a whole range of different types of Galician folklore: e.g., customs and beliefs concerning the human life cycle from birth through death, festivals, games, folk medicine, myths and myth-based beliefs and superstitions, omens, magic and witchcraft, popular religion, prayers, and literary folklore such as tales, ballads, proverbs, and riddles.

332. TAYLOR, Anya. "'The Incantation of this Verse': How Valid was the Magical Analogy?" *FForum*, VI:2 (April, 1973), 87-102.

Examines the use of metaphor, personification, and symbol, primarily by Romantic poets, to give their poetry magical power, and points out through a comparison with primitive poetry certain factors which distinguish this poetry from true magical incantation.

333. TAYLOR, Archer. *Comparative Studies in Folklore: Asia-Europe-America*. Taipei: The Orient Cultural Service, 1972. 439 pp. (*Asian Folklore and Social Life Monographs. Vol. XLI.*)

Reprints articles previously published in American and European journals on the folklore of Asia, America, and Europe. Includes articles on general problems in the study of folklore and comparative studies of riddles, proverbs, proverbial sayings, gestures, and tales.

334. TERRERA, Guillermo Alfredo. *El caballo criollo en la tradición argentina*. B.A.: Círculo Militar, 1969. 484 pp. illus.

Includes among other themes such subjects as proverbs, songs, stories, legends, superstitions, and vocabulary about horses.

335. THIGPEN, Kenneth. "Rumanian Folklore of the New Year." *FForum*, VI:3 (July, 1973), 160-164.

Describes the folklore and ritual behavior observed during Christmas and New Year in Rumania. Refers to Rumanian scholarship concerned with these observances.

336. THOMSON, Peggy. "Old-style Farming Suits These Sisters." *Smithsonian* (Washington, D. C.), III:12 (March, 1973), 42-46.

Describes the old-time style of life of two elderly sisters who live atop Branch Mountain in West Virginia and have a thriving business in weaving by hand. Includes good photographs.

337. TOLG, Clarence. *The Lore of Uncle Fogy: Reminiscences, Philosophy, and Some Practical Advice from a Fine Old Gentleman*. Minneapolis: Munsingwear, 1971. 134 pp.

Presents items of philosophy, recollection, and helpful advice given by Clarence Tolg on special tape recordings and over WCCO Radio, Minneapolis, Minnesota, from 1951 until recently. Topics include weather, birds, household hints, cooking, etc.

338. TYLER, Ronnie C. "Photography and Texas Traditions." In *ORTF*. Pp. 21-29.

Describes the photographic exhibitions of the Amon Carter Museum of Western Art in Fort Worth, Texas, and shows the importance of photography in recording traditions. Contains photographs.

339. VALLEJOS, Beatriz, and FLURY, Lázaro. *El agua y el viento en el folklore: conferencias dictadas en el Ateneo Folklórico de Cosquín*. N. p.: V Simposio Nacional de Folklore, 1972. 23 pp.

In "La influencia del viento en la creación popular" Flury discusses wind lore in various countries and concentrates on folklore about the wind in Argentina. Vallejos in "Influencia del viento y del agua en el folklore" poetically describes the Paraná River and its influence upon folklore.

340. VARAS REYES, Victor. *Ch'ajmidas*. La Paz: Empresa Editora "Universo," 1972. 327 pp.

A collection of short chapters or articles, most of them previously published elsewhere. Some, particularly those found in the first section entitled "Apuntes folklóricos," deal briefly with folklore of various kinds (e.g., *coplas*, the trickster Urdimalas, Christmas customs, fiestas, etc.).

341. VICKERY, John. *The Literary Impact of the Golden Bough*. Princeton, New Jersey: Princeton University Press, 1973. x, 435 pp.

Studies the impact upon modern literature of Sir James Frazer's important 19th-century book on mythology, ritual, etc. Four modern writers, Eliot, Yeats, Lawrence, and Joyce, receive most attention.

342. VLACH, John M., ed. *Studies in Yoruba Folklore*. Bloomington, Indiana, 1973. iv, 76 pp. (*FForum, Bibliographic and Special Series, No. 11.*)

A collection of papers on Yoruba folklore by Lida M. Belt, Gerald Cashion. G. D. Hall, Janet Langlois, Mary Arnold Twining, and John M. Vlach. Contains a foreword by Wande Abimbola and an unannotated bibliography on Africa in general, on the Yoruba, and on the New World Negro. These papers have been listed separately in the present bibliography.

343. WALKER, Roger M. *Estoria de Santa María Egiçiaca*. Exeter, England: University of Exeter, 1972. xlvi, 31 pp. (*Exeter Hispanic Texts I.*)

An edition of a 14th-century Spanish manuscript in the library of El Escorial that contains prose texts about the life of Santa María Egiçiaca, nine in number. Some of them are direct translations from the French. Several of the documents in this manuscript are chivalresque stories.

344. WEST, James L. W., III. "Early Backwoods Humor in the Greenville *Mountaineer*, 1826-1840." *Mississippi Quarterly* (State College, Mississippi), XXV:1 (Winter, 1971-1972), 69-82.

Surveys backwoods humor in the Greenville, South Carolina, *Mountaineer*. Genres included: tales of ring-tailed roarers and frontier fighters, sketches about courtship and marriage, religious humor, and stories about Davey Crockett. Gives an annotated bibliography of the pertinent items.

345. WIDDOWSON, J. D. A. "Figures Used for Threatening Children, I: A Newfoundland Example." *Lore and Language, The Journal of the Survey of Language and Folklore* (Sheffield, England), No. 7 (July, 1972), 20-24.

Recalls a person named Louis Mousae, an old Frenchman who before his death in 1918 was a figure who terrified children in Daniel's Harbour, Newfoundland. Parents used him as a means of controlling children's behavior. Contains communications from informants who feared him in their childhood.

346. WIGGINS, William H., Jr. "Jack Johnson as Bad Nigger: The Folklore of His Life." *Black Scholar* (Sausalito, California), II (1971):5, pp. 35-46.

Treats Jack Johnson, the first Negro heavyweight boxing champion, as a folk hero who displayed many of the characteristics of the "bad nigger" frowned upon by white society (e.g., fearlessness, defiance, sexual virility, etc.).

347. WIGGINTON, Eliot, ed. *Foxfire 2: Ghost Stories, Spring Wild Plant Foods, Spinning and Weaving, Burial Customs, Corn Shuckin's, Wagon Making and More Affairs of Plain Living*. Garden City, N.Y.: Doubleday and Co., 1973. 410 pp. illus.

A sequel to *The Foxfire Book* published in 1972. The work of high school students of Rabun Gap, Georgia, the many short articles contain a considerable amount of material of interest to folklorists. Most of it appeared earlier in the quarterly magazine, *Foxfire*.

348. WILEY, Bell I. "The Common Soldier of the Civil War." *Civil War Times Illustrated* (Gettysburg, Pennsylvania), XII:4 (July, 1973), 1-64.

An entire special issue of the journal is devoted to studying and characterizing Civil War soldiers from both the North and the South. Folklore *per se* does not play a large role, but folklorists interested in Civil War lore will find passing mention of traditional customs, games, beliefs, songs, jokes, etc. Includes many drawings and photographs.

349. WILSON, William A. "Folklore and History: Fact amid the Legends." *Utah Historical Quarterly* (Salt Lake City), XLI:1 (Winter, 1973), 40-58.

Defends the value of folklore studies for an understanding of culture, history, and attitudes. Gives many textual examples of tales and songs, many of them oriented toward Utah, Mormons, etc. Includes photographs.

350. WREN, Robert M. "Youthful Traditions Score at Kaduna." *Africa Report* (N.Y.), XVIII:1 (January-February, 1973), 36-37.

Reports with satisfaction on the All-Nigeria Festival of the Arts held at Kaduna from December 9-16, 1972. Notes the many traditional arts such as dancing, singing, masks and costumes, etc. that made up the festival.

351. YERIAN, Margaret, and YERIAN, Cameron. "The Children of Vaitogi Call the Shark and the Turtle." *Fate: True Stories of the Strange and the Unknown* (Highland Park, Illinois), XXVI (1973):1, pp. 49-56.

The authors report on having personally witnessed the appearance of a shark and a turtle in the sea when children on the Samoan island of Tutuila performed a song-ritual. The sea dwellers are said to be ancient mythical visitors who returned to the sea with a promise to come back whenever the ritual was performed.

352. ZAMBONI, Olga Mercedes, and RODRÍGUEZ, Antonio Hernán. *Misiones en imágenes y leyendas.* Posadas, Argentina: Instituto Superior del Profesorado "Antonio Ruiz de Montoya," 1971. 43 pp.

Only the second part, "Hacia una compresión del folklore espiritual de Misiones" by Rodríguez, is of interest to folklorists. It includes versions of some myths and legends and various beliefs and superstitions. Sources are not indicated.

353. ZORA CARVAJAL, F. *Tacna, historia y folklore.* Segunda edición aumentade y corregida. Tacna, Perú: Editorial Santa María, 1969. 466 pp.

A jumbled miscellany of brief articles or sketches about historical incidents and figures along with a section called "Del folklore tacneño" (pp. 157-288) that contains a small amount of genuine folklore (e.g., tales, beliefs, local traditions, superstitions, etc.). Though the author does not know what folklore is, the book should not be ignored entirely by folklorists interested in the Tacna area.

B PROSE NARRATIVE

[See also numbers 11, 15, 17, 22, 30, 65, 74, 76, 78, 85, 92, 94, 95, 99, 102, 103, 104, 106, 108, 114, 117, 120, 125, 126, 127, 128, 133, 138, 141, 143, 148, 149, 152, 153, 156, 161, 163, 167, 168, 169, 173, 179, 181, 182, 185, 189, 190, 196, 201, 202, 207, 210, 211, 216, 217, 222, 223, 229, 234, 235, 241, 247, 248, 250, 254, 255, 257, 266, 267, 272, 273, 275, 279, 281, 282, 284, 286, 288, 291, 301, 306, 307, 309, 311, 315, 319, 323, 324, 327, 331, 333, 334, 343, 344, 347, 349, 352, 562, 613, 616, 662, 679, 682, 832, 840, 844, 846, 856, 882, 901, 955, 959, 1007, 1043, 1045, 1061, 1100, 1180, 1199, 1223, 1239.]

354. ADAMS, Edward. *Congaree Sketches: Scenes from Negro Life in the Swamps of the Congaree and Tales by Tad and Scip of Heaven and Hell with Other Miscellany*. N.Y.: Kraus Reprints, 1971. 116 pp.

Reissue of the 1927 edition (Chapel Hill: The University of North Carolina Press). Presents in dialect 54 tales, religious sketches, and poems collected from Negroes of lower Carolina. An introduction by Paul Green notes advancements made by Negroes since emancipation.

355. AGEE, Hugh. "Ghost Lore from Sevier County, Tennessee." *TFSB*, XXXIX:1 (March, 1973), 8-10.

Relates legends of house ghosts and mysterious lights told by Mrs. Ruth Maples of Sevierville, Tennessee.

356. AGOGINO, George A., STEVENS, Dominique E. and CARLOTTA, Lynda. "Doña Marina and the Legend of La Llorona." *Anthropological Journal of Canada* (Quebec, Quebec), XI (1973):1, pp. 27-29.

Seeks to identify *La Llorona* (The Crying Woman) of Mexican and Spanish American legendary tradition with the historical Doña Marina, an Indian woman who was the mistress of Hernán Cortés and an important figure in the conquest of Mexico.

357. AINSWORTH, Catherine Harris. "American Folktales from the Recent Wars." *NYFQ*, XXIX:1 (March, 1973), 38-49.

Gives texts of five folktales that have in common the fact that they were told by soldiers or sailors of World War II or more recent years. Informant data, motif numbers, and some commentary are provided.

358. ALEXANDER, John. "Tales from North Carolina." *AFFword*, II:4 (January, 1973), 17-20.

Gives four orally collected texts about episodes in North Carolina or about North Carolinians in California. One is about Tom Dooley.

359. ARMSTRONG, Benjamin G. "Reminiscences of Life among the Chippewa (Part III)." *Wisconsin Magazine of History* (Madison, Wisconsin), LVI:1 (Autumn, 1972), 37-58; "Part IV," 2 (Winter, 1972-1973), 140-161.

Armstrong's account of life among the Chippewa Indians about one hundred years ago contains one legend about the coming of the white men and some other information of possible interest to folklorists (e.g., beliefs, ceremonies, some aspects of verbal behavior, pictographs, etc.). A photographic insert (pp. 52-53) about making a birch-bark canoe is also informative.

360. ARRENDONDO, Art. "La Llorona in Flagstaff." *AFFword*, II:4 (January, 1973), 21-28.

Gives sixteen orally collected texts of stories having to do with *La Llorona*, the "Weeping Woman" of Mexican tale tradition. Three are from Mexico, three are from Arizona towns other than Flagstaff, and ten are from Flagstaff.

361. BABCOCK, Wilfred. "Story of the Canteen that Eddie Rouchon Told Me." *AFFword*, I:4 (January, 1972), 21-22.

Text of a western tale about a man driven mad by thirst on the desert.

362. BAGDANAVIČIUS, Vytautas. *Cultural Wellsprings of Folktales*. N.Y.: Maryland Books, 1970. 196 pp.

A Lithuanian theologian, philosopher, and folklorist studies the folktales of Lithuania and of many other areas as literary entities but also as sources of historical and theological information of value to the study of cultural development.

363. BARRERAS, Ramona. "Spanish-American Belief Tales." *AFFword*, II:4 (January, 1973), 3-16.

Gives eighteen texts of some tales or simply statements of belief that were orally collected by the author among relatives and friends. They deal with the evil-eye, the power of twins to cause muscular cramps or other pains, and various forms of witchcraft.

364. BARRIGA LÓPEZ, Franklin. *Leyendas y tradiciones de Cotopaxi*. Latacunga, Ecuador: Editorial "Pío XII" (Ambato, Ecuador), 1970. 127 pp. illus.

Offers literary versions of some tales and legends associated with the author's native Latacunga. No sources are indicated and folkloric content is small, but folklorists interested in the region should perhaps look at the book.

365. BARRIONUEVO, Alfonsina. *Los dioses de la lluvia*. Lima: Editorial Universo, n.d. 291 pp. illus.

Offers highly literary sketches about myths and legends of Peru, descriptions of some fiestas and dances, and numerous excellent photographs, mostly in color.

366. BASCOM, William. "African Dilemma Tales: An Introduction." In *African Folklore*. Pp. 143-155.

Analyzes and defines the African dilemma tale distinguishing it from other forms of the folktale and delineating types and versions.

367. BASCOM, William. "Cinderella in Africa." *JFI*, IX:1 (June, 1972), 54-70.

Shows how using the Aarne-Thompson type index and the Thompson motif index aids in answering questions of limited time-depth about an African Cinderella tale. Includes the text of a Hausa tale in English translation.

368. BASTIN, Bruce. "The Devil's Goin' to Get You." *NCFJ*, XXI:4 (November, 1973), 189-194.

Gives orally collected texts of four North Carolina tales about the appearance of the devil before people who do things like playing the banjo or going to the movies on Sunday. Analyzes motifs.

369. BEDE, Cuthbert, coll. and illus. *The White Wife; with Other Stories, Supernatural, Romantic and Legendary*. Norwood, Pa.: Norwood

Editions, 1972. xii, 252 pp.

Reissue of the 1865 edition (London: Sampson Low, Son, and Marston). Offers 47 tales, mostly ghost tales, fairy tales, and the like "collected during the past four years . . . from the very interesting Western Highland district, Cantire, or Land's-end. . . ." Cuthbert Bede is the pseudonym of Edward Bradley.

370. BELLA, José M. "Origen y difusión de la leyenda de Pedro Telonario y sus derivaciones en el teatro del siglo de oro." *Revista de Filología Española* (Madrid), LV (1972): Cuadernos 1-2, 51-59.

Examines the use of a medieval saint's legend by two 17th-century Spanish dramatists, Mira de Amescua and Felipe Godínez, who wrote religious plays (i.e., *autos sacramentales*) about it.

371. BEN-AMOS, Dan. "Two Benin Storytellers." In *African Folklore*. Pp. 103-114.

Discusses changes in the storytelling event performed at the "okpobhie," a secular festival of the Bini of midwest Nigeria. Interviews with two storytellers, one urban and one rural, show the changing instrumentation, performance style, beliefs, role, etc. of the narrators.

372. BERNIER, Hélène. *La fille aux mains coupées (conte-type 706).* Québec: Les Presses de l'Université Laval, 1971. xi, 190 pp. (*Les Archives de Folklore, 12.*)

Using a historico-geographic approach the author analyzes written and oral versions of Aarne-Thompson tale type 706 in Canada and elsewhere in the world. Includes a lengthy appendix, bibliography, a glossary, an index map, and charts.

373. BETTRIDGE, William Edwin, and UTLEY, Francis Lee. "New Light on the Origin of the Griselda Story." *Texas Studies in Literature and Language* (Austin), XIII:2 (Summer, 1971), 153-208.

A scholarly study of Boccaccio's literary tale of the patient Griselda, source of many folktales (Aarne-Thompson Type 887). Looks into possible oral folktale sources for Boccaccio's creation of the Griselda story in the *Decameron*.

374. BIANCHI, Diane. "Mountain Legend in Eastern Kentucky." *KFR*, XIX:3 (July-September, 1973), 58-78.

Gives twenty orally collected texts of narratives gathered in Evarts, Kentucky. They are personal accounts about experiences in the mines and union activities, tales about ghosts and corpses, murder stories, etc. Informant and collecting data are provided and William Hugh Jansen offers copious commentaries that include identification of motif numbers.

375. BLAFFER, Sarah C. *The Black-Man or Zinacantan, a Central American Legend; Including an Analysis of Tales Recorded and Translated by Robert M. Laughlin.* Austin: University of Texas Press, 1972. xvi, 194 pp. illus.

Determines the cultural significance of the Mayan mythological trickster demon *h'k'al* and its possible prototype, the bat, by using a structuralist approach modified by historical considerations. Stories and beliefs collected from the Tzotzil Maya by Robert M. Laughlin plus earlier ethnological and historical data provide the basis for the analysis. Includes illustrations, tables, maps, and a bibliography.

376. BRETT, Bill. "Horse Penning: Southeast Texas, 1913." In *ORTF*. Pp. 117-120.

Retells a story of horse running and penning told by a cowhand from southeast Texas.

377. BRETTEVILLE, Christian. "Ivo Caprino: The Wizard of Snarϕya." *American Scandinavian Review* (N.Y.), LXI:4 (December, 1973), 353-358.

Tells about Norwegian film producer Caprino who since 1948 has been making motion pictures with puppets. His most important films have been based on Norwegian folktales. Includes photographs.

378. BREWER, J. Mason. "More of the Word on the Brazos." In *ORTF*. Pp 91-99.

Presents live tales in dialect form collected for but not used in the author's *The Word on the Brazos*, a book published in 1953 containing black folk stories.

379. BUCHAN, Peter. *Ancient Scottish Tales*. Darby, Pa.: Norwood Editions, 1973. 64 pp.

Reprints a collection of fourteen selected Scottish tales collected by Peter Buchan and published in 1908 (Peterhead, Scotland). An introduction by John A. Fairley defends the collection and transcription work of Peter Buchan and prints some letters written from Buchan to Charles Kirkpatrick Sharpe concerning this tale collection.

380. CALOGERAS, Roy C. "Lévi-Strauss and Freud: Their 'Structural' Approaches to Myths." *American Imago* (Detroit, Michigan), XXX:1 (Spring, 1973), 57-79.

A psychiatrist examines and compares Lévi-Strauss's and Freud's "structural" approaches to myths pointing out similarities and differences and criticizing both. Studies the Oedipus myth and the Asdiwal myth in considerable detail.

381. CARSON, Gerald. "Fantastic Animals Prowl Tall Timber of Our Mythology." *Smithsonian* (Washington, D.C.), III:5 (August, 1972), 20-25.

An article for the general reader about fantastic animals in folklore of the U.S. Ranges from accounts of early explorers to modern tall-tale tradition.

382. CASTELO BRANCO, Renato. *Pré-história brasileira: fatos e lendas*. São Paulo: Quarto Artes Editôra, 1971. 191 pp. illus.

A significant part of the book deals with beliefs and legends about lost cities in the jungle, Amazon warriors, footprints of St. Thomas, etc. The author suggests that they may contain some historical truths.

383. CLARE, Warren. "The Slide-Rock Bolter, Splinter Cats and Paulski Bunyanovitch." *Idaho Yesterdays* (Boise, Idaho), XV:3 (Fall, 1971), 2-8.

Deals with the creation of Paul Bunyan stories by author-newspaperman James Stevens in the mid-1920's. Also treats some tall tales about fantastic animals.

384. CLARK, Carol. "Communications: 'My Grandmother Told Me the Story About . . . ,' Folklore in a Secondary Short Story Unit." *FForum*, VI:4 (October, 1973), 245-250.

Advocates a program for using folklore to teach 7th to 10th graders about stories and storytelling.

385. CLARKE, Kenneth W. *Uncle Bud Long: The Birth of a Kentucky Folk Legend*. Lexington, Kentucky: University Press of Kentucky, 1973. 78 pp.

Studies folktales about Uncle Bud Long and his family who lived in Clark's Landing, Warren County, Kentucky, from around 1900 to 1919. From orally collected materials the author reconstructs the life of the family and the community. Relates stories about Long to universal folk motifs and studies the legend-making process.

386. COLBY, B. N. "Analytical Procedures in Eidochronic Study." *JAF*, LXXXVI:339 (January-March, 1973), 14-24.

Performs an eidochronic analysis (i.e., an analysis of "the sequence of narrative ideas") and discovers generative rules of some Eskimo folktales. Opposes the universal application of Propp's functions, holding that such units and their sequence are culture-specific.

387. COLBY, B. N. "A Partial Grammar of Eskimo Folktales." *AA*, LXXV:3 (June, 1973), 645-662.

Seeks to provide through a methodology which resembles that used by Propp to provide a partial generative grammar of covert but empirically discoverable narrative elements in Eskimo folktales. Includes charts, notes, and bibliography.

388. CORDERO Y TORRES, Enrique, and others. *Leyendas de la Puebla de los Angeles*. México: Fotolitográfica Leo, 1972.

A collection of literarily retold legends and tales from the region of Puebla and other areas of Mexico. They are by Cordero y Torres and thirteen other writers. Many are in poetic form and all are far removed from possible folk origins.

389. CROWLEY, Daniel J. *Folktale Research in Africa*. Accra: Ghana Universities Press, 1971. 19 pp.

A lecture delivered at the University of Ghana in 1971. Reviews briefly the history of folktale scholarship, enumerates the volume of tales and other narrative materials recorded for African peoples, and notes some problems to be resolved in preparing an African Tale Type Index. Contains a bibliography.

390. CUNNINGHAM, Keith. "The Forest Dale Exodus." *AFFword*, II:3 (October, 1972), 11-16.

Gives three accounts, two of them orally collected texts, of the settlement and abandonment around 1880 of a Mormon town, Forest Dale, Arizona. Notes differences in style and emotional content in the different versions of the historical episode. Includes photographs.

391. DAEMMRICH, Horst. "The Infernal Fairy Tale: Inversion of Archetypal Motifs in Modern European Literature." *Mosaic* (Winnipeg, Manitoba), V (1972):3, pp. 85-95.

Treats inversions of three basic motifs (the Rite of Spring, the Quest for Life, and Spiritual Rebirth) as used by some modern European writers in order to show man's existential anguish as he lives in an absurd world.

392. DASENT, George Webbe. *Popular Tales from the Norse*. Detroit: Grand River Books, 1971. cli, 443 pp.

Reissue of the 1888 edition (Edinburgh: David Douglas). Presents in English translation the collection of Norse tales by M. M. Asbjörnsen and Moe. An introductory essay discusses the origin and diffusion of popular tales, and an appendix discusses and presents thirteen African "Ananzi stories" from the West Indies.

393. DAVIS, Hubert J. "Old Devil Tyree Gets Religion." *NCFJ*, XXI:2 (May, 1973), 73-76.

Presents a tall tale from southwest Virginia about a servant of the devil whose encounter with some snakes results in his conversion.

394. DE CARO, Rosan Jordan. "A Note about Folklore and Literature (The Bosom Serpent Revisited)." *JAF*, LXXXVI:339 (January-March, 1973), 62-65.

Criticizes an article by Daniel R. Barnes ("The Bosom Serpent: A Legend in American Literature and Culture") in which literary variants are more thoroughly analyzed than folkloric variants and their contents. Offers analyses of the function of "vaginal serpent" legends found among Mexican-American women in West Texas.

395. DEVOTO, Daniel. *Introducción al estudio de Don Juan Manuel y en particular de «El Conde Lucanor». Una bibliografía.* Madrid: Editorial Castalia, 1972. 505 pp.

A very scholarly annotated bibliography of over a thousand titles about Juan Manuel, Spanish prose writer of the fourteenth century who draws upon *exempla* and folktales for subjects of his own writings.

396. DORSON, Richard M. "Esthetic Form in British and American Folk Narrative." In *MLFS*. Pp. 305-321.

Determines the main genres of Anglo-American oral prose tradition. Examines the applicability to stories from this tradition of Axel Olrik's laws for European tales, focusing on a Highland Scottish, an urban American, and a Swedish-American immigrant narrative.

397. DOW, James R. "'Ah,' He Says, 'I've Heard of You.' 'Oh,' I said, 'No Doubt!' Status Seeking through Story Telling." *NYFQ*, XXIX:2 (June, 1973), 83-96.

Tells about a southern Indiana storyteller, Benjamin Kuhn of Hartsville, Indiana, and his repertoire. Gives a few texts and speculates on the reasons why Kuhn tells tales, particularly certain stories that suggest a desire for personal recognition.

398. DURRENBURGER, E. Paul. "Rats, Cats, and Abandoned Fields." In *HandH*. Pp. 157-163.

Investigates the story behind an abandoned rice field in Northwestern Thailand inhabited by spirits; also one about the existence of so many rats in Mak Com Pae Village.

399. EBERHARD, Wolfram. *Chinese Fables and Parables: A Catalogue.* Taipei: Oriental Cultural Service, 1971. xv, 166 pp. (*Asian Folklore and Social Life Monographs, Vol. XV.*)

Abstracts in English 514 ancient and modern Chinese "yü yen" (fables and allegorical anecdotes) found in three recent collections printed in Taiwan and Communist China. The introduction discusses the sources and makes a comparative analysis of these collections.

400. EDELMAN, Prewitt. "Working Back: The New Physics and Pueblo Mythology." *Southwest Review* (Dallas, Texas), LVIII:3 (Autumn, 1973), 302-306.

Points out curious parallels between theories of contemporary relativist physics and Pueblo Indian emergence myths, space and time concepts, etc.

401. FEER, Michael. "'The Skunk and the Smallpox': Mythology and Historical Reality." *Plains Anthropologist* (Lincoln, Nebraska), XVIII:59 (February, 1973), 33-39.

Establishes the data of an etiological myth collected by Marius Barbeau among the Wyandot Indians in 1911. It deals with the origins and treatment of smallpox and apparently had its origin about 1815 when the Wyandot were at Sandusky, Ohio. Includes bibliography.

402. FERNÁNDEZ, James W. "Equatorial Excursions: The Folklore of Narcotic Inspired Visions in an African Religious Movement." In *African Folklore*. Pp. 341-361.

Shows how the drug-induced visions of the Fang Bwiti cult reflect origin and migratory legends of these people.

403. FERRIS, William R., Jr. "Folklore and Racism." *JFSGW, IV*:1 (Spring, 1973), 1-6.

Seeks to show how folklore reflects attitudes about white-black relationships. Offers examples of stories that show white racism and one example of a story that attests to black resistance to white violence.

404. FERRIS, William R., Jr. "Ray Lum: Muletrader." *NCFJ*, XXI:3 (September, 1973), 105-119.

Presents the transcript of an extended narrative given by Lum, a muletrader and auctioneer from Vicksburg, Mississippi. Includes a preliminary comment on his life and also a photograph.

405. FIORE, Silvestro. "The Western Adventure of Oriental Man: Echoes of Ancient Near Eastern Legends in Medieval Arabic and Celtic Literature." *Studies in Medieval Culture* (Kalamazoo, Michigan), IV/1 (1973), 36-43.

Notes that the oldest myths of the Orient associate the Occident with ideas of the entrance to the Nether World. Finds echoes of such concepts in two widely separated but similar medieval texts: the "City of Brass" tale of the Arabian Nights and the Irish "Imram" of *Maelduin's Voyage*.

406. FRATTO, Toni Flores. "On Going in Circles: A Comment on Köngäs Maranda's 'Five Interpretations.'" *JAF*, LXXXVI:342 (October-December, 1973), 390-391.

Contributes some comments and additional ideas to Elli Köngäs Maranda's "Five Interpretations of a Melanesian Myth" in *JAF*, LXXXVI (1973), 3-13.

407. FROBENIUS, Leo, comp. *African Nights: Black Erotic Folk Tales*. Translated by Peter and Betty Ross. N.Y.: Herder and Herder, 1971. 284 pp.

Presents in English translation forty tales of an erotic nature selected from *Das Schwarze Dekameron*, a collection of African tales made by the German ethnologist Leo Frobenius and published in 1910. Contains a glossary.

408. GARRETT, Roland. "The Notion of Language in Some Kiowa Folktales." *Indian Historian* (San Francisco), V:2 (Summer, 1972), 32-37, 42.

Gives the texts of six Kiowa tales or legends and then analyzes them in order to set forth the subtlety and power of language as used in such oral literature.

409. GASTER, Moses, trans. *The Chronicles of Jerahmeel or The Hebrew Bible Historiale*. N.Y.: Ktav Publ. House, 1971. cxii, 341 pp.

Reprints a translation published in 1899 (London: Oriental Translation Fund) and adds a prolegomenon and bibliography (124 pp.) by Haim Schwarzbaum. Provides a translation into English of Hebrew Apocryphal legend texts that were compiled by Eleasar ben Asher the Levite in the 14th century.

410. GIZELIS, Gregory. "A Neglected Aspect of Creativity of Folklore Performers." *JAF*, LXXXVI:340 (April-June, 1973), 167-172.

Holds that the "real creation" of new stories by a narrator as opposed to "re-creation" and "limited creation" has been neglected by folklorists. Cites examples of real creativity from fieldwork among Greeks in Philadelphia.

411. GONZÁLEZ REBOREDO, José M. *El folklore en los castros*

gallegos. Santiago de Compostela: Universidad de Santiago de Compostela, 1971. 102 pp. (*Monografías de la Universidad de Santiago de Compostela, Vol. V.*)

Studies legends connected with ruins of castles and other fortifications in Incio, Galicia (Spain). Discusses the significance in popular history and mythology of stories about previous inhabitants or builders of the castles and the social function of treasure legends. Presents transcriptions of the legends collected.

412. GRANJA, Fernando de la. "Nuevas notas a un episodio del «Lazarillo de Tormes»." *Al-Andalus* (Madrid-Granada), XXXVI (1971): Fasc. 1, pp. 223-237.

Continuing a longstanding debate about the origins of the "House of Death" episode in the Spanish picaresque novel *Lazarillo de Tormes*, the author adduces new evidence that the story came from Arabic folklore.

413. GREENBERG, Andrea. "Drugged and Seduced: A Contemporary Legend." *NYFQ*, XXIX:2 (June, 1973), 131-158.

Considers the problem of defining legend and then seeks to arrive at a definition by inductive means through analysis of eight texts of a contemporary legend that circulates among female college freshmen and sophomores. It concerns the girl who is drugged and raped at a fraternity party. Gives the texts and notes.

414. GRINDAL, Bruce T. "The Sisala Trickster Tale." *JAF*, LXXXVI:340 (April-June, 1973), 173-175.

Suggests the Sisala children of northern Ghana identify with the trickster in trickster tales.

415. GUIRMA, Frederic. *Tales of Mogho; African Stories from the Upper Volta*. N.Y.: Macmillan, 1971. xii, 113 pp. illus.

Retells in English seven *soalema* (i.e., amusing tales) and one *kibare* (a legend) from Mossi people of West Africa. Contains a glossary and illustrations.

416. HALLENBECK, Cleve, and WILLIAMS, Juanita H. *Legends of the Spanish Southwest*. Ann Arbor: Gryphon Books, 1971. 342 pp. illus.

Reissue of the 1938 edition (Glendale, Calif.: The Arthur H. Clark Co.). Retells colonial Spanish legends of New Mexico, Texas, Arizona, California, etc. An introduction reviews the history of the colonization. Includes a bibliography, illustrations, and a map.

417. HANSEN, William F. *The Conference Sequence: Patterned Narration and Narrative Inconsistency in the Odyssey*. Berkeley: University of California Press, 1972. 61 pp. (*University of California Publications: Classical Studies, VIII.*)

Compares and analyzes conference scenes in Homer's *Odyssey* and argues that the much debated narrative inconsistencies are due to oral composition.

418. HARING, Lee. "A Characteristic African Folktale Pattern." In *African Folklore*. Pp. 165-179.

Studies the motifeme sequences in three African, one Jamaican, and one Afro-American narrative and reviews theories of structural analysis applicable to such texts.

419. HARRIS, Joel Chandler. *Daddy Jake the Runaway and Short Stories Told After Dark by "Uncle Remus."* Freeport, N.Y.: Books for Libraries Press, 1972. 198 pp. illus.

Reissue of the 1889 edition. Contains a short story about a runaway slave and thirteen Uncle Remus stories.

420. HARRIS, Joel Chandler. *Stories of Georgia*. Spartanburg, S.C.: Reprint Co., 1972. 315 pp. illus.

Reissue of the 1896 edition (N.Y.: American Book Co.). Recounts events of Georgia history and legend from the time of discovery and settlement to the Reconstruction Period. Contains illustrations.

421. HEDGES, James S. "Attributive Mutation in Cherokee Natural History Myth." *NCFJ*, XXI:3 (September, 1973), 147-154.

Classifies the means by which animals receive attributes in Cherokee myths collected and published in 1900 by James Mooney. Treats circumstantial, punitive, revenge, design, personal deficiency, reward, and gift mutations.

422. HOGAN, Moreland H., Jr. "A New Analogue of the *Shipman's Tale*." *Chaucer Review* (University Park, Pennsylvania), V (1971):3, pp. 245-246.

Suggests that an obscene joke told by a college student in South Carolina may be a modern-day version of Chaucer's Tale.

423. HUGGINS, Edward. *Blue and Green Wonders, And Other Latvian Tales*. N.Y.: Simon and Schuster, 1971. 128 pp. illus.

Retells ten Latvian wonder tales. An afterword comments upon prevalent themes, beliefs, symbols, and the style of Latvian tales. Drawings are by Owen Wood.

424. HULL, Eleanor, comp. *The Cuchullin Saga in Irish Literature; Being a Collection of Stories Relating to the Hero Cuchullin*. N.Y.: AMS Press, 1972. lxxix, 316 pp.

Reissue of the 1898 edition (London: David Nutt). Presents translations or adaptations of translations of fourteen tales belonging to the Gaelic Cuchullin Cycle. Contains notes to the tales and a lengthy introduction which discusses literary, historical, and mythological aspects of the saga. Includes maps and charts.

425. HURREIZ, Sayyid. "Afro-Arab Relations in the Sudanese Folktale." In *African Folklore*. Pp. 157-163.

Outlines the narrative genres of Sudanese tribes showing that folktales of the Sudan reflect Afro-Arab contact.

426. JAGENDORF, M. A. *Folk Stories of the South*. N.Y.: Vanguard Press, 1972. xx, 355 pp. illus.

A collection of 95 literarily retold tales, anecdotes, myths, etc. gathered in eleven southern states. There are perfunctory notes for each story, but the book is non-scholarly in its overall approach and is intended primarily as entertainment for the general reader.

427. JAMESON, Mrs. [Anna Brownell]. *Legends of the Madonna as Represented in the Fine Arts*. Detroit: Gale Research Co., 1972. lxxv, 344 pp. illus.

Reissue of the New Edition of 1890 (London: Longmans, Green, and Co.). An introduction deals with the general theme of the Virgin Mary in art and then there are sections on "Devotional Subjects" and "Historical Subjects." Certain legendary material enters the discussions, but the book is more about art than about legends. Includes many illustrations.

428. JANSEN, William Hugh. "A Content-Classification of a Random Sample of Legends." *KFQ*, XVI:2 (Summer, 1971), 81-107.

Defines "legend" and "local legend" and among 211 narratives collected in Kentucky distinguishes "purely local legends," "localized legends," and "non-localized narratives." Classifies them according to content (i.e. ghostly manifestations, local characters, origins of names, idioms, family sayings, etc.) giving examples for each category.

429. JANSEN, William Hugh. "The Surpriser Surprised: A Modern Legend." *FForum*, VI:1 (January, 1973), 1-24.

Analyzes 28 U.S. variants of a modern legend about a naked person or persons who are surprised with a party.

430. JASON, Heda. "Structural Analysis and the Concept of the 'Tale-type.'" *ARV, Journal of Scandinavian Folklore* (Stockholm), XXVIII (1972), 36-54.

Examines the consequences of Propp's analysis of folktales for Aarne's concept of a "tale type" by setting forth a structural analysis of fourteen texts of Aarne-Thompson Type 881A and Jason Type No. 881* B. Shows the Aarne's type "disintegrates" under Proppian analysis and proposes the concept of a "tale-field" to reflect the relations between concrete texts. Contains charts.

431. JECH, Jaromír. "A Bohemian Medieval Fable on the Fox and the Pot." In *MLFS*. Pp. 275-289.

Examines and compares four exempla and epic versions of the fable of the fox and the pot in medieval Bohemian manuscripts. Presents the texts in Czech with English translation and in Latin.

432. JEFFREY, Adi-Kent Thomas. *Ghosts in the Valley; True Haunting in the Delaware Valley*. New Hope, Pa.: New Hope Art Shop, 1971. 96 pp.

Retells forty ghost legends from the Delaware Valley of Pennsylvania.

433. JIMÉNEZ BORJA, Arturo. *Imagen del mundo aborigen*. Lima: n.p., 1973. 72 pp. illus.

Offers literarily retold versions of about sixty legends and tales collected in various parts of Peru between 1930 and 1950. An introductory essay discusses the Indian view of the world as seen in such tales and in accounts drawn from early chronicles. Includes some drawings.

434. JUSTIN, Dena. "From Mother Goddess to Dishwasher." *Natural History* (N.Y.), LXXXII:2 (February, 1973), 40-45.

A non-scholarly but entertaining essay which seeks to show how women have been debased and subjugated to men in folk tradition from pre-historic times to the present. Draws mostly upon myths and folktales for evidence.

435. KINCAID, C. A. *Deccan Nursery Tales or Fairy Tales from the South*. Detroit: Grand River Books, 1971. xiii, 135 pp.

Reissue of the 1914 edition (London: Macmillan and Co., Limited). Translates and retells for English readers twenty Marathi tales of Hindu deities.

436. KOTZIN, Michael C. *Dickens and the Fairy Tale*. Bowling Green, Ohio: Bowling Green University Popular Press, 1972. 123 pp. illus.

Examines the influence of fairy tales on the writings of Charles Dickens. Lists published translations into English of folklore collections showing in what form tales were available to the English of Dickens' time.

437. KREISLER, Nicolai Alexander von. "An Aesopic Allusion in the *Merchant's Tale*." *Chaucer Review* (University Park, Pennsylvania), VI:1 (Summer, 1971), 30-43.

Deals with an apparently inexplicable passage of the "Merchant's Tale" which seems to be an allusion to an Aesopic anecdote that Chaucer must have known from oral tradition.

438. KRISS, Marika. *Werewolves, Shapeshifters, and Skinwalkers*. Los Angeles: Sherbourne Press, 1972. 143 pp. illus.

Surveys the history of shapeshifting and beliefs about it in mythology and legend. Includes many legends, but the work is intended for a popular audience.

439. KROEBER, A. L. *More Mohave Myths*. Berkeley: University of California Press, 1972. 182 pp. illus. (*Anthropological Records, Vol. 27.*).

Supplements the author's Mohave myth collections published in 1948 and 1951. Presents the English texts of eleven Mohave myths providing informant data and describing the telling situation as well as analyzing and determining the itinerary of the tales. Contains charts and photographs.

440. KRUGOVOY, George. "A Motif from Old Russian *Vita Sanctorum* in Arthurian Romance." *Canadian Slavonic Papers, Revue Canadienne des Slavists* (Ottawa, Ontario), XV:3 (Autumn, 1973), 351-373.

Compares an episode in *La Queste del Saint Graal* and the story of the murder of Prince Boris as told in three medieval Russian texts. Notes similarities and interrelationships between the two traditions due perhaps to oral transmission.

441. LACOURCIÈRE, Luc. "Le ruban qui rend fort (Conte-type 590)." *Les Cahiers des Dix* (Montreal), XXVI (1971), 235-297.

Said to be about French-Canadian folklore.

442. LANDÍVAR U., Manuel A. "Contribución a mitos y leyendas en el Azuay y Cañar." *Revista del Instituto Azuayo de Folklore* (Cuenca, Ecuador), No. 4 (Noviembre, 1971), 101-120.

Gives thirteen texts of pre-Hispanic myths, legends, and beliefs that were tape recorded in field investigation. Includes informant data and vocabulary in some cases.

443. LANGFORD, Beverly Young. "History and Legend in William Faulkner's 'Red Leaves.'" *Notes on Mississippi Writers* (Hattiesburg, Mississippi), VI:1 (Spring, 1972), 19-24.

Offers some evidence that Faulkner's short story, "Red Leaves," was probably based on an Indian legend.

444. LEEMING, David Adams. *Mythology; The Voyage of the Hero*. Philadelphia, N.Y., Toronto: J. B. Lippincott Company, 1973. vii, 338 pp.

In a popularizing style and approach the author discourses briefly on the nature of myth and surveys myth scholarship in a fairly perfunctory way and then groups in eight sections texts from mostly literary but occasionally folkloric sources. They represent eight stages in man's life (e.g., birth, childhood, trial and quest, death, resurrection, etc.) as viewed in narratives about mythic heroes from all over the world. Each section is followed by a brief commentary on the texts and heroes treated therein. There is a useful bibliography and an index.

445. LEMLEY, Marian. "Two Tales from Lincoln County." *NCFJ*, XXI:1 (April, 1973), 25-26.

Presents the texts of two legends told by Thomas Wehunt of Lincolnton, N.C. One concerns the appearance of a strange light and the other that of a ghost.

446. LEVY, Howard S.,trans. and ed. *Korean Sex Jokes in Traditional Times*. Washington, D.C.: The Warm-Soft Village Press, 1972. 263 pp. (*Sino-Japanese Sexology Classics Series, Vol. III.*)

Offers a collection of over two hundred sex jokes (actually most of them are tales) translated into English. They are taken from documents that date from the late 15th to the 17th century. Includes notes and commentaries, a glossary of sex terms, and an index.

447. LIEBERMAN, José. *Leyendas indígenas*. B.A.: Centro Editor de

América Latina, 1972. 116 pp. illus.

Surveys various aspects of Indian legends in Argentina and comments upon them. Generally the contents of legends are simply summarized and few real texts are given. Includes numerous photographs.

448. LIEBERMAN, Marcia R. "'Some Day My Prince Will Come': Female Acculturation through the Fairy Tale." *College English* (Urbana, Illinois), XXXIV:3 (December, 1972), 383-395.

Holds that fairy tales serve to condition girls to accept traditional sex-typed social roles by acculturating them to be passive and submissive to male dominance.

449. LINTON, E. Lynn. *Witch Stories*. Detroit: Grand River Books, 1971. iv, 428 pp.

Reissue of the 1861 edition (London: Chapman and Hall). Compiles stories about witches in Scotland and England taken from sources in the British Museum and other public libraries. A brief introduction discusses the social background and legendary stories of witchcraft in Scotland.

450. LUNDMAN, Della. "My Kin Knew Jesse James." *AFFword*, I:2 (July, 1971), 18-20.

A verbatim transcription by Colleen Quiner of an interview with Della Lundman of Wyoming, who claims that her grandparents knew Jesse James. Her account about James contains many elements characteristically found in tales about outlaw-heroes.

451. LUOMALA, Katharine. "The Ear-Flyers and Related Motifs in the Gilbert Islands and Its Neighbors." *JAF*, LXXXVI:341 (July-September, 1973), 260-271.

Examines the Ear-Flyer motif contained in narratives from the islands of Beru and Nauru and relates it to the Ear-Sleeper motif found elsewhere. Posits a diffusion of the elements associated with the motif from Melanesia to these Micronesian and Polynesian islands.

452. MACCULLOCH, J. A. *The Childhood of Fiction: A Study of Folk Tales and Primitive Thought*. Ann Arbor, Michigan: Gryphon Books, 1971. xi, 509 pp.

Reissue of the 1905 edition (London: John Murray). Studies folktales as primitive romantic and imaginative literature. Seeks out origins of tales, considers incidents and themes, and attempts to interpret all this. Includes a bibliographical appendix and an index.

453. MACDONALD, Regina Harrison. "The Order of Things: An Analysis of the Ceramics from Santarem, Brazil." *Journal of the Steward Anthropological Society* (Urbana, Illinois), IV:1 (Fall, 1972), 39-57.

Studies some figures on ceramics from Santarem, Brazil, that were produced by the now extinct Tapajo Indians. Seeks to interpret their world view by relating the figures of caymans, toads, birds, etc. to myths still current among the Warrau people, a people of Arawakan and Carib stock. Includes drawings and bibliography.

454. MCNEIL, Norman L. "Origins of 'Sir Patrick Spens.'" In *HandH*. Pp. 65-72.

Reviews the orgin theories for the Scottish ballad of "Sir Patrick Spens" holding that the ballad has undergone many regionalizations.

455. MAKARIUS, Laura. "The Crime of Manabozo." *AA*, LXXV:3 (June, 1973), 663-675.

Analyzes Algonkin Manabozo trickster myths in order to ascertain the message that they are supposed to convey (i.e., ritual violation of taboo to obtain magical power). Includes copious notes and a bibliography.

456. MANDEL, Jerome. "Lancelot and Tristan: 'The Prince as Bird.'" *Studies in Medieval Culture* (Kalamazoo, Michigan), IV/1 (1973), 141-146.

Analyzes Chrétien de Troyes' adaptation of a well known folktale for use in the *Charrette*, where he presents a love tryst between Lancelot and Guenievre.

457. MANRIQUE DE LARA, G. *Leyendas y cuentos populares españoles*. Barcelona: Editorial Bruguera, 1971. 223 pp.

Retells 25 legends and 26 tales from Spanish tradition. Also discusses genre differences, qualities of narrators, literary worth of such narratives, etc.

458. MARANDA, Elli Köngäs. "Five Interpretations of a Melanesian Myth." *JAF*, LXXXVI:339 (January-March, 1973), 3-13.

Gives the text of a Melanesian myth and interprets it in terms of myth-and-ritual theory, cultural reflection, Malinowskian analysis, Freudian and Jungian symbolism, and structuralism. Shows the interpretations to be complementary to one another.

459. MARANDA, Pierre, comp. *Mythology: Selected Readings*. Harmondsworth, England, and Baltimore: Penguin Books, 1972. 320 pp.

Selects from previously published articles and books significant studies of myth published between 1923 and 1969 by many scholars. Considers metaphor, myth and language, field studies of myth, myths in societies and cultures, and the semantics of myth. Contains a bibliography.

460. MARHOEFER, Barbara. *Witches, Whales, Petticoats and Sails: Misadventures from Three Centuries of Long Island History*. Port Washington, N.Y.: I. J. Friedman Division of Kennikat Press, 1971. xiii, 206 pp. illus.

Creates from historical accounts stories about people and their lives as soldiers, sailors, etc. on Long Island from the Colonial and Revolutionary period to modern times. Some of the events are told as legends of the area, but the author here tries to "correct" inaccurate traditional accounts.

461. MATTHEWS, Cornelius. *The Enchanted Moccasins and Other Legends of the Americans* [sic] *Indians*. N.Y.: AMS Press, 1970. vi, 338 pp. illus.

Reissue of the third edition (N.Y.: G.P. Putnam's Sons). Contains 26 literarily retold tales and legends based upon the compilation originally made by Henry R. Schoolcraft.

462. MAYNADIER, Gustavus Howard. *The Wife of Bath's Tale: Its Sources and Analogues*. N.Y.: AMS Press, 1972. xii, 222 pp.

Reissue of the 1901 edition (London: David Nutt). Studies English analogues in such forms as ballad, tale, and romance and investigates Irish, Norse, French, and German parallel incidents to Chaucer's *Wife of Bath's Tale*.

463. MILLER, Elaine K. *Mexican Folk Narrative from the Los Angeles Area*. Austin and London: University of Texas Press, 1973. xx, 388 pp. illus. (*Publications of the American Folklore Society, Memoir Series, Vol. 56*.)

An exemplary collection of orally collected legends and tales gathered in 1966-1967 in and around Los Angeles. Sixty-two legend texts are given under the following headings: Religious Narratives (9 texts), The Return of the Dead (24 texts), Buried Treasures (8 texts), *Duendes* (7 texts), and Miscellaneous Legendary Narratives (5 texts). Twenty-two additional texts of traditional tales are also provided, most of them Tales of Magic. Each large section is preceded by a scholarly commentary and individual texts are accompanied by collecting data, a summary of tale content in English, and analysis of tale type and motif numbers. There is also a section dedicated to Biographies of Informants and another that contains indexes of tale types and motifs along with a vocabulary. Finally, there is an exhaustive bibliography.

464. MILLER, Francis Trevelyan. *Hero Tales from American Life*. Ann Arbor: Gryphon Books, 1971. xv, 454 pp. illus.

Reissue of the 1909 edition (N.Y.: Christian Herald). Relates one hundred stories from American legend and history which tell of an act of bravery on the part of an individual. The tales are designed to promote patriotism.

465. MITCHELL, Roger. "Micronesian Folklore and Culture Change." *JFI*, IX:1 (June, 1972), 28-44.

Compares previously collected and recently obtained folktales, legends, and myths from various peoples of the Micronesian Islands and shows the significance and function of folklore to the younger generation in a technologically advancing society.

466. MURDOCH, Brian. "The River that Stopped Flowing: Folklore and Biblical Typology in the Apocryphal Lives of Adam and Eve." *SFQ*, XXXVII:1 (March, 1973), 37-51.

Examines the motif of the Jordan River's stopping its flow as Adam does penance in the river, a motif found in various Jewish and Christian texts examined here that date from the 1st century B.C. to the 14th century A.D. Treats problems raised by the appearance of this phenomenon at the penance of Adam and also at the nativity of Christ.

467. MUSICK, Ruth Ann. "The Helpful Ghost." *NCFJ*, XXI:2 (May, 1973), 55-57.

Presents the texts of three legends from West Virginia about helpful ghosts. Holds that in most legends ghosts are helpful rather than harmful to living man.

468. NAITO, Hiroshi. *Legends of Japan*. Rutland, Vt.: C. E. Tuttle Co., 1972. 111 pp. illus.

Retells 22 tales and humorous anecdotes selected from the Japanese *Konjaku Monogatari* and other literary collections.

469. NEWBIGGING, Thomas. *Fables and Fabulists: Ancient and Modern*. Ann Arbor, Michigan: Gryphon Books, 1971. 152 pp.

Reissue of the 1895 edition (London: Elliot Stock). Defines and outlines characteristics of the fable, concentrating upon Aesop's Fables and stories about Aesop. Also discusses Hindu, Arabian, and Persian fables and examines the work of European fabulists.

470. NEWCOMB, Franc (Johnson). *Navajo Bird Tales Told By Hosteen Clah Chee*. Wheaton, Illinois: Theosophical Pub. House, 1970. xiii, 125 pp. illus.

Retells for children sixteen Navajo folktales collected by the author. Illustrations were drawn by Na-Ton-Sa-Ka.

471. NICOLSON, John. *Some Folk-Tales and Legends of Shetland*. Norwood, Pa.: Norwood Editions, 1973. 93 pp.

Reissue of the 1920 edition (Edinburgh: Thomas Allan & Sons). Contains literary versions of folktales and other folklore. There are sections on The Trows (i.e., the *peerie* or little folk), Traditions and Legends, Superstitions, Guddiks, etc. Includes some riddles and a glossary.

472. NOSS, Philip A. "Description in Gbaya Literary Art " In *African Folklore*. Pp. 73-101.

Describes and provides examples of narrative devices, including ideophones, names, imagery, narrative description, and allusion used by the Gbaya people of Cameroun and the Central African Republic. Also gives suggestions for translating such expressions.

473. ODUM, Howard Washington. *Cold Blue Moon: Black Ulysses Afar Off*. N.Y.: Kraus Reprint, 1972. 278 pp.

Reissue of the 1931 edition (Indianapolis: The Bobbs-Merrill Company). Gives an impressionistic description of certain aspects of slavery and changes in the South during and after the Civil War. Incorporates occasional anecdotes, ghost stories, and other Negro narratives written in dialect form.

474. OINAS, Felix. "Tarinat kansan itsenähautaamisesta" ["Legends of Peoples' Self Burial"]. In *Kalevalaseuran Vuosikirja, Vol. LIII: Karjala—Idän ja lännen silta*. Porvoo and Helsinki, 1973. Pp. 137-145.

Treats migratory legends told in Karelia, Russia, and Siberia, about the self-burial of the Chuds, "Pans," "Volots," etc. for the purpose of escaping from approaching enemies, mostly Russians. Abyssinian parallels are given.

475. O SÚILLEABHÁIN, Seán. "Etiological Stories in Ireland." In *MLFS*. Pp. 257-274.

Presents abstracts of seventeen origin legends found in Ireland but not purely of Irish origin or provenance.

476. OWEN, Elias. *Welsh Folk-lore: A Collection of the Folk-tales and Legends of North Wales*. Norwood, Pa.: Norwood Editions, 1973. xii, 359 pp.

Reissue of the 1896 edition. (Oswestry and Wrexham: Woodall, Minshall, and Co.). Presents a collection of legends and tales collected from old people and clergy in Welsh parishes. Includes stories about fairies, mythic animals, Satan, ghosts, witches and conjurors, superstitions about animals, death portents, and charms.

477. "The Oxford Solar Myth: A Contribution to Comparative Mythology." *FForum*, VI:2 (April, 1973), 68-74.

Reprints an unsigned article printed in an 1870 issue of *Kottabos* published by Trinity College, University of Dublin, and supposedly written by Rev. Dr. Richard Frederick Littledale. Satirizes the solar mythology theory of Max Müller by analyzing philologically the name of Max Müller and other scholars in terms of a solar myth.

478. PAREDES-CANDIA, Antonio. *Cuentos populares bolivianos*. La Paz: Ediciones Isla, 1973. 391 pp.

Contains an introduction which discusses the folktale as a subject for scientific study by folklorists and then offers texts of folktales from many areas of Bolivia. Includes legends and traditions, animal tales, ghost stories, tales of Urdimalas, outlaw tales, etc.

479. PARKER, Everett. *The Secret of No Face (An Ireokwa Epic)*. Healdsburg, California: Native American Publishing Co., 1972. 174 pp. illus.

Retells literarily a series of myths and legends that are said to come from orally preserved narrative tradition of the Seneca Indians They are the story of Cornhusk Doll's passage through life and her discovering the secret of her place in the universe.

480. PARKS, Lillian V. "Black Jests from Virginia." *JFSGW*, IV:1 (Spring, 1973), 18-20.

Offers eight orally collected humorous stories gathered from a black informant in Newport News, Virginia.

481. PAULL, Michael R. "The Influence of the Saint's Legend Genre in the *Man of Law's Tale.*" *Chaucer Review* (University Park, Pennsylvania), V (1971):3, pp. 179-194.

Shows how Chaucer adapts the saint's-legend genre in order to create an exemplary tale that illustrates a God-ordered Christian universe.

482. PEARCE, T. M. *Stories of the Spanish Southwest: Cuentos de los niños chicanos. In English and Spanish.* Albuquerque, New Mexico: Published by the author, 1973. x, 54 pp.

Six tales that are told among Chicanos in the southwest. Texts are given in English and Spanish on facing pages. Translations are by Catherine Delgado Espinosa.

483. PEARSALL, Erin Anne. "The Legend of Swann's Cut." *NCFJ*, XXI:2 (May, 1973), 64-69.

Discusses the evolution and function of one version of an explanatory legend current in Swann's Point, North Carolina. The legend contains the Thompson motif of a "race won by trickery" (J11).

484. PELLIZZARO, Siro M., ed. and trans. *Cultura shuar, una civilización desconocida.* Cuenca, Ecuador: Editorial "Don Bosco," 197?. 82 pp. illus.

Literarily retold myths and legends of many types but mostly origin myths gathered and translated apparently by a missionary among an Indian group of eastern Ecuador. No information is given about the group nor are any sources indicated. Includes numerous drawings that illustrate the myths.

485. PENNINGTON, Lee, and PENNINGTON, Joy, colls. "Two Tales from Bloody Harlan." *Appalachian Journal* (Boone, North Carolina), I:2 (Spring, 1973), 139-142.

Gives texts of two orally collected monster tales from Harlan, Kentucky, "Monster on Black Mountain" and "The Giant Man."

486. PENTIKÄINEN, Juha. "Belief, Memorate, and Legend." *FForum*, VI:4 (October, 1973), 217-241.

Prints a translation by Josephine Lombardo and W. K. McNeil of "Grenzprobleme zwischen Memorat und Sage" from *Temenos,* 3 (1968), 136-167. Comprehensively reviews and evaluates Scandinavian and Central European scholarship that distinguishes between legend and memorate. Contains charts.

487. POSTON, Glenda. "Tall Tales from Perquimans County." *NCFJ*, XXI:1 (April, 1973), 40-47.

Presents a transcript of several tall tales told by Ray Hollowell of Bear Swamp, North Carolina.

488. POTTER, Murray Anthony. *Sohrab and Rustem: The Epic Theme of a Combat between Father and Son; A Study of Its Genesis and Use in Literature and Popular Tradition.* N.Y.: A. M. S. Press, 1972. xii, 234 pp.

Reissue of the 1902 edition (London: David Nutt). Studies the father vs. son theme in art literature, popular literature, folklore, American Indian tales, and other sources from all over the world.

489. RANKE, Kurt. "Oral and Literary Continuity." *FForum*, VI:3 (July, 1973), 127-138.

A translation by Josephine Lombardo, W. K. McNeil, and Richard C. Sweterlitsch of an article in *Kontinuität. Festschrift für Hans Moser*, ed. by Hermann Bausinger and Wolfgang Brückner (Berlin: Erich Schmidt,

1969). Ranke defends his position that there is a definite continuity of tradition, citing legends which support the contention.

490. REICH, Rosalie, trans. *Tales of Alexander the Macedonian*. N.Y.: KTAV Publishing House, 1972. xiii, 143 pp.

Presents in Hebrew transcription and English translation legends about Alexander the Great from *Sefer Hazichronot*, a collection compiled by Eleazer, son of Asher ha-Levi about 1325 A. D. Notes analogues in Middle English literature and parallels between Solomon and Alexander in Hebrew legend. Identifies Thompson motif numbers and offers a bibliography and glossary.

491. RÍO, Daniel A. del. "The Princess and the Three Volcanoes." *Américas*, XXV:5 (May, 1973), 8-9.

A literary retelling of an Inca legend about the origin of three volcanoes and an island on the border between Bolivia and Peru (i.e., Illimani, Mururata, Huayna Potosí, and the island of Sumac Huayta in Lake Titicaca).

492. RIVERA DE BIANCHI, Mabel. "Mitología de los pueblos del Chaco, según visión de los autores de los siglos XVII y XVIII." *AI*, XXXIII:3 (Julio-Septiembre, 1973), 695-733.

Surveys various myths from the Chaco region of Argentina and Paraguay and notes versions of these which are to be found in five early chronicles of the area. They deal with stars and the heavens, the destruction of the world, supernatural beings, etc. Includes a chart and bibliography.

493. ROBE, Stanley L., ed. *Amapa Storytellers*. Berkeley, Los Angeles, London: University of California Press, 1972. xiv, 108 pp. illus. (*University of California Publications, Folklore Studies:25*.)

Offers fifteen orally collected texts of folktales gathered in 1959 in Amapa, Nayarit (Mexico). An introduction gives information about the village, its inhabitants, tale-telling customs, and informants. Texts are accompanied by brief summaries of their content in English along with detailed notes that identify tale types, indicate motif numbers, and give leads to other versions of each tale. There is an extensive bibliography, and registers of tale types and motifs as well as a vocabulary are provided.

494. ROBE, Stanley L. *Index of Mexican Folktales, Including Narrative Texts from Mexico, Central America, and the Hispanic United States*. Berkeley, Los Angeles, London: University of California Press, 1973. xxiii, 276 pp.

An excellent and important index of approximately 150 *Hispanic* tale texts based upon the Aarne-Thompson system of tale-type classification. Tales of purely indigenous origin are not treated. Includes an introduction, bibliography, and an index of the classification of tales which makes up the body of the book (pp. 1-228).

495. RODRÍGUEZ DE LA FUENTE, Mercedes. "Historia y leyenda de San Román de Moroso." In *PIHS(I)*, 131-141.

Along with some historical data about the monastery of San Román de Moroso in the province of Santander (Spain), the author offers texts of two local legends about the monastery.

496. ROSENBERG, Bruce A. "*The Cherry-Tree Carol* and *The Merchant's Tale*." *Chaucer Review* (University Park, Pennsylvania), V (1971):4, pp. 264-276.

Points to possible influence of the story known as *The Cherry-Tree Carol* upon *The Merchant's Tale* and indicates the forms in which Chaucer might have known it.

497. RUSSELL, Nellie N. *Gleanings From Chinese Folklore*. Detroit: Singing Tree Press, 1972. 169 pp. illus.

Reissue of the 1915 edition (N.Y.: Fleming H. Revell Co.). Contains eleven Chinese tales recorded by Nellie N. Russell, an American missionary to Peking in the early 1900's. Also includes some of her personal remembrances about life in China.

498. SALOMON, Brownell. "'Don Diego' and the Befouling of St. Paul's Cathedral." *American Notes and Queries*, (New Haven, Connecticut), X:9 (May, 1972), 138-142.

Speculates on the origin of the 17th-century English joke tradition that dramatists often used about a Spaniard who defiled St. Paul's Cathedral by defecating in it. Suggests that Don Diego never existed and ties the story to probable oral folklore of the period.

499. SAUGNIEUX, J., ed. *Légendes du desert chilien*. Recueillies par B. Tolosa, traduites et presentées par J. Saugnieux. Paris: Ed. Hispano-Americanas, 1973. 47 pp. (*Publications de l'Institut d'Etudes Brésiliennes et Latino-Américaines de l'Université Lyon, II*.)

A translation of Bernardo Tolosa, *Leyendas de tierra adentro* (Antofagasta: Imp. El Salar, 1970, 43 pp.). Contains eighteen texts of tales and legends from the Atacama region of Chile.

500. SCHEUB, Harold. "The Art of Nongenile Mazithathu Zenani, A Gcaleke Ntsomi Performer." In *African Folklore*. Pp. 115-142.

Examines the narrative techniques and artistry of a South African Xhosa storyteller and diviner Nongenile Mazithathu Zenani. Focuses upon her performance of several dramatic narratives called "ntsomi."

501. SCHMITZ, Nancy. *La Mensongère (conte-type 710)*. Québec: Les Presses de l'Université Laval, 1972. xiv, 310 pp. (*Les Archives de Folklore, 14*.).

Offers a historico-geographic study in depth of Aarne-Thompson tale types 710A and 710B in Canada and elsewhere in the world (mainly Ireland). Includes voluminous appendices containing tale texts and a questionnaire used in research, a copious bibliography, a glossary, an index, and maps.

502. SCHWARZ, Herbert T. *Elik and Other Stories of the MacKenzie Eskimos*. Toronto: McClelland and Stewart, 1970. 79 pp. illus.

Presents in English ten legends and tales recently collected from seven MacKenzie Eskimo informants. Discusses the lives of the story-tellers and the circumstances of the collector's finding them. Presents a photograph of each.

503. SCHWARZBAUUM, Haim. "The Zoologically Tinged Stages of Man's Existence." *Folklore Research Center Studies* (Hebrew University of Jerusalem), III (1972), 267-290.

Studies versions of AT Types 173 and 828, "Men and Animals Readjust Span of Life," found in Hebrew, modern Jewish, Spanish, Bulgarian, Polish, and ancient Greek folklore and literature.

504. SEVERS, J. Burke. *The Literary Relationships of Chaucer's* Clarke's Tale. Hamden, Connecticut: Archon Books, 1972. ix, 371 pp.

Reissue of the 1942 edition (New Haven: Yale University Press). A scholarly literary study of the Griselda story and its sources, this work takes note in passing of some folktale sources of Chaucer's tale.

505. SHAW, Mary, ed. *According to Our Ancestors; Folk Texts from Guatemala and Honduras*. Norman, Oklahoma: Summer Institute of

Linguistics, University of Oklahoma, 1971. 510 pp. illus.

Offers a collection of texts of tales, legends, and first-person accounts collected by eighteen linguistic teams working in Guatemala and Honduras. Most are given in various Indian languages with a free translation into English. There are some comparative notes in an introduction and bibliography. Most of the texts should be of interest to folklorists.

506. SIGNORILE, Vito. "Acculturation and Myth." *Anthropological Quarterly* (Washington, D.C.), XLVI:2 (April, 1973), 117-134.

An anthropologist considers various interpretations of myths and explores their function as part of the acculturative-assimilative processes for individuals and for groups. Distinguishes different types of "validation" within this context. Includes notes and bibliography.

507. SIMON, Bill. "The Time We Hung the Indian." *AFFword*, II:3 (October, 1972), 7-10.

A personal narrative about participation in a hanging that took place on the Yavapai Indian Reservation near Prescott, Arizona, in 1929. The text is transcribed in oral style and has a few folkloric elements.

508. SIMPSON, Jacqueline, ed. and trans. *Icelandic Folktales and Legends*. Berkeley and Los Angeles: University of California Press, 1972. viii, 206 pp.

Presents 85 Icelandic folk legends and tales in English translation selected mainly from the first three chapters of Jón Árnason's *Islenzkar Þjóðögur og Aefintýri*. Notes the earliest known occurences in Iceland of particular stories and gives Aarne-Thompson and Christiansen type numbers. Contains a bibliography.

509. SKINNER, Charles M. *Myths and Legends of Our New Possessions and Protectorate*. Ann Arbor, Michigan: Gryphon Books, 1971. 354 pp.

Reissue of the 1900 edition (Philadelphia: L. B. Lippincott). Assembles and rewrites many tales, legends, myths, historical accounts, etc. from various places in the Caribbean and other parts of Spanish America, Hawaii, the Philippines, and other islands of the Pacific Ocean. The work is very unscholarly and no sources or bibliography are given.

510. SMITH, Jo Sherrin. "Two Legends from Western North Carolina." *NCFJ*, XXI:1 (April, 1973), 35-36.

Relates two legends heard in various versions from residents of western North Carolina. One concerns the treasure left behind after a post-Civil War "kingdom" of blacks broke up. The other concerns a hunting cabin ghost in the Pisgah National Forest.

511. SOLAND, Craig. "Ghost Stories from Cottage II." *AFFword*, III:2 (July, 1973), 1-24.

Offers 36 texts of tales orally collected from five informants aged 12 to 16 of Anglo, Negro, and Mexican-American backgrounds who were inmates at the Arizona Youth Center, a juvenile detention facility in Tucson, Arizona. There are devil stories, ghost stories, strange animal tales, and some versions of *La Llorona* (i.e., the Crying Woman tale of Mexican tradition). The author provides analysis (includes Thompson motif numbers) and commentary.

512. SORUCO, Cristina. "La narrativa popular de Valle Grande (Provincia de Jujuy)." *Etnía* (Olivarría, Argentina), No. 13 (Enero-Junio, 1971), 5-24; No. 14 (Julio-Diciembre, 1971), 20-38.

Transcriptions of 42 tales of various kinds orally collected in the towns of Valle Grande and Valle Colorado, Jujuy (Argentina). Aarne-Thompson motif numbers and informant data are provided.

513. SPERRY, Margaret, trans. *Scandinavian Stories*. N.Y.: Franklin Watts, 1971. 287 pp.

An anthology of literarily translated and retold tales, some of them folktales, from the five Scandinavian countries. Intended for general readers, young and old alike.

514. STAHL, Sandra. "Structuralism and Three Finnish Runes." *FForum*, VI:1 (January, 1973), 25-39.

Argues for the recognition and study of structural pattern in folk narrative genres and charts the structure of three Finnish runes using a modification of the model of Claude Brémond. Contains charts and a bibliography.

515. STANSEL, David B., Jr. "Unique Experiences at the Maco Light." *NCFJ*, XXI:1 (April, 1973), 18-22.

Relates six versions of a legend about the appearance of a ghostly lantern on the railroad tracks near Maco, North Carolina.

516. STERN, S.M., and WALZER, Sofie, trans. *Three Unknown Buddhist Stories in an Arabic Version*. Columbia, S.C.: University of South Carolina Press, 1971. 38 pp.

Presents in Arabic text and English translation three stories from Ibn Bābūya's excerpt of the Bombay text of *The Book of Balawhar and Būdāsf*. Traces the stories' translation history and shows the transfer to the West into Christian tradition of these Buddha legends.

517. STEVENS, James R. *Sacred Legends of the Sandy Lake Cree*. Toronto: McClelland and Stewart, 1971. xii, 144 pp. illus.

Presents rewritten legends of the Anishinabek Indians of Northwestern Ontario. Also includes customs and superstitions, some tales, and a discussion of the history and life of these Cree Indians. Drawings are by Carl Ray.

518. STONE, James H. "Lamar Fontaine's Civil War Tales." *TFSB*, XXXIX:4 (December, 1973), 107-110.

Discusses and considers the authenticity of stories about the legendary exploits of Lamar Fontaine, a Confederate soldier from Texas and Mississippi. Reprints a New York *Sun* reporter's interview with Fontaine as it appeared in the *Daily Clarion-Ledger* of Jackson, Miss., on April 11, 1896.

519. STROSS, Brian. "Social Structure and Role Allocation in Tzeltal Oral Literature." *JAF*, LXXXVI:340 (April-June, 1973), 95-113.

Demonstrates how the social structure of the Tenejapa Tzeltal of Chiapas, Mexico, is reflected directly, not symbolically, in their oral literature. Contains the translated texts of ten stories. Includes photographs.

520. STOUFF, Faye, and TWITTY, W. Bradley. *Sacred Chitimacha Indian Beliefs*. Pompano Beach, Florida: Twitty and Twitty, Inc., 1971. 79 pp. illus.

Said to contain 21 myths and two poems orally collected from Chitimacha Indian informants of south-central Louisiana.

521. STURDZA, Iona, comp. *Fairy Tales and Legends from Romania*, trans. by Iona Sturdza and others. N.Y.: Twayne Publishers, 1972. 333 pp. illus.

Presents in English translation thirteen folktales and six stories written in folktale style selected from collections of Romanian folktales and literature.

522. SULLIVAN, Philip E. "Buh Rabbit: Going through the Changes." *Studies in Black Literature* (Fredericksburg, Virginia), IV:2 (Summer, 1973), 28-32.

Seeks to interpret the characters of Uncle Remus stories and of their analogs in African folklore in terms of black psychological responses to black social conditions in the U.S.

523. SÜMER, Faruk, UYSAL, Ahmet E., and WALKER, Warren S., trans. and eds. *The Book of Dede Korkut, A Turkish Epic*. Austin and London: University of Texas Press, 1972. xxiii, 212 pp. illus.

The first English translation of an epic about the Oghuz, a Turkish people. It dates from no later than 1332, comprises a prologue and twelve legends mostly in prose but containing some verse, and is based on traditional materials. The translators-editors provide an introduction, notes, and a bibliography. There are photographs and a map.

524. TAYLOR, Archer. "The Anecdote: A Neglected Genre." In *MLFS*. Pp. 223-228.

Reviews known collections and studies of the anecdote and distinguishes it from other genres.

525. TAYLOR, Deborah. "Traditional Tales from Salter Path." *NCFJ*, XXI:1 (April, 1973), 10-14.

Presents the texts of four stories, including one ghost legend and two local seacoast legends, told by David Merle of Salter Path, Carteret County, N.C.

526. TETEL, Marcel. *Marguerite de Navarre's* Heptameron: *Themes, Language, and Structure*. Durham, North Carolina: Duke University Press, 1973. 217 pp.

A highly literary study of the *Heptameron*, which is an important 16th-century French work that often draws on folk narrative tradition. In this study, however, little attention is paid to the folkloristic aspects of the work.

527. THOMPSON, Stith. "Unfinished Business: The Folktale." In *MLFS*. Pp. 213-221.

Discusses methods of studying folktales focusing especially upon problems of comparative historic-geographic study.

528. TRAVELLER BIRD. *The Path to Snowbird Mountain: Cherokee Legends by Traveller Bird (Tsisghwanai)*. N.Y.: Farrar, Straus and Giroux, 1972. 87 pp. illus.

Retells sixteen legends and stories of the Eastern Cherokee Indians.

529. UTLEY, Francis Lee. "Five Genres in the Clerk's Tale." *Chaucer Review* (University Park, Pa.), VI:3 (Winter, 1972), 198-228.

A literary analysis of the Griselda tale as told by Chaucer, but the author ties the story to folktale sources (Aarne-Thompson tale type 425) as well as literary ones.

530. VANCE, Zebulon Baird. "Indian Legend." *NCFJ*, XXI:2 (May, 1973), 51-52.

Reprints a retelling of a Cherokee serpent-killing legend published in the *North Carolina University Magazine* in March of 1852 by Zebulon Vance, a popular military and political figure of North Carolina.

531. VIGGIANO ESAIN, Julio. *Leyendas cordobesas..* Córdoba, Argentina: Dirección General de Historia, Letras y Ciencias, 1970. 124 pp. illus.

Contains 127 literary versions of legends from the Córdoba region of Argentina grouped into three categories: cosmogonical, heroic, and etiological legends.

532. VON FRANZ, Marie Louise. *An Introduction to the Interpretation of Fairy Tales*. N.Y.: Spring Publications, 1970. 73 pp.

Examines fairy tales, legends, and myths as archetypal stories, outlines a method of psychological interpretation of fairy tales, and analyzes some of them.

533. WALKUP, Lucy. "A Collection of Folklore from the Flagstaff, Arizona, Area." *AFFword*, II:4 (January, 1973), 29-40.

Offers texts of orally collected folklore. There are sections on tall tales, folk etymologies for place names, stories of and about Indians (i.e., origin myths, legends, etc.), stories of cock fighting, and miscellaneous tales. Informant data are given.

534. WILGUS, D.K., and ROSENBERG, Bruce A. "A Modern Medieval Story: 'The Soldier's Deck of Cards.'" In *MLFS*. Pp. 291-303.

Studies recent versions of Aarne-Thompson Type 1613 in church sermons and on recordings in the U.S. Distinguishes different versions of the exemplum and refers to its history in European tradition. Presents the texts of several sermons and recordings.

535. WILKERSON, Frank. "The Haunted Tribe." *Alberta Historical Review* (Calgary, Alberta), XX:2 (Spring, 1972), 3-12.

A story, published originally in 1880, that relates an encounter with six Indians on horseback who are said to be spirits of some Cree Indians murdered by Blackfeet.

536. WOODLEY, Edward C. *Legends of French Canada*. N.Y.: Benjamin Blom, Inc., 1971. 105 pp. illus.

Reissue of the 1931 edition (Toronto). Retells twelve French-Canadian legends selected from previous collections in French and English.

537. YANAN, Eileen. *Coyote and the Colville*. Omak, Washington: St. Mary Mission, 1971. 76 pp. illus.

Contains a collection of Okanagon Indian legends about the trickster Coyote. They are from the Colville Indian Reservation. Includes maps.

538. ZÁRATE PLASENCIA, Fidel A. *Los cuentos contumacinos del tío Lino*. Lima: La Floralia del Inca, 1970. 81 pp.

A collection of literary tales of popular flavor which I list only because a few of them are versions of genuine folktales and might be of interest to folktale scholars (e.g., the Tar-Baby story, some animal tales, etc.).

539. ZELLER, Joan. "The Legends of John Wilhelm." *JOFS*, II:2 (August, 1973), 43-46.

Gives six orally collected legends that relate how a child named John Wilhelm died in 1875. The cause of death seems to vary in accordance with the need to exercise control over the behavior of children in differing situations.

C   SONG–GAME–DANCE

[See also numbers 6, 11, 22, 23, 39, 54, 66, 76, 78, 89, 92, 98, 99, 100, 102, 106, 109, 119, 122, 126, 128, 130, 138, 139, 141, 142, 149, 153, 161, 163, 164, 165, 167, 173, 175, 176, 177, 179, 187, 189, 191, 200, 202, 203, 207, 210, 211, 213, 216, 222, 223, 229, 230, 232, 233, 235, 238, 246, 248, 255, 256, 257, 259, 263, 266, 268, 273, 275, 277, 280, 281, 282, 290, 293, 295, 296, 304, 306, 307, 309, 310, 311, 313, 314, 315, 316, 318, 319, 331, 332, 334, 340, 348, 349, 350, 354, 462, 519, 523, 763, 808, 812, 817, 825, 832, 843, 861, 863, 893, 917, 922, 935, 939, 947, 1045, 1055, 1069, 1093, 1149, 1153, 1210, 1227.]

540. ABERCRONBY, John. *The Pre-and Proto-Historic Finns, Both Eastern and Western, with the Magic Songs of the West Finns.* 2 vols. N.Y.: AMS Press, 1972, illus.

Reissue of the 1898 edition (London: D. Nutt). Volume One reconstructs Finnish pre- and proto-history from Neolithic times to the Middle Ages by means of craniology, archaeology, ethnography, and philology, and analyzes the beliefs of the Western Finns. Volume Two contains a literal translation into English of 639 magic songs or charms from the *Suomen Kánsan muinaisia Loitsurunoja* edited by Lönnrot. Contains maps, a bibliography, and numerous illustrations.

541. ABERNETHY, Francis Edward. "Singing All Day and Dinner on the Ground." In *ORTF*. Pp. 131-140.

Discusses the themes of the music and the singing traditions of Sacred Harp singers in an East Texas community. Contains photographs.

542. ABRAMS, W. Amos. "Della Adams Bostic: Sweet Singer of Old Songs." *NCFJ*, XXI:3 (September, 1973), 132-146.

Reports the discovery of an 1824 manuscript of songs and tells of meeting Della Adams Bostic, a singer of folksongs, in Mooresboro, N.C., in 1938. Gives the words of seven of her songs and includes photographs.

543. ABRAMS, W. Amos. "Pure Coincidence—If Not, Why Not?" *NCFJ*, XXI:4 (November, 1973), 177-180.

Relates how an 1825 manuscript of a Virginia version of "Sweet Sally" (Child 295) happened to fall into the author's possession. Gives the text (no music) of the song in question.

544. ADAMS, Kenneth. "The Metrical Irregularity of the *Cantar de Mío Cid*: A Restatement Based on the Evidence of Names, Epithets and Some Other Aspects of Formulaic Diction." *Bulletin of Hispanic Studies* (Liverpool, England), XLIX:2 (April, 1972), 109-119.

Reviews scholarship about the regularity or irregularity of meter in the Spanish epic, the *Cantar de mío Cid*, discusses problems related thereto, and considers the possibility of using supposedly regular forms of formulaic diction like names or epithets to attack the problem. However, these too seem to be syllabically irregular.

545. AKPABOT, Samuel. "Standard Drum Patterns in Nigeria." *Journal of the New African Literature and the Arts* (N.Y.), Nos. 13-14

(1972 [pub. September, 1973]), 49-52.

Describes drums and the composition of drum orchestras used for ritual worship and festival occasions. Briefly analyzes drum rhythms in different parts of Nigeria.

546. ÁLVAREZ BLÁZQUEZ, Xosé M.ª *Cantares de cego*. Vigo: Edicións Castrelos, 1972. 48 pp. illus.

Offers a collection of ballad texts and other songs from Galicia of the kind that are sung by blind street-singers. Includes reproductions of the illustrations that head the broadsides of chapbooks that contain texts. There is also a prologue that studies this genre of popular song.

547. ANDERSON, John Q. "'The Gatesville Murder': The Origin and Evolution of a Ballad." In *HandH*. Pp. 73-81.

Compares two versions of a ballad written about a murder in Gatesville, Texas, in 1899. Examines the facts behind the ballad and the process of ballad making. Presents the words of both versions.

548. ANDERSON, John Q. "'Miller Boy', One of the First and Last of the Play-Party Games." *NCFJ*, XXI:4 (November, 1973), 171-176.

Gives words and music of "Miller Boy" as the author knew it in play-parties in the Texas Panhandle as late as the mid-1930's. Describes typical play-parties of that period and the changing circumstances that led to their decline.

549. ARMISTEAD, S. G. "A Mozarabic Ḫarǧa and a Provençal Refrain." *Hispanic Review* (Philadelphia), XLI:2 (Spring, 1973), 416-417.

Calls attention to a refrain in an old Provençal poem that appears to be derived from a Mozarabic *ḫarǧa* If this is so, the lines represent an unusual echo of popular poetry in this kind of exquisitely artistic troubadour verse.

550. ARMISTEAD, Samuel G., HASSAN, Iacob M., and SILVERMAN, Joseph H. "La *Literatura oral del ladino* de Damián Alonso García: sobre una reciente chapucería romancística." *Sefarad*, XXXII (1972):2, pp. 451-474.

A scholarly review-article that in masterful fashion documents the unscholarly methods and questionable procedures found in Alonso García's recent work on Judeo-Spanish ballads.

551. ASCH, Moses, DUNSON, Josh, and RAIM, Ethel, eds. *Anthology of American Folk Music*. N.Y.: Oak Publications, 1973. 118 pp. illus.

Offers melodic and textual transcriptions of 48 songs from a Folkways recording entitled *Anthology of American Folk Music*. The recordings were originally made in the early 1920's by such artists as Uncle Dave Macon, the Carter family, and others. Also includes interviews with Moses Asch and Frank Walker.

552. AVERILL, Patricia. "Media Review: Delta International Records." *JOFS*, II:2 (August, 1973), 53-55.

Discusses the place of polka music in folk tradition and identifies record companies, mostly small ones, that produce polka records.

553. BABAD, Harry, comp. *Roll Me Over*. N.Y.: Oak Publications, 1972. 143 pp. illus.

Gives words, music, and notes for 107 songs of lechery and drunkenness plus three sacreligious songs. Besides Elizabethan, Scottish, Irish, and American songs, there are some that were recently collected at the University of Illinois. Includes illustrations, bibliography, and a discography.

554. BAL Y GAY, Jesús. "Panorama de la música popular gallega."

Grial (Vigo), No. 41 (Xulio-Setembre, 1973), 345-350.

A reprinting of an article published in Argentina in 1940. Seeks to characterize the folk music of Galicia in historical and geographical terms and then describes some specific types of folksongs, dances, and musical instruments.

555. BALFOUR, David. *Ancient Orkney Melodies*. Norwood, Pa.: Norwood Editions, 1973. x, 88 pp. illus.

Reissue of a work published in 1885 (Edinburgh: Ballantyne, Hanson and Co.). Gives words, music, and notes for 36 songs and ballads collected mostly around the Orkney Islands of Scotland.

556. BARKER, T. Steven. "Games Our Parents Hated." *NCFJ*, XXI:1 (April, 1973), 37-39.

Describes dangerous bicycle tricks, war games, and Halloween tricks played by young boys in Durham, North Carolina.

557. BARRETT, William Alexander. *English Folk-songs: Collected, Arranged, and Provided with Symphonies and Accompaniments for the Pianoforte*. Darby, Pa.: Norwood Editions, 1973. 95 pp.

Reissue of the 1891 edition (London and N.Y.: Novello, Ewer and Co.). Presents words, music and brief notes for 54 songs collected in England. The book is designed as a songbook, not a study of folklore.

558. BECKER, Paula. *Let the Song Go On: Fifty Years of Gospel Singing with the Speer Family*. Nashville, Tenn.: Impact Books, 1971. 175 pp. illus.

Presents a life history of three generations of the Tom Speer family, traveling gospel singers originally from Alabama. Contains many photographs of the family.

559. BELL, Thelma Harrington. "The Hickory Pole, A Ballad of the Blue Ridge." *Appalachian Journal* (Boone, North Carolina), I:3 (Autumn, 1973), 199-202.

Gives words only of a humorous narrative song in ballad style as sung by an informant in Transylvania County, North Carolina.

560. BERGER, Donald Paul, comp. *Folk Songs of Japan*. N.Y.: Oak Publications, 1972. 152 pp. illus.

A songbook which presents music, Japanese texts, transliterations, and translations into English of 54 Japanese folksongs. Each song is accompanied by notes and there is a general introduction.

561. BERRUETA, Mariano D. *Del cancionero leonés*. Segunda edición. León: Imprenta Provincial, 1971. 353 pp. illus.

A second edition of a book first published in 1941. Offers words without music of a large collection of Leonese folkloric songs, mostly *coplas* but also including some traditional ballads (i.e., *romances*) and other types of popular songs. Includes some commentary and several photographs, but no informant data.

562. BIEBUYCK, Daniel. "The Epic as a Genre in Congo Oral Literature." In *African Folklore*. Pp. 257-273.

Describes the mode of presentation, social context, form, style, and content of the heroic epics of Bantu speaking peoples of the Congo. Deals with both prose and poetry.

563. BIRD, Charles "Heroic Songs of the Mande Hunters." In *African Folklore*. Pp. 275-293.

Describes the training and social position of bards and discusses hunters' songs that are sung in the Mande, a region at the headwaters of the Niger River. Analyzes a particular heroic song entitled *Kambili*.

564. "Black Music, Where It's At and Where It's Going." *Africa Report* (N.Y.), XVIII:1 January - February, 1973), 12-18, 20-24.

Offers a transcription of comments on black music made by Ray Barretto, Lazarus E. N. Ekwueme, Leonard Goines, Jonas Gwangwa, Carman Moore, and Michael Babatunde Olatunji during a round-table discussion at Brooklyn College on November 27, 1972. Deals with black music in very broad terms. Folk music and the music of blacks in various parts of Latin America are treated in the discussion. Includes photographs.

565. BLACKING, John. "Deep and Surface Structures in Venda Music." In *1971 YIFMC*. Pp. 91-108.

Holds that Venda music reflects not only musical conventions and traditions but also cognitive and social processes (i.e., non-musical structures) that underlie all aspects of the Venda culture of northern Transvaal (Africa).

566. BOAZ, Peggy Bradley. "Take It Off; Knock It Off; or Let the Crows Pick It Off." *TFSB*, XXXIX:3 (September, 1973), 77-78.

Discusses variations of a children's game called Club Fist which is played in North Carolina and Kentucky.

567. BOOMSLITER, Paul C., CREEL, Warren, and HASTINGS, George S., Jr. "Perception and English Poetic Meter." *PMLA, Publications of the Modern Language Association of America* (N.Y.), LXXXVIII:2 (March, 1973), 200-208.

Presents results of perception tests that support the theory that meter in English exists in the mind of the listener. Testing is based on unled choral responses. Indirectly important to folklorists interested in metrical variation in ballads and other forms of poetic expression.

568. BOSWELL, George W. "A Note on the Barring of 3/2 Tunes." *KFR*, XIX:1 (January-March, 1973), 11-13.

Criticizes Cecil Sharp's faulty barring of some tunes and his use of unnecessary sharps and flats in his *English Folk Songs from the Southern Appalachians*. Presents portions of the texts and music as examples.

569. BOSWELL, George W. "The Operation of Popular Etymology in Folksong Diction." *TFSB*, XXIX:2 (June, 1973), 37-58.

Discusses and gives examples of regional pronunciation, grammar, usage, and folk etymology as extracted from the texts of 859 ballads and songs in the author's Middle Tennessee collection.

570. BOSWELL, George W. "A Song to Sing." *KFR*, XIX:1 (January-March, 1973), 15-16; 3 (July-September, 1973), 87-88.

In the first installment gives words and music of orally collected versions of "Pretty Polly"; in the second, "Storms on the Sea."

571. BRAND, Oscar. *Songs of '76: A Folksinger's History of the Revolution*. N.Y.: M. Evans, 1972. xiv, 178 pp. illus.

Tells the story of the North American Revolution and gives words and music of 63 topical or narrative songs about conditions or events. The words are mostly from old manuscripts or printed sources but almost all have been edited, set to new music, and copyrighted by the author.

572. BRANDON, William, ed. *The Magic World: American Indian Songs and Poems*. N.Y.: William Morrow and Co., 1971. 145 pp.

Contains 82 poems, songs, and short tales representing 36 tribal groups going back as far as the Mayas. Selections are from older oral traditions, but the approach is very literary and it is clear that the texts have sometimes been adapted and reworked.

573. BRONSON, Bertrand H. "Are the Modes Outmoded?" In *1972 YIFMC*. Pp. 23-31.

The author replies to criticism by Norman Cazden (see item No. 581 below) of his employment of conventional modal terminology in analyzing British-American traditional song-tunes.

574. BRONSON, Bertrand Harris. *The Traditional Tunes of the Child Ballads, IV, Ballads 245 to 299.* Princeton, N.J.: Princeton University Press, 1972. 576 pp.

Presents the traditional music for variants of Child ballads 245 to 299. Also contains the word texts, notes, and a bibliography.

575. BUCHAN, David. *The Ballad and the Folk.* London-Boston: Routledge and Kegan Paul, 1972. xii, 326 pp. illus.

Examines the stanzaic character and narrative structures of the ballads of northeastern Scotland and studies the effect of social change and literacy upon this ballad tradition. Draws upon Lord's theory of oral-formulaic composition. Contains charts, a map, and a bibliography.

576. BUCHNER, Alexander. *Folk Music Instruments of the World.* N.Y.: Crown Publishers, 1972. 292 pp.

Offers several hundred excellent plates of musical instruments from all over the world. There are commentaries on the various instruments, though some of them (at least those dealing with Spain) are sometimes inaccurate.

577. CANTÓN, Darío. *Gardel, ¿a quién le cantás?* B.A.: Ediciones de la Flor, 1972. 219 pp.

A sociologist analyzes the words of Argentine tangos that were in the repertoire of the popular singer, Carlos Gardel, in order to gain insights into the values of the singer of tangos and his cosmovision. Compares these to the conception of the world found in *Martin Fierro*, the gaucho poem of José Hernández.

578. CARNEIRO, Edison. *Capoeira.* Rio de Janeiro: Ministério da Educação e Cultura, Campanha de Defesa do Folclore Brasileiro, 1971. 8 pp. (*Cadernos de Folclore, 14.*)

Describes a Brazilian game-demonstration of the art of self-defense that apparently had its origins in Angola but today exists in Brazil as a kind of traditional exercise of skill among friends or sportsmen. Includes a brief glossary of terms used.

579. CARROLL, Ginger A. "Stick Dance." *Alaska Journal* (Anchorage, Alaska), II:2 (Spring, 1972), 28-33.

Describes the "Stick Dance," an Athapascan Indian ceremonial ritual celebrated today only in the villages of Nulato and Kaltag. Includes photographs.

580. CARVALHO, Ilmar. "O choro carioca; perspectiva sóciohistórica." *Revista de Cultura Vozes* (Rio de Janeiro), LVI:9 (Novembro, 1972), 53-57.

Treats the rise of a typical musical group known as a *choro* which became popular in the Rio de Janeiro area around 1880. Its popularity began to decline about 1925, but the *choro* still is a part of Cariocan tradition.

581. CAZDEN, Norman. "A Simplified Mode Classification for Traditional Anglo-American Song Tunes." In *1971 YIFMC.* Pp. 45-78.

Criticizes the use of church modes to classify folk tunes and proposes examining tunes and tune families using larger structural frameworks called *genera*.

582. CHILD, Francis James. *Letters on Scottish Ballads from Professor Francis J. Child to W. W., Aberdeen*. Darby, Pa.: Norwood Editions, 1972. 37 pp.

Reissue of the 1930 edition (Aberdeen: The Bon-Accord Press). Prints 37 letters from Francis Child to William Walker of Aberdeen, Scotland, written between December of 1890 and August of 1896. Most are about Child's interest in the MS. volumes of ballad texts compiled by Peter Buchan and housed in the British Museum.

583. CLAYTON, Lawrence. "'The Last Longhorn': A Poetic Denouement of an Era." *SFQ*, XXXVII:2 (June, 1973), 115-122.

Explicates "The Last Longhorn," a folk ballad from John A. Lomax's *Cowboy Songs and Other Frontier Ballads*. Shows how it accurately reflects the historical situation of 1885-1887, years which saw the death of the Old West era of longhorn cattle raising.

584. "Clayton McMichen Talking." *Old Time Music* (London), No. 1 (Summer, 1971), 8-10; No. 2 (Autumn, 1971), 13-15; No. 3 (Winter, 1971-1972), 14-15, 19.

A transcription of an interview with McMichen who discusses his early country-music group that performed on radio broadcasts beginning in 1921 and also treats many other subjects related to his long career in performing "folk" or "hillbilly" music.

585. COHEN, Anne, and COHEN, Norm. ' Tune Evolution as an Indicator of Traditional Musical Norms." *JAF*, LXXXVI:339 (January-March, 1973), 37-47.

Studies changes in fourteen Tin Pan Alley songs published between 1860 and 1910 as they entered folk tradition. Attempts to determine the process by which they were changed to fit folk style. Gives bibliographic and discographic data for the tunes analyzed.

586. COHEN, Norm. "'Casey Jones': At the Crossroads of Two Ballad Traditions." *WF*, XXXII:2 (April, 1973), 77-103.

Examines the evolution of folksongs about railroadman Casey Jones showing that versions of this ballad were found both in the Anglo-American vulgar ballad tradition and in the blues ballad tradition. The writers of the popular vaudeville song of "Casey Jones" seem to have borrowed from both traditions.

587. COHEN, Norm. "Fiddling Sid Harkreader." *JEMFQ*, VIII, Part 4 (Winter, 1972), No. 28, pp. 189-193.

Discusses the life and career of Tennessee fiddler Sid Harkreader and comments upon his association with other country musicians, such as Uncle Dave and Grady Moore. Includes picture reproductions and a preliminary discography of his 1927 and 1928 recordings on Paramount.

588. COHEN, Norm. "Folk Music on Records." *WF*, XXXII:3 (July, 1973), 217-223.

Lists and describes critically some recent recordings of folksongs and instrumental music from England, Scotland, and Ireland. Also includes brief notice of a few recordings from Puerto Rico, Spain, and other countries.

589. COHEN, Norm, and MEADE, Guthrie. "The Sources of Old Time Hillbilly Music. I: Child Ballads." *JEMFQ*, IX, Part 2 (Summer, 1973), No. 30, pp. 56-61.

Discusses the sixteen Child ballads found on hillbilly records from 1925 to 1948 and presents a discography of recordings.

590. COLÍN, Mario, comp. *El corrido popular en el Estado de México*.

México: Biblioteca Enciclopedia del Estado de México, 1972. xxiv, 556 pp. illus.

Presents the verses of more than 130 Mexican *corridos* dating from the 1800's to the present. Contains previously published essays on the *corrido* written by Salvador Novo, Andrés Henestrosa, Daniel Moreno, Arturo Martínez Cáceres, and José Agustín. Reproduces some *corrido* broadsides.

591. COLLINS, Fletcher, Jr., ed. *Alamance Play-Party Songs and Singing Games*. Norwood, Pa.: Norwood Editions, 1973. 61 pp.

Reissue of the mimeographed edition of 1940 (Elon College, North Carolina). A collection (words and music) of 45 play-party songs, singing games, cumulative songs, rhyming games, and children's songs. Includes directions for their performance, an introduction, and a small bibliography.

592. COLLINSON, Francis. "Scottish Folkmusic: An Historical Survey." In *1971 YIFMC*. Pp. 34-44.

Discusses the two broad Scottish folk music traditions, the Gaelic and the Lowland, and notes the history of collecting and scholarship in the field. Considers the folksong as a living Scottish tradition.

593. CONE, James H. *The Spirituals and the Blues: An Interpretation*. N.Y.: The Seabury Press, 1972. 152 pp.

Studies Negro spirituals and blues songs as expressions of black experience. The focus is primarily on socio-religious aspects of the songs with less attention to their music.

594. "Conversation with Clark Kessinger." *Old Time Music* (London), No. 3 (Winter, 1971-1972), 4-8.

An interview given at Charleston, West Virginia, in which Kessinger talks about learning to be a fiddler, making records in the 1920's, playing for radio stations, etc.

595. COOKE, Peter R. "Ludaya—A Transverse Flute from Eastern Uganda." In *1971 YIFMC*. Pp. 79-90.

Concerns an unusual type of flute found among the Gisu people of Eastern Uganda. Discusses one player's repertory.

596. CORTAZAR, Augusto Raúl. "'Martín Fierro' a la luz de la ciencia folklórica (fundamentos teóricos y propuestas de investigación)." Separata of *Logos* (B.A.), No. 12 (1972). 20 pp.

A most illuminating discussion of the relationship of José Hernandez' famous gaucho poem to folklore. Points to folkloric influences in the literary formulation of the poem and also to its importance as a source of folklore. Discusses many possible subjects for fruitful research.

597. COUTINHO FILHO, F. *Violas e repentes; repentes populares em prosa e verso, pesquisas folclóricas no nordeste brasileiro*. 2ª edição melhorada. São Paulo: Editora Lectura em convénio com o Instituto Nacional do Livro, 1972. 333 pp. illus.

A book about popular singers, of the northeastern part of Brazil and their songs. Notes genres of songs cultivated by such singers, identifies the principal artists, relates many episodes about their lives, mostly in the 1930's-1950's, and gives hundreds of examples of song texts (no music). Includes drawings, photographs, and indexes.

598. CRAIGIE, W. A. *The Icelandic Sagas*. Millwood, N.Y.: Kraus Reprint Co., 1973. 120 pp.

Reissue of the 1913 edition (Folcraft, Pa.: Folcroft Library Editions). Deals with the origin of sagas, types of sagas, etc.

599. CUNNINGHAM, Keith. "Do-It-Yourself Records Revisited."

FForum, VI:I (January, 1973), 40-43.

Revises advice offered in *FForum*, I:3 (September, 1968) describing the entire procedure for making a record of the music of folk performers.

600. CUNNINGHAM, Keith. "Notes and Queries." *AFFword*, II:4 (January, 1973), 47-48.

Gives a version of an orally collected sentimental ballad known as "Black Sheep."

601. CUNNINGHAM, Keith. "Notes and Queries: A Rare Old Cowboy Song." *AFFword*, I:2 (July, 1971), 23-34.

Seeks informants who know a cowboy song that is a version of Laws' No. N42, "Pretty Fair Maid." Gives words only of "The Cowboy and the Maiden."

602. DALYELL, John Graham. *Musical Memoirs of Scotland, with Historical Annotations and Numerous Illustrative Plates.* Norwood, Pa.: Norwood Editions, 1973. xii, 300 pp. illus.

Reissue of the 1849 edition (Edinburgh: Thomas G. Stevenson). Studies Scottish musical instruments (e.g., bagpipe, organ, bells, guitar, lute, harp, etc.), discusses techniques of playing, and describes the music played. Includes numerous illustrations from old manuscripts.

603. DANKER, Frederick E. "Country Music and the Mass Media: The Johnny Cash Television Show." *Popular Music and Society* (Bowling Green, Ohio), II:2 (Winter, 1973), 124-144.

Traces the history and problems of the Johnny Cash Show, which ran from 1969-1971. Deals with formats, singing styles, guest artists, etc. and includes discussion of Cash's use of folk materials.

604. *Danzas folklóricas de Guatemala.* Guatemala: Dirección General de Cultura y Bellas Artes, Departamento de Arte Folklórico Nacional, 1971. 38 pp. illus.

Shows on charts and a map the various folk dances found in Guatemala. There is a brief introduction about the history of dances, masks and costumes used, musical instruments, types of dances, etc. Includes many illustrations.

605. DAVIS, Martha Ellen, comp. *Music and Dance in Latin American Urban Contexts: A Selective Bibliography.* Brockport, N.Y.: Dept. of Anthropology, SUNY-Brockport, 1973. 20 pp. (*Urban Anthropology Bibliographies No. 1.*)

An annotated bibliography of 42 items published between 1957 and 1972 dealing with traditional and popular music and dance in or near urban centers in Latin America and the southwestern part of the U.S.

606. DAVIS, Ronald L. "Early Jazz: Another Look." *Southwest Review* (Dallas, Texas), LVIII:1 (Winter, 1973), 1-13; 2 (Spring, 1973), 144-154.

Surveys early jazz, particularly in the New Orleans and Chicago areas. Discusses influences, music, jazz musicians, etc.

607. DEAN, Michael Cassius, comp. *Flying Cloud, and One Hundred and Fifty Other Old Time Songs and Ballads of Outdoor Men, Sailors, Lumber Jacks, Soldiers, Men of the Great Lakes, Railroadmen, Miners, etc.* Norwood, Pa.: Norwood Editions, 1973. 146 pp.

Reissue of the 1922 edition (Virginia, Minnesota: The Quickprint). Presents words only to 152 traditional and popular but written North American songs. Many seem to concern Ireland, but no information is given about any of them.

608. DEL RÍO, Amelia Agostini de, ed. *Flores del romancero.*

Englewood Cliffs, N.J.: Prentice-Hall, Inc., 1970. viii, 276 pp.

An edition of ballad texts for use in Spanish classes. Includes traditional ballads of folk tradition and also poems in *romance* form by named poets of the 15th to the 17th century. There are explanatory footnotes and some brief essays about each ballad cycle or epic legend.

609. DÍAZ ROIG, Mercedes. "Un rasgo estilístico del romancero y de la lírica popular." *Nueva Revista de Filología Hispánica* (México), XXI (1972):1, pp. 79-94.

Studies an enumerative pattern consisting of three elements which appears in modern popular lyric poetry (i.e., *coplas*). Traces it back in various forms to traditional epic poems and ballads.

610. DICKENS, Gloria. "Childhood Songs from North Carolina." *NCFJ*, XXI:1 (April, 1973), 4-9.

Gives words only of twelve songs of parody, word-play, and profanity collected in a dormitory at North Carolina State University.

611. DOERFLINGER, William Main, comp. *Songs of the Sailor and Lumberman*. N.Y.: Macmillan Company; London: Collier-Macmillan Ltd., 1972. xxiii, 374 pp. illus.

A revised and updated second edition of a book first published in 1951 under the title *Shantymen and Shantyboys*. Offers words and music of around 150 songs, many of them orally collected. Gives informant data, commentaries, comparative notes, extensive bibliography, an index, and both photographs and drawings.

612. DUMAS, Danielle, trans. and ed. *Chants flamencos, coplas flamencas*. Paris: Aubier Montaigne, 1973. 236 pp.

An introduction surveys in fairly brief form (pp. 7-72) the salient facts about flamenco singing (i.e., history, cultural factors, singers, music, literary form and style, structure, etc.). There follows a section of texts without music of Spanish *coplas* with French translations on facing pages. Includes notes, charts, and a glossary.

613. DUMÉZIL, Georges. *From Myth to Fiction; The Saga of Hadingus*. Translated by Derek Coltman. Chicago and London: University of Chicago Press, 1973. xii, 253 pp.

A translation of Dumézil's *Du myth au roman: La Saga de Hadingus et autres essais* (1970). The book is a series of analytical chapters on various aspects of the *Saga of Hadingus* based on mythic sources and written by the Danish poet Saxo. Besides the very scholarly work itself there are seven appendices, each of which is itself a separate but related study (e.g., "Njördr, Nerthus, and the Scandanavian Folklore of Sea Spirits").

614. EBERHARD, Wolfram. *Taiwanese Ballads: A Catalogue*. Taipei: Oriental Cultural Service, 1972. ix, 171 pp. illus. (*Asian Folklore and Social Life Monographs, Vol. XXII*.)

Abstracts in English two hundred Chinese folk ballads printed in small booklets between 1927 and the 1960's. Most are in Min-nan language and circulated among farmers and lower class people in Taiwan.

615. ECKSTROM, Fannie Hardy, and SMYTH, Mary Winslow. *Minstrelsy of Maine: Folk-Songs and Ballads of the Woods and the Coast*. Ann Arbor: Gryphon Books, 1971. xvi, 390 pp.

Reissue of the 1927 edition (Boston and N.Y.: Houghton Mifflin Company). Contains unedited transcriptions of the words to over 125 Maine folksongs and ballads. Identifies informants, gives song sources, and discusses the folk aesthetic, the social functions of the singer, and other matters concerning balladry.

616. EDMONSON, Munro S., trans. *The Book of Counsel: The Popol Vuh of the Quiche Maya of Guatemala.* New Orleans: Tulane University, 1971. xvii, 273 pp. (*Middle American Research Institute, Publication 35.*)

Offers a new poetic translation of the *Popel Vuh* along with an introduction. The original Quiche text and the English translation are presented side by side with notes at the bottom of the page. Includes a bibliography and an index.

617. EMMERSON, George S. *Rantin' Pipe and Tremblin' String: A History of Scottish Dance Music.* Montreal: McGill-Queen's University Press, 1971. xv, 278 pp. illus.

Focuses upon the dance, the dancers, and the occasions for dancing in Scotland from the Middle Ages to the present. Also discusses musical instruments which accompany dance and some aspects of Scottish music. Contains pictures, a bibliography, and musical notation of tunes.

618. EMMERSON, George S. *A Social History of Scottish Dance; Ane Celestial Recreatioun.* Montreal: McGill-Queen's University Press, 1972. xv, 352 pp. illus.

Studies the dance tradition of Scotland, tracing the cultural history of Scotland and the history of dancing in the courts and among the people of Scotland and England from the Middle Ages through the 18th century. Discusses in detail Scottish dance style, Highland Games dancing, folk reels, the high dances, the jig and hornpipe, and country dancing. Contains illustrations, diagrams, some musical notations, and a bibliography.

619. ERDELY, Stephen, and CHIPMAN, Robert A. "Strip-Chart Recording of Narrow Band Frequency Analysis in Aid of Ethnomusicological Data." In *1972 YIFMC.* Pp. 119-136.

A technical paper that reports on a method of analyzing sound waves with sophisticated electronic laboratory equipment. The efforts are designed to improve on existing methods of transcribing music. Includes tables, charts, musical transcriptions, and notes.

620. FAKHR AL-DĪN GURGĀNĪ. *Vīs and Rāmīn* (transl. by George Morrison). N.Y.: Columbia University Press, 1972. xix, 357 pp.

Translates into English the Persian epic *Vīs o Rāmīn* composed between A.D. 1040 and 1054 by Fakhr al-Dīn Gurgānī from Pahlavī sources. The introduction discusses the historical background of the composition and its possible relationship to the romance of Tristan and Isolde.

621. FERRIS, William R., Jr. "The Ballad in Gaelic Literature." *KFR*, XIX:1 (January-March, 1973), 3-6.

Tries to account for the absence of the ballad form in Gaelic literature. Attributes the lack to the isolation of Ireland from European thought, to the dominance of the bardic school which produced lengthy heroic poems but disdained folk poetry, and to an Irish predilection for lyric poetry.

622. FERRIS, William R., Jr. "Folk Song and Culture: Charles Seeger and Alan Lomax." *NYFQ*, XXIX:3 (September, 1973), 206-218.

Discusses problems of studying folksongs in the context of their culture and shows how ethnomusicologists have dealt with some of them. Considers particularly the contributions of Charles Seeger and Alan Lomax, with special attention to the latter's work in cantometrics. Includes bibliography.

623. FORCADAS, Alberto. "El Romancero español, Lope de Vega, Góngora y Quevedo, y sus posibles resonancias en «Sonatina» de Rubén

Darío." *Quaderni Ibero-Americani* (Torino, Italia), No. 41 (Dicembre, 1972), 1-6.

Seeks to show that Rubén Darío's famous poem "Sonatina" probably draws more than most critics had supposed from thoroughly Spanish sources such as traditional ballads and ballads by art poets.

624. FOSTER, George Murphy. *Pops Foster: The Autobiography of a New Orleans Jazz-Man as Told to Tom Stoddard.* Berkeley: University of California Press, 1971. xxii, 208 pp. illus.

Transcribes interviews with double-bass jazz player George "Pops" Foster in which Foster discusses his past, New Orleans' life in the early 1900's, and his playing for bands in New York and elsewhere. Contains a discography, a bibliography, and many photographs. An introduction by Bertram Turetsky describes playing technique and Ross Russell offers a brief general history of jazz.

625. FRENK ALATORRE, Margit. "Un desconocido cantar de los comendadores, fuente de Lope." In *Homenaje a William L. Fichter.* Madrid: Castalia, 1971. Pp. 211-222.

Points to a 15th-century folksong as a source for Lope de Vega's play *Los comendadores de Córdoba.*

626. FRYE, Ellen. "Children's Rhythm Games from New York City." *WF*, XXXII:1 (January, 1973), 54-56.

Presents the words of five rhythm games collected from children of east and central Harlem in 1966.

627. FRYE, Ellen. *The Marble Threshing Floor: A Collection of Greek Folksongs.* Austin and London: University of Texas Press, 1973. xvi, 327 pp. (*Publications of the American Folklore Society, Memoir Series, Vol. 57.*)

Offers a collection of 110 orally recorded Greek folksongs grouped according to region. Words and music are given along with English translations and brief notes that include informant data, musical analysis, commentary on context, etc. Includes also a general introduction, some photographs, a glossary, a bibliography, and an index of first lines and titles.

628. FUENTES, Rumel. "Corridos de Rumel." *El Grito* (Berkeley, California), VI:3 (Spring, 1973), 3-40.

Words and music of thirteen new *corridos* (i.e., narrative songs) written by Fuentes about recent events of interest to Chicanos in the United States. There is an introduction in Spanish with English translation and explanatory introductions to each individual song, also in Spanish and English.

629. GARRENTON, Valerie. "Children's Games." *NCFJ*, XXI:1 (April, 1973), 27-31.

Describes physical games, guessing or party games, and hopping games recalled from the author's childhood and collected in 1972 from fourth graders in Raleigh, N.C. Contains diagrams.

630. GARVIN, Richard M. and ADDEO, Edmond. *The Midnight Special: The Legend of Leadbelly.* N.Y.: Bernard Geis Associates, 1971. 312 pp.

Reconstructs in biographical novel form the life of black guitarist-singer Huddie Ledbetter from Louisiana. Interviews with people who knew Leadbelly, including John Lomax, other musicians, and prison officials, were used as sources.

631. GERSON-KIWI, Edith. "Drone and 'Dyaphonia Basilica.'" In *1972 YIFMC*. Pp. 9-22.

Studies the *bourdon* or drone type of polyphony (known also as *dyaphonia basilica*) in both Eastern and Western music as part of a general reorientation concerning the origins and true nature of Western polyphony. Includes notes and musical examples from India, Persia, Iraq, Morocco, and Spain.

632. GIFFONI, Maria Amália Correa. "Considerações históricas sôbre as danças sociais no Brasil." *Revista do Arquivo Municipal* (São Paulo, Brasil), XXXIII (1971):182, pp. 125-161.

Offers an interesting historical survey of dancing on various social levels in Brazil. Though it deals mostly with salon dances and foreign dances that were brought into Brazil at different periods in history, there is some attention to the dances of Negroes and other folk groups.

633. GIFFONI, Maria Amâlia Corrêa. "Tradições brasileiras—III—Serenatas." *Boletim Bibliográfico, Biblioteca Municipal Mário de Andrade* (São Paulo), XXX (Abril-Junho, 1972), 7-18.

Surveys and describes the customs and practices surrounding various types of serenades, mostly street serenades, in many different places in Brazil. This is a third article in a series on folklore begun in *Revista do Instituto Histórico e Geográfico de São Paulo* in 1970.

634. GONZÁLEZ ECHEGARAY, María del Carmen. "Danzas para el día del Corpus en la Villa de Reinosa." In *PIHS (I)*, 175-179.

Prints and comments upon two contracts from the year 1604 with dancers who were to perform in the Corpus Christi celebrations in a town of La Montaña (Spain).

635. GOODWYN, Frank. "Ballads Old and New: The Metamorphosis of the Little Old Log Cabin." *JFSGW*, IV:1 (Spring, 1973), 13-17.

Shows how a late 19th-century song, *The Little Old Log Cabin in the Lane*, has spawned a large number of similar songs adapted to different conditions or differing occupations (i.e., *The Little Old Sod Shanty on My Claim, The Little Red Caboose Behind the Train, Little Joe the Wrangler*, etc.). Gives words only of versions of the four songs just named.

636. GOWER, Herschel. "Wanted: The Singer's Autobiography and Critical Reflections." *TFSB*, XXXIX:1 (March, 1973), 1-7.

Urges the collection of informants' life histories, noting the scant treatment given singers' lives by various ballad and folksong collectors.

637. GOWER, Herschel, and PORTER, James. "Jeannie Robertson: The 'Other' Ballads." *Scottish Studies* (University of Edinburgh), XVI (1972), Part Two, 139-159.

Presents words and music of ten non-Child ballads from the repertory of Jeannie Robertson, a major Scottish ballad singer, and analyzes the songs and her performance. Tunes were collected by Hamish Henderson.

638. GREBE, María Ester. "El kultrún mapuche: un microcosmo simbólico." *RMC*, Año XXVII:123-124 (Julio-Diciembre, 1973), 3-42.

Studies the signification, the mythical context, and the social and ritual functions of the *Kultrun*, a shamanic drum used by the Mapuche people of the Province of Cautín in Chile. Also examines the distribution, construction, and music of the instrument. Includes words of a song, photographs and drawings, and a bibliography.

639. GREEN, Archie. "Commercial Music Graphics." *JEMFQ*, VIII: Part 4 (Winter, 1972), No. 28, pp. 196-202; IX:Part 1 (Spring, 1973), No. 29, pp. 18-23; Part 2 (Summer, 1973), No. 30, pp. 62-66.

Listed above are Nos. 23-25 of a continuing series. No. 23 reproduces and discusses graphic representations of the singing cowboy; No. 24 reproduces four items documenting the appearance of folksongs on campus; and No. 25 reproduces and discusses three items concerning some recordings of sacred music.

640. GREGOR, Walter. *Counting-Out Rhymes of Children*. Norwood, Pa.: Norwood Editions, 1973. 32 pp.

Reissue of the 1891 edition. Presents counting-out rhymes collected in northeastern Scotland. An introduction surveys the uses of lots by Jewish, Chinese, Greek, Roman, and Scottish people, speculates as to the origin of counting-out rhymes, and discusses form and classification of the collected rhymes.

641. GRIFFIS, Ken. "The Charlie Quirk Story and the Beginning of the Beverly Hill Billies." *JEMFQ*, VIII:Part 4 (Winter, 1972), No. 28, 173-178.

Discusses the life and career of guitarist and country singer Charlie Quirk of Humphrey, N.Y., focusing especially upon his association with the popular Beverly Hill Billies who performed on Beverly Hills and Los Angeles radio stations in the late '20's. Contains photographs.

642. GRIFFIS, Ken. "The Ken Maynard Story." *JEMFQ*, IX:Part 2 (Summer, 1973), No. 30, 67-69.

Reviews the career of Ken Maynard, the first singing cowboy of the movies, using information obtained in a 1968 interview with him.

643. GRIFFITH, James. "Old Time Fiddle Contests in Arizona." *AFFword*, II:3 (October, 1972), 3-6.

Reports the existence of three fiddlers' contests in Tucson, Bisbee, and Payson, Arizona. Describes them and notes the importance of such contests for the preservation of fiddling as an art.

644. GRONOW, Pekka. "Popular Music in Finland: A Preliminary Survey." *Ethomusicology*, XVII:I (January, 1973), 52-71.

Surveys historical and sociological aspects of various kinds of popular music in Finland during the 19th and 20th centuries. There is a section on "Folk Music in a Period of Change" (pp. 53-56). Includes a bibliography.

645. GROVER, Carrie B. *A Heritage of Songs*. Norwood, Pennsylvania: Norwood Editions, 1973. 216 pp.

Offers words and music (musical transcriptions by Ann L. Griggs) of 140 folksongs from Nova Scotia along with commentary and an introduction by the author, who learned the songs from her parents.

646. GUERRA GUTIÉRREZ, Alberto. *La picardía en el cancionero popular*. La Paz: Ediciones Isla, 1972. 59 pp.

Offers some *copla* texts without music along with brief commentary. They range from political satire and humorous commentaries to obscenities.

647. GUTIÉRREZ, Electra, and GUTIÉRREZ, Tonatiuh. "La danza ritual de los voladores." *Mexico Quarterly Review* (Puebla, México), IV:2 (1973), 27-38.

Deals with the history of the ritual dance of the *voladores* (i.e., flyers) and its present-day status in the eastern part of Mexico. The text of the article appears in Spanish on pp. 27-32. On pp. 33-38 there is an English translation by Coley Taylor.

648. HEIM, Michael. "Moravian Folk Music: A Czechoslovak Novelist's View." *JFI*, IX:1 (June, 1972), 45-53.

Prints from a modern Czech novel by Milan Kundera entitled *The Joke* a portion that was omitted in the published English edition but is important for its deliberations on folklore and folk music. The novel text includes the tunes of some folk music.

649. HELLMANN, John M., Jr. "'I'm a Monkey': The Influence of the Black American Blues Argot on the Rolling Stones." *JAF*, LXXXVI: 342 (October-December, 1973), 367-373.

Discusses reasons why the argot of blacks was attractive to Mick Jagger and the Rolling Stones and notes the influence of Jagger and his group upon the youth of the counter culture.

650. HOLLAND, William E. "Formulaic Diction and the Descent of a Middle English Romance." *Speculum* (Cambridge, Mass.), XLVIII:1 (January, 1973), 89-109.

Examines in a scholarly way the diction of all of the five known manuscripts of a single metrical romance, *Arthour and Merlin*, in order to determine the extent to which oral variation may have affected the text over a period of several centuries. Includes copious notes.

651. HOLYOAK, Van. "Lone and Painted Cottage." *AFFword*, I:3 (October, 1971), 24-25.

Words without music of a narrative cowboy song as sung by Holyoak.

652. HOOD, Mantle. *The Ethnomusicologist*. N.Y.: McGraw-Hill Book, 1971. xii, 386 pp. illus.

A textbook which outlines the work of the ethnomusicologist. Treats transcription and notation, organology, field and laboratory methods, and communications. Upholds a contextual approach to the study of music in all cultures. Contains pictures, diagrams, and musical notations.

653. HOSTETTLER, Agnes. "Symbolic Tokens in a Ballad of the Returned Lover." *WF*, XXXII:I (January, 1973), 33-38.

Compares English (Child 252 and 263) versions of the ballad of "The Returned Lover" with German versions of "Die Liebesprobe" and finds the German ballads differ in the symbolic significance of the ring and in the added symbolic use of the veil.

654. "Huelva: la orilla del folklore hispanoamericano." *Mundo Hispánico* (Madrid), XXVII:307 (Octubre, 1973), 48-51.

Photographs and brief commentary to report on a Latin American song festival held in the city of Huelva (Spain). Various "folk" groups from different countries of Latin America participated.

655. IVES, Edward Dawson. *Lawrence Doyle: The Farmer-Poet of Prince Edward Island; A Study in Local Songmaking*. Orono: University of Maine Press, 1971. xviii, 269 pp. (*University of Maine Studies, No. XCII*.)

Studies and presents the words and music to the local songs of Lawrence Doyle sung by informants in the northern part of King's County, Prince Edward Island. Discusses Doyle's life, the style of his songs, and occasions for singing them. Also studies other songmakers in the area. Contains maps and a bibliography.

656. JASEN, David A. *Recorded Ragtime, 1897-1958*. Hamden, Connecticut: Archon Books, The Shoe String Press, 1973. viii, 155 pp.

A discography of ragtime recordings preceded by an introduction that deals with the genre's history, its origins in folk music, composers, performers, etc. Besides the main discography there is a listing of composers and their works, a bibliography, and an index of performers

657. JOHN, Teri. "A Collection of Jump Rope Rhymes." *NCFJ*, XXI:1 (April, 1973), 15-17.

Presents the words to jump rope rhymes, some told by a second grader in Raleigh, N.C. and some recalled by older girls from their childhood in widely scattered areas of the U.S.

658. JOHNSON, Kinchen, ed. and trans. *Folksongs and Children-Songs from Peiping.* 2 vols. Taipei: Orient Cultural Service, 1971. 428 pp. (*Asian Folklore and Social Life Monographs, XVI and XVII.*)

Presents 214 folksongs, verses, and children's rhymes in Chinese and English prose translation without music. The material was collected in Peking in the 1930's.

659. JOHNSON, Martha, and BURTON, Thomas. "The Vitality of the Ballad Tradition in Beech Mountain." *TFSB*, XXIX:2 (June, 1973), 33-34.

Presents the results of an interview with ballad singer Benjamin Franklin Jones and members of his family from Beech Mountain, North Carolina. Gives Child and Laws numbers of some ballads but no texts.

660. JOHNSTON, Thomas F. "Integration, Status, Redefinition, and Conciliation at Tsonga Beer-Drink Singsongs." *FForum*, VI:3 (July, 1973), 149-159.

Examines the occasions and social functions of beer-drink songs among the Tsonga of Africa. Shows that in situations of higher stress there is greater prescription severity for song performance. Includes the words to some songs.

661. JOHNSTON, Thomas F. "Tsonga Children's Folksongs." *JAF*, LXXXVI:341 (July-September, 1973), 225-240.

Examines the social uses of children's songs among the African Tsonga peoples. Presents words and music of twenty songs that occur within children's stories. Offers analysis of the music, an interval count chart, etc.

662. JONES, Bessie, and HAWES, Bess Lomax. *Step it Down: Games, Plays, Songs, and Stories from the Afro-American Heritage.* N.Y.: Harper and Row, 1972. xxi, 233 pp.

A collection of Negro folklore as remembered by informant Bessie Jones from her childhood in Dawes, Georgia. Includes: Baby Games and Plays, Clapping Plays, Jumps and Skips, Singing Plays, Ring Plays, Dances, House Plays and Home Amusements, Outdoor Games, Songs and Stories. Mrs. Jones provides excellent commentary and Mrs. Hawes sets each piece in its historical and functional setting. Intended for use in schools the book has notes to parents and teachers, annotations, a selected bibliography, a discography, and an index.

663. JONES, Harold G., III. "El cancionero español (*Cod. Reg. Lat. 1635*) de la Biblioteca Vaticana." *Nueva Revista de Filología Hispánica* (México), XXI (1972):2, pp. 370-392.

Describes an important 16th-century manuscript in the Library of the Vatican which contains texts of Spanish ballads and songs (i.e., *coplas, villancicos*, etc.). Catalogues the compositions contained therein and gives comparative notes.

664. JONES, Loyal. "The Minstrel of the Appalachians: Bascom Lamar Lunsford at 91." *JEMFQ*, IX:Part 1 (Spring, 1973), No. 29, 2-8.

Presents a sketch of the life of Bascom Lamar Lunsford, a folksinger and fiddler from North Carolina, who is known for his large repertory and for directing some Appalachian folk festivals. Quotes Lunsford's comments on ballads, song collecting, instruments, and playing techniques. Includes a discography and photographs.

665. JORDAN, David K. "Anti-American Children's Verses from Taiwan." *WF*, XXXII:3 (July, 1973), 205-209.

Gives texts of some verses used by children in Taiwan as catcalls to passing Americans.

666. [JÓRIO, Amaury, and ARAÚJO, Hiram.]. *Escolas de samba em desfile; vida, paixão e sorte*. Rio de Janeiro: Poligráfica Editora, 1969. 320 pp. illus.

Marginal to real folklore, the samba schools described here in great detail are organized city groups scattered through Brazil. They cultivate samba dancing partly for cultural reasons and partly as a tourist attraction.

667. JOYNER, Charles W. "The Repertory of Nancy Jones as a Mirror of Culture in Scotland County." *NCFJ*, XXI:3 (September, 1973), 89-97.

Analyzes the repertory of Nancy Jones, a folksinger from Scotland County, N.C. Examines her stylistic approach to Afro-American religious songs and Anglo-American songs and discusses the social function and meaning of her children's and love songs. Presents words and music of two songs and words only of some others.

668. KAEPPLER, Adrienne. "Acculturation in Hawaiian Dance." In *1972 YIFMC*. Pp. 38-46.

Describes and contrasts traditional *hula* dancing, which is rooted in poetry, and the *hula* dancing that developed after the coming of Europeans to Hawaii and more recently the arrival of tourists. Includes words and music of a traditional song and a photograph.

669. KAHN, Ed. "International Relations, Dr. Brinkley, and Hillbilly Music." *JEMFQ*, IX, Part 2 (Summer, 1973), No. 30, 47-55.

Tells of the career of the popular quack medical doctor and radio broadcaster, Dr. John R. Brinkley of Kansas, who established a powerful radio station on the Mexican border to avoid FCC regulations. His activities included presenting such popular hillbilly performers as the Pickard family and the Carter family. Includes photographs.

670. KAUFFMAN, Robert. "Shona Urban Music and the Problem of Acculturation." In *1972 YIFMC*. Pp. 47-56.

Studies Shona urban music in the Salisbury and Bulawayo area of Africa and notes the acculturation of outside European, North American, and South African influences. Suggests that such influences are important but that they seem not to eliminate the traditional processes of Shona music making.

671. KOHT, Halvdan. *The Old Norse Sagas*. Millwood, N.Y.: Kraus Reprint Company, 1971. 191 pp.

A reissue of the 1931 edition (N.Y.: W.W. Norton and Co.). Deals with the origin of the sagas, kinds of sagas, the art of the sagas, their historical value, the methods by which they were transmitted, etc.

672. KOLINSKI, Mieczyslaw. "A Cross-Cultural Approach to Metro-Rhythmic Patterns." *Ethnomusicology*, XVII:3 (September, 1973), 494-506.

Points out difficulties of applying specifically Western concepts to non-Western musical styles in both art and folk music and suggests a broadly conceived approach based upon the findings of Gestalt psychology. Includes musical examples and some references.

673. KOON, William Henry. "Ragtime on Records: Classic and Country." *TFSB*, XXXIX:1 (March, 1973), 11-13.

Reviews recent recordings and reissues and discusses the history of ragtime music.

674. KOON, William Henry. "The Songs of Ken Maynard." *JEMFQ*, IX:Part 2 (Summer, 1973), No. 30, 70-77.

Presents the words of eight cowboy songs on test pressings for

Columbia recordings made by singing movie cowboy Ken Maynard. Notes the probable sources and recordings made by other performers of the same songs. Contains a discography and illustrations.

675. KOSHIYAMA, Alice Mitika. *Análise de conteúdo da literatura de cordel: presença dos valores religiosos*. São Paulo: Universidade de São Paulo, 1972. 159 pp.

Analyzes quantitatively the contents of sixteen pamphlets or booklets of popular verses (i.e., *literatura de cordel*) from Northeastern Brazil in order to ascertain popular attitudes toward religion, social problems, politics and political leaders, moral and ethical values, etc. Over two-thirds of the volume consists of reproductions of the texts studied.

676. KRAUSS, Joanne. "Love and Death and the American Ballad: A Morphology of 'Ballads of Family Opposition to Lovers.'" *FAUFA*, Nos. 4-5 (1972-1973), 91-100.

Offering a classification based on syntagmatic structural analysis, the author finds three types of American ballads where lovers meet opposition from parents or other relatives. Essays some interpretation of the themes detected in the analysis. Includes notes, an appendix, and a bibliography.

677. KRAVITT, Edward F. "The Ballad as Conceived by Germanic Composers of the Late Romantic Period." *Studies in Romanticism* (Boston), XII:2 (Spring, 1973), 499-515.

Discusses art ballads for solo voice and piano written by German composers of the 19th century. Not about folklore, but the author shows an awareness of the relationship between such ballads and folk traditions. Includes music.

678. KRISHNASWAMI, S. *Musical Instruments of India*. Boston: Crescendo Pub. Co., 1971. 102 pp. illus.

Discusses the origin of Indian musical instruments and traces the history of their use. Lists and describes in detail 59 wind, string, and percussion instruments. Also notes techniques for playing and provides pictures for each of these instruments.

679. KUNENE, Daniel P. "Metaphor and Symbolism in the Heroic Poetry of Southern Africa." In *African Folklore*. Pp. 294-320.

Explains phrases of praise found in southern African heroic poetry by relating them to cultural-symbolic contexts. Focuses upon "the idea of containing" in mythology, tales, etc.

680. KURATH, Gertrude Prokosch, and GARCIA, Antonio. *Music and Dance of the Tewa Pueblos*. Santa Fe: Museum of New Mexico Press, 1970. viii, 309 pp. illus.

Gives dance notations, musical scores, and texts for Tewa religious ceremonies. Analyzes the music and dance of the ceremonies and discusses Tewa society, beliefs, and geographical environment. Contains a bibliography, photographs, and drawings.

681. LANDÍVAR U., Manuel A. "Contribución al folklore poético en el Azuay." *Revista del Instituto Azuayo de Folklore* (Cuenca, Ecuador), No. 4 (Noviembre, 1971), 121-180.

Offers words without music of 217 field-collected song texts from Azuay (Ecuador), most of them four-line *coplas*. Includes classificatory indexes.

682. LANGMUIR, Gavin I. "The Knight's Tale of Young Hugh of Lincoln." *Speculum* (Cambridge, Mass.), XLVII:3 (July 1972), 459-482.

Studies events and the tradition of Jewish ritual murder as related to the events surrounding the death of Hugh of Lincoln in 1255. The legend of Hugh of Lincoln enters Chaucer's prioress' tale and also Anglo-Norman ballad literature.

683. LAWS, G. Malcolm, Jr. *The British Literary Ballad: A Study in Poetic Imitation*. Carbondale, Illinois: Southern Illinois University Press, 1972. 180 pp.

Studies the evolution of literary balladry from folk ballads and broadside ballads prior to the 18th centry. Contains four main sections: "Literary Ballad Styles," "Literary Ballad Subjects," "The Archaic Literary Ballad," and "Humorous Literary Ballads and Parodies."

684. LEDANG, Ola Kai. "On the Acoustics and the Systematic Classification of the Jaw's Harp." In *1972 YIFMC*. Pp. 95-103.

Surveys different types of jaw's harps, considers theories that have been propounded about the instrument, and by means of electronic sound spectographs seeks to establish a new general outlook on the acoustical and musical properties of the jaw's harp. Includes drawings.

685. "La lengua alemana como mediadora de otras poesías: La poesía de los esquimales." *Humboldt* (Munich), Año XIV (1973):50, pp. 97-104.

Gives German translations of some Eskimo songs from collections by such people as Franz Boas, Peter Freuchen, *et al.* Some are folkloric in character. A commentary that accompanies the collection discusses their place in Eskimo tradition. Includes drawings.

686. LEWIN, Olive. "Jamaica's Folk Music." In *1971 YIFMC*. Pp. 15-22.

Treats Jamaican folk music as rooted in both native Indian and African traditions. Holds that the ritual, ceremonial, social, functional, and recreational roles of traditional music in Africa are found also in Jamaica.

687. "Library of Congress Recordings." *Old Time Music* (London), No. 1 (Summer, 1971), 23-24; No. 2 (Autumn, 1971), 21-22; No. 3 (Winter, 1971-1972), 24.

A continuing list in alphabetical order of folk music recordings held by the Library of Congress.

688. LIMA, Rossini Tavares de. *Romanceiro folclórico do Brasil*. São Paulo, Brasil: Irmãos Vitale, 1971. 112 pp.

Gives words and music of twenty Brazilian *romances* (i.e., ballads), many in multiple versions and all orally collected. Most are from São Paulo. Includes introductory comments about each ballad family, a general introduction, and bibliography.

689. LIST, George. "El conjunto de gaitas de Colombia, la herencia de tres culturas." *RMC*, XXVII:123-124 (Julio-Diciembre, 1973), 43-54.

Studies contributions made to a Colombian folk ensemble by Spanish, African, and Amerindian cultures. Conclusions are based on the musical instruments played and the form of the texts sung.

690. LIST, George. *Ensayos sobre etnomusicología*. México: Ediciones del Conservatorio Nacional de Música, 1973. Diverse pagination [160 pp].

A series of lectures given at the Conservatorio Nacional de Música, Mexico City, in August, 1971. Discusses the history and development of ethnomusicology, fieldwork, transcription and classification of traditional music, musical acculturation, and relations between melody and text in song.

691. LOGSDON, Guy. "Speedy West." *JEMFQ*, IX, Part 2 (Summer, 1973), No. 30, 78-83.

Discuss the career and instrumental techniques of famous country and western guitarist from Missouri, Speedy West. Includes photographs and a discography.

692. LOMAX, Alan. "Brief Progress Report: *Cantometrics–Choreometrics Projects*." In *1972 YIFMC*. Pp. 142-145.

Reports on progress thus far on ambitious long-term projects being carried out at Columbia University to study world-wide song performances and dance performances by new methods of analysis known by the coined terms of *cantometrics* and *choreometrics*.

693. LÓPEZ GORGE, Jacinto. "Los intelectuales y el cante flamenco." *EL*, No. 519 (1 julio, 1973), 10-14.

Offers a transcription of tape-recorded comments about current attitudes toward flamenco singing as expressed by six Spanish intellectuals (i.e., writers, an investigator of the subject, poets, etc.) in a round-table discussion. They perceive that intellectuals are turning increasingly toward flamenco and Spanish folkloric traditions in general.

694. LOVELL, John, Jr. *Black Song: The Forge and the Flame: The Story of How the Afro-American Spiritual Was Hammered Out*. N.Y.: Macmillan Company; London: Collier-Macmillan Ltd., 1972. xviii, 686 pp. illus.

A huge volume that studies Afro-American spirituals past and present and in the part that is of most interest to folklorists seeks their origins in black folksongs. But the study also treats themes, singers who perform or have performed spirituals, the spiritual as a world phenomenon, etc. Includes almost fifty pages of bibliography in source notes; also indexes and many photographs.

695. MCARTUR, Enrique S. "Los bailes de Aguacatán y el culto a los muertos." *Estudios Centro Americanos* (San Salvador), XXVII:283 (Mayo, 1972), 255-271.

Notes several types of traditional group dances that are performed in Aguacatán (Guatemala) and then examines the reasons for dancing (principally out of fear of the dead who are supposed to be liberated by such dancing). Also analyzes the "structure" of the dances (i.e., preparations, making contact with the dead, obtaining costumes etc.).

696. MCDANIEL, John N. "Giuseppe Cocchiara's 'The Revolt of Poetry.'" *TFSB*, XXXIX:4 (December, 1973), 119-128.

Presents a translation into English of Chapter 8 of Italian folklorist Giuseppe Cocchiara's *Storia del Folklore in Europa* published in 1952. Deals with the pre-romantic growth of appreciation for the poetry of the folk in England, focusing upon MacPherson's *Ossian* and Percy's *The Reliques of Ancient English Poetry*.

697. MCDONALD, James J. "Principal Influences on the Music of the Lilly Brothers of Clear Creek, West Virginia." *JAF*, LXXXVI:342 (October-December, 1973), 331-344.

Offers a brief historical survey of the rise of hillbilly music of various types and styles during the 20th century and then traces the career of the Lilly Brothers group of singer-instrumentalists from 1925-1970. Includes an appendix.

698. MCDOWELL, John H. "Cultural Evolution and the Singing, Dancing Throng: An Objective Approach to Intellectual History." *FAUFA*, Nos. 4-5 (1972-1973), 1-9.

Reviews the development of the theory of ballad origins which held that the earliest ballads were produced communally by singing and dancing throngs. Seeks to show how it was a natural outgrowth of the intellectual and cultural climate of the late 19th and early 20th centuries.

699. MADELUNG, A. Margaret Arent. *The Laxdoela Saga: Its Structural Patterns*. Chapel Hill: University of North Carolina Press, 1972. xiii, 258 pp.

A very scholarly and detailed literary study of the Icelandic *Laxdoela Saga*. Analyzes its plan and stylistic characteristics and delves into many aspects of the work that relate to its oral or folkloric sources. Includes appendices, bibliography, and indexes.

700. MAGALHÃES, Celso de. *A poesia popular brasileira. Introdução e notas de Braulio do Nascimento*. Rio de Janeiro: Divisão de Publicáções e Divulgáção, 1973. 113 pp. illus.

Republishes with an excellent introduction, notes, and commentary a series of ten articles said to be the first published in Brazil on folkloric poetry and song. They appeared in 1873 in *O Trabalho*, a newspaper of Recife, and dealt mostly with traditional ballads (i.e., *romances*). Includes plates and indexes.

701. MAKEBA, Miriam, comp. *The World of African Song*. Chicago: Quadrangle Books, 1971. 119 pp. illus.

Presents words, music, and English translations of 24 songs, some of them traditional songs or folksongs of recent origin, collected from the Zulu and Xhosa peoples. An introduction by Solomon Mbabi-Katana discusses the form and function of African folksong, African musical instruments, and the singer's role. Contains many illustrations and a discography.

702. MALONE, Bill C. "From Folk to Hillbilly to Country: The Coming of Age of America's Rural Music." In *ORTF*. Pp. 101-116.

Traces the history of American rural music from its local appeal and folk roots in the rural South to its national popularity. Focuses upon the careers of outstanding muscians past and present. Contains photographs.

703. MARTÍNEZ GARCÍA, Gabriel. "Una referencia poco conocida de Federico García Lorca, a las añadas de Asturias." *Boletín del Instituto de Estudios Asturianos* (Oviedo, España), Año XXVII:79 (Mayo-Agosto, 1973), 389-401.

With some observations of the famous poet Federico García Lorca as a point of departure, the author comments upon Spanish lullabies and their unusual characteristics. Deals particularly but not exclusively with those from Asturias. Gives words and music of several examples.

704. MESSENGER, Betty. "Picking Up the Linen Threads: Some Folklore of the Northern Irish Linen Industry." *JFI*, IX:1 (June, 1972), 18-27.

Discusses songs and rhymes in circulation from 1900 to 1940 in the spinning mills of counties in Ulster, Ireland. Gives the words of some songs and rhymes.

705. MISIEWICZ, Roger. "Sacred Harp Notes." *Old Time Music* (London), No. 3 (Winter, 1971-1972), 20-21.

A brief discussion of fa-sol-la singing as found mainly in the southern U.S. Takes note of recordings and some hymnals that can be purchased.

706. MOYLE, Alice M. "Sound Films for Combined Notation: The Groote Eylandt Field Project, 1969." In *1972 YIFMC*. Pp. 104-118.

Reports on techniques, problems, results, etc. of the Groote Eylandt Field Project which obtained sound films of northern Australian aboriginal dancing from which notations (transcriptions) of complete dance items and their related songs were made. Includes words and music of examples, photographs, and drawings.

707. MULLEN, Patrick B. "Folk Songs and Family Traditions." In *ORTF*. Pp. 49-63.

Comments upon and presents the words of six ballads sung and written down by the author's grandfather, who had moved from Arkansas to Southeast Texas in the early 1900's. Notes analogues and discusses the context and function of the songs.

708. MUÑOZ V., Milina. "Juegos de salón: Penitencias. Los aguinaldos. La baraja o juego de naipes." *RCF*, IV:10 (1966-1969), 85-105.

Describes some twenty or thirty parlor games, penalties, etc. said now to be falling into disuse. There is a special section of Christmans games (i.e., *aguinaldos*) and another on various card games.

709. NELSON, Donald Lee. "The Ohio Prison Fire." *JEMFQ*, IX, Part 2 (Summer, 1973), No. 30, 42-45.

Gives a historical account of the 1930 prison fire in Columbus, Ohio, in which 250 people died. Shows its impact upon the public as manifested in recorded "event ballads" written by Carson J. Robison and Bob and Charlotte Miller. Presents the words to the songs and an illustration.

710. NELSON, Donald Lee. "Ridgel's Fountain Citians." *JEMFQ*, IX, Part 1 (Spring, 1973), No. 29, 8-9.

Reviews the brief career of a four-member string band founded by fiddler Leroy R. Ridgel which sang and recorded hillbilly music in Knoxville, Tennessee, between 1927 and 1930. Includes a discography and a photograph.

711. NELSON, Donald Lee. "The Crime at Quiet Dell." *JEMFQ*, VIII, Part 4 (Winter, 1972), No. 28, 203-210.

Gives an account of a heinous murder in West Virginia in 1931 and discusses two hillbilly event ballads concerning it written by A. H. Grow and Leighton D. Davies and by Bob Miller. Contains pictures, the words to one song, and the music and words to the other.

712. NELSON, Donald Lee. "Okeh 45303." *JEMFQ*, VIII, Part 4 (Winter, 1972), No. 28, 194-195.

Reviews the life and career of Charles Mumford Bean, country fiddler from Itawamba County, Mississippi, who with his band made a recording on the Okeh label in 1928. Contains photographs.

713. NELSON, Donald Lee. "The Sinking of the *Vestris*." *JEMFQ*, IX, Part 1 (Spring, 1973), No. 29, 10-14.

Relates the accounts of the steamship *Vestris'* sinking in the Atlantic Ocean in November, 1928. Presents the words to "event ballads" composed by Carson Robison, Dempsey Jones, and an unknown composer. Discusses the possible reasons why these songs about the disaster did not enter tradition. Includes a discography and illustrations.

714. *1971 Yearbook of the International Folk Music Council*, ed. by Charles Haywood. Manufactured in Canada: UNESCO, 1972. 203 pp.

Contains nine main articles on folk music and song by Samuel Baud-Bovy, John Blacking, Norman Cazden, Francis Collinson, Peter R. Cooke, Olive Lewin, Hugh Shields, Erich Stockmann, and Walter Wiora. These are listed separately in this bibliography. Some shorter notes have not been listed above.

715. *1972 Yearbook of the International Folk Music Council*, ed. by Charles Haywood. Manufactured in Canada: UNESCO, 1973. 200 pp. illus.

Contains eleven main articles on folk music and song by Bertrand H. Bronson, Robert A. Chipman and Stephen Erdely, Edith Gerson-Kiwi, Aldrienne L. Kaeppler, Robert Kauffman, Ola Kai Ledang, Alice M. Moyle, Poul Rovsing Olsen, Mosunmola Omibiyi, E. Thomas Stanford, and Bonnie C. Wade. These are listed separately in this bibliography as are some briefer contributions by Charles Haywood, Alan Lomax, and Luis Felipe Ramón y Rivera.

716. NOEBEL, David. "New Work on Folk Music Verifies Crusade's Stand." *Christian Crusade Weekly* (Tulsa, Oklahoma), XII:29 (May 28, 1972), 1, 6.

Calls attention to R. Serge Denisoff's recent book, *Great Day Coming: Folk Music and the American Left* (1971), as proof that much urban folk music has been inspired by the Communist Party. Holds that Denisoff's book confirms the findings of Noebel's own work, *Rhythm, Riots, and Revolution* (1966).

717. OHRLIN, Glenn. "Selections from the Hell-Bound Train." *MSF*, I:2 (Summer, 1973), 55-68.

From a collection of cowboy and rodeo songs by Glenn Ohrlin (*The Hell-Bound Train*, scheduled for publication by the University of Illinois Press) come some samples of Arkansas material with commentary and line drawings. Words and music are given for "Old Time Cowboy," "Pride of the Prairie," "The Texas Rangers," "Button Willow Tree," and "The Sweeter the Breeze Number 1." Includes a biblio-discography of these songs by Harlan Daniel.

718. "Okeh 45000 Series." *Old Time Music* (London), No. 1 (Summer, 1971), 25-26; No. 2 (Autumn, 1971), 23-24.

Lists recordings in this famous series of "folk" or "country" music issued under the Okeh label.

719. OMIBIYI, Mosunmola. "Folk Music and Dance in African Education." In *1972 YIFMC*. Pp. 87-94.

Discusses problems of African folk music and dance and their acceptance in the modern world. Considers their place in the curriculum in African education.

720. O'NEILL, Francis. *Irish Minstrels and Musicians, with Numerous Dissertations on Related Subjects*. Darby, Pa.: Norwood Editions, 1973. viii, 497 pp. illus.

Reissue of the 1913 edition (Chicago: The Regan Printing House). Gives biographies of traditional Irish musicians known from ancient times to the 1800's, including pipers, fiddlers, harpers, pipemakers, fluters, warpipers, music collectors, etc. Also provides examples of Irish folk tunes and texts and traces the history of some instruments. A new introduction is by Barry O'Neill. Contains illustrations, diagrams, and a bibliography.

721. PARK, John O. "'The Kosciusko Bootlegger's Gripe': A Ballad as History and Argumentation." *MSF*, I:1 (Spring, 1973), 27-32.

Presents the text of a protest song written by Negro bootleggers of Kosciusko, Mississippi, to lament their imprisonment in the 1930's. Relates it to information received in an interview with the arresting sheriff.

722. PEACOCK, Kenneth. *A Garland of Rue: Lithuanian Folksongs of Love and Betrothal*. Ottawa: National Museum of Man, 1971. 60 pp, (*Publications in Folk Culture, No. 2.*)

Gives music and words in Lithuanian and English of 28 folksongs pertaining to the "mating cycle" collected in Toronto and other urban centers of southern Ontario in 1967-1968. Includes informant data, commentary, and an introduction in English and French. Also includes four flexidiscs that contain recordings of all the songs.

723. PEARSON, Barry. "The Late Great Elmore James." *KFQ*, XVII:4 (Winter, 1972), 162-172.

Reviews the career and studies the music of Elmore James, blues singer-guitarist from Mississippi.

724. PENNA, Mario. "Las *Rimas* de Béquer y la poesía popular." *Revista de Filología Española* (Madrid), LII (1969):1-4, pp. 187-215.

Studies the relationship between folk poetry and the poems of Gustavo Adolfo Bécquer (1836-1870). Suggests caution in drawing conclusions about similarities between Bécquer's work and certain lines that seem to be folkloric because the main collections of Spanish folk poetry were made *after* Bécquer's death. Some lines of his poems may have passed into oral tradition.

725. PIKE, Gustavus D. *The Singing Campaign for Ten Thousand Pounds; or the Jubilee Singers in Great Britain*. Freeport, N.Y.: Books for Libraries Press, 1971. xiv, 272 pp. illus.

Reissue of the 1875 edition (American Missionary Association). Reports the experiences of and the reception given to the Fisk University Jubilee Singers in England, Ireland, and Scotland in 1873 and 1874 on a tour designed to earn money for this Negro University. Presents the words, the music, and a brief discussion of the "slave songs" sung by the Jubilee Singers.

726. PORRATA, Francisco E. *Incorporación del romancero a la temática de la comedia española*. N.Y.: Plaza Mayor Ediciones, 1972. 200 pp.

Treats 16th-century Spanish dramatists before Lope de Vega who drew inspiration for their works from traditional ballad literature. There is, however, little that is new in this book.

727. "A Preliminary Vernon Dalhart Discography. Part IXa: Plaza Recordings." *JEMFQ*, VIII, Part 4 (Winter, 1972), No. 28, 212-216; "Part IXb: Plaza Recordings," and "Part X: American Record Corporation Recordings." IX, Part 1 (Spring, 1973), No. 29, 15-17; "Part XI: Paramount Recordings." Part 2 (Summer, 1973), No. 30, p. 83.

A continuation of the Dalhart discography that has been running for several years in *JEMFQ*.

728. RAMÓN y RIVERA, Luis Felipe. "Maypole Songs from the Atlantic Coast of Nicaragua." In *1972 YIFMC*. Pp. 137-142.

Describes briefly a Maypole dance observed in the city of Bluefields, Nicaragua, among native blacks who are English speakers. Includes three musical examples of songs that accompany the dance.

729. *Relaciones poéticas sobre las fiestas de toros y cañas*, edited by Antonio Pérez y Gómez. 6 vols. [and still continuing]. Cieza, España: ". . . la fonte que mana y corre. . . " [i.e., Valencia: Artes Gráficas Soler], 1971-1973. (*El ayre de la almena, textos literarios rarísimos*, XXIX, XXXI-XXXV.).

A very important series of facsimile editions of old chapbooks printed from the 17th through the 19th centuries and containing narrative or descriptive poems about festivals of various kinds where bullfighting or equestrian sports took place. Many are in popular or semi-popular form (e.g., *romance* or ballad form) and students of folk poetry or Spanish fiestas will find the series of great value. Vols. I and IV contain works from the Library of Antonio Pérez Gómez; Vols. II, III, and V are from the Library of the Hispanic Society of America; and Vol. VI is from the National Library of Madrid.

730. RESTREPO DUQUE, Hernán. *Lo que cuentan las canciones: Cronicón musical*. Bogotá: Impreso por Tercer Mundo, 1971. 256 pp.

Traces the historical development of national music and song in Colombia dealing mainly with various instrumental and singing groups of concerts, records, radio, etc. mostly before about 1950. Some of the material has to do with folkloric songs, though most does not.

731. RICH, Kirby. "Our Own Music." *Mountain Life and Work* (Clintwood, Virginia), XLVIII:11 (December, 1972), 3-14.

Deals with mountain music from the time of Cecil Sharp's collecting of folksongs until the present day. Includes interviews with some folk musicians and a representative of the Southern Folk Festival.

732. RICHMOND, W. Edson. "Paris og Helen i Trejeborg: A Reduction To Essentials." In *MLFS*. Pp. 229-243.

Examines Scandinavian broadside texts of a ballad about Helen of Troy and shows that they contain two very popular medieval narratives in localized form.

733. RIMBAULT, Edward F. *Musical Illustrations of Bishop Percy's Reliques of Ancient English Poetry. A Collection of Old Ballad Tunes, etc.* Norwood Editions: Norwood, Pa., 1973. xii, 119 pp.

Reissue of the 1850 edition (London: Cramer, Beale, and Co.). A collection of tunes for some of Percy's ballads as taken from old books and manuscripts. Gives 74 tunes with a brief commentary on each.

734. RODNITZKY, J. L. "The Mythology of Woody Guthrie." *Popular Music and Society* (Bowling Green, Ohio), II:3 (Spring, 1973), 227-243.

Seeks to assay different interpretations of Woody Guthrie as a "protest" folksinger, predecessor of counter culturists, etc. Includes notes.

735. ROGERS, Edith. "'Sofía mía' en el contexto europeo." *RDTP*, XXVIII (1972): Cuadernos 3-4, pp. 275-281.

Notes the existence in New Mexico of a *romance, Sofía mía*, that seems to be related to various ballads of northern European tradition (e.g., *Lord Thomas* and *Fair Annet* in Britain) for which no counterparts have been discovered in Spanish peninsular tradition.

736. ROSS-JONES, Margaret. "Devil Dancers of Yare." *Américas*, XXV:6-7 (June-July, 1973), 12-13.

Describes superficially the performance of the Devil Dancers who are a feature of the Corpus Christi celebration in the town of Yare, Venezuela. Includes photographs.

737. RUEDA, Manuel. *Conocimiento y poesía en el folklore*. Santo Domingo: Instituto de Investigaciones Folklóricas de la Universidad Nacional Pedro Henríquez Ureña, 1971. 63 pp.

An essay which treats some of the basic problems of folklore theory and then analyzes stylistic and thematic aspects of some Dominican songs, ballads, prayers, and verbal conjurations.

738. SCHAFER, William J. "Indian Intermezzi ('Play It One More Time, Chief!')." *JAF*, LXXXVI:342 (October-December, 1973), 382-387.

Discusses the Indian-song fad that characterized popular music in the U.S. in the first decade or two of the 20th century. Seeks to analyze certain psychological aspects of the songs and gives an appendix that lists author, title, publisher, and date of 88 songs.

739. SCHMIDT, Henry. "The Huapango: A Dithyrambic Festival." In *HandH*. Pp. 147-156.

Discusses the music, dance, and verse of the mestizo *huapango* as it is performed in east-central Mexico. Includes a discography and the words to some *coplas*.

740. SCHWENDINGER, Robert J. "The Language of the Sea: Relationships Between the Language of Herman Melville and Sea Shanties of the 19th Century." *SFQ*, XXXVII:1 (March, 1973), 53-73.

Examines the similarity in tone, symbols, figurative language, and subject matter used in the writings of Herman Melville and in 19th-century sea shanties. Gives the texts of some shanties.

741. SEEGER, Pete. *The Incompleat Folksinger*. Ed. by Jo Metcalf Schwartz. N.Y.: Simon and Schuster, 1972. viii, 596 pp. illus.

Presents a collection of articles, letters, record liners, etc. and new material written by Seeger. Includes a history of the American folk music revival, a discussion of the contributions of folk and protest songs to American song tradition, guidelines for singing, methods of playing certain instruments, etc. Includes words and music of some songs.

742. SERRANO MARTÍNEZ, Celedonio. *Coplas populares de Guerrero*. México: Mario Colín, 1972. 334 pp. illus.

Presents *coplas* of the state of Guerrero (México) arranged thematically and gives information about the performers of the songs. Discusses the age, logic, classification, and singing forms of the *coplas* and gives some musical examples, but does not provide music for the main collection. Contains a short bibliography.

743. SHARPLES, Ian. "Old Time Today." *Old Time Music* (London), No. 3 (Winter, 1971-1972), 9-13.

Takes note of about 25 superior LP recordings of old-time music made within the past ten years.

744. "Shelley Lee Alley: A Discography." *JEMFQ*, IX:Part 1 (Spring, 1973), No. 29, 33-37.

Presents a discography of the recordings of Shelly Lee Alley, a pop music and western swing musician who appeared as a violinist and vocalist on radio stations in Texas in the 1920's and 1930's.

745. SHIELDS, Hugh. "Singing Traditions of a Bilingual Parish in North-West Ireland." In *1971 YIFMC*. Pp. 109-119.

Discusses folksinging customs in the Donegal parish of Glencolumbkille, where both Gaelic and English are used. Considers the stylistic aspects of some recently collected songs.

746. SIMON, Billy. "How I Rassled Out a Tune to 'Border Affair.'" *AFFword*, I:3 (October, 1971), 8-9.

The cowboy author and folksinger tells how he learned the song "Border Affair" from a book. Gives words and music of his version of the song.

747. SMITH, Colin, ed. *Poema de mío Cid*. Oxford, England: Clarendon Press, 1972. xcviii, 184 pp.

Offers a new edition of the famous Spanish epic poem. The edition of the text itself has some changes over previous readings of the unique MS, but most important is the scholarly introduction wherein the editor calls into question many of the conclusions and opinions of the great Spanish medievalist scholar Ramón Menéndez Pidal.

748. SMITH, John D. "Popular Images in the Poetry of Manuel Machado." *Kentucky Romance Quarterly* (Lexington, Kentucky), XX (1973):3, pp. 291-302.

Deals with the influence of popular poetry, particularly *coplas*, upon the poems of the 20th-century Spanish poet, Manuel Machado.

749. SOONS, Alan. "Spanish Ballad and News-Relation in Chapbook Form: The Index of a Mentality." *Kentucky Romance Quarterly* (Lexington, Kentucky), XX (1973):1, pp. 3-17.

Traces the history of the chap-book tradition in Spain from the appearance of printing to the 19th century and notes the kinds of literary genres (e.g., ballads, prose accounts of newsworthy events, etc.) and subjects that attracted publishers of chap-books.

750. SORDO SODI, Carmen. *Manuel M. Ponce, iniciador de la etnomúsica en México*. Oaxaca, México: Ediciones de la Universidad Autónoma «Benito Juarez», 1973. 29 pp.

A paper delivered in Oaxaca in March, 1973, honoring Manuel M. Ponce, composer and collector of Mexican popular and Indian songs. Treats his pioneering work in ethnomusicology and contains interviews that discuss his compositions. Presents the music to his "Cuatro Danzas Mexicanas" and portions of other works.

751. SPIELMAN, Earl V. "An Interview with Eck Robertson." *JEMFQ*, VIII:Part 4 (Winter, 1973), No. 28, 179-187.

Gives a transcription of an interview with traditional rural fiddler Eck Robertson, who began recording in 1922. Contains a photograph.

752. STANFORD, E. Thomas. "The Mexican Son." In *1972 YIFMC*. Pp. 66-86.

A useful compendium of information about not only the types of music known as the *son* in various parts of Mexico but many other terms associated with songs, dances, musical instruments, etc. (e.g., *baile, danza, mariachi, huapango, vihuela, sesquialtera*, and many others.).

753. STARK, Richard B., PEARCE, T. M., and COBOS, Rubén. *Music of the Spanish Folk Plays in New Mexico*. Santa Fe: Museum of New Mexico Press, 1969. viii, 359 pp. illus.

Gives words and music of songs from Mexico, New Mexico, and Colorado that are sung as part of the Christmas shepherd-nativity plays, *Los pastores* and *El niño perdido*. T. M. Pearce presents a text of *Los pastores* from Las Palomas, New Mexico. Rubén Cobos writes on the poetic forms used. Includes photographs and maps.

754. STARLING, Nair. *A trova e o folclore*. Rio de Janeiro— Guanabara: Editora Pongetti, 1973. 59 pp.

Offers some *trova* texts and comments upon them. They are generally grouped according to subject matter or some key word. Sources are given only for some of literary origin.

755. STAVIS, Barrie. *The Man Who Never Died: A Play About Joe Hill*. South Brunswick, N.J.: A.S. Barnes, 1972. 157 pp. illus.

A play about the execution of Joe Hill, Swedish-American migratory worker, writer of labor protest songs, and martyr-hero of the working class in the early 1900's. The introduction was written by Pete Seeger. Contains the words and music of seven songs and photographs from play productions.

756. STEVENSON, Robert. "English Sources for Indian Music until

1882." *Ethnomusicology*, XVII:3 (September, 1973), 399-442.

An excellent historico-bibliographic study that surveys sources in English about North American Indian music from 1585 to 1882. Quotes at length from many commentaries and provides numerous musical examples, copious notes, and a good bibliography.

757. STEVENSON, Robert. "Written Sources for Indian Music until 1882." *Ethnomusicology*, XVII:1 (January, 1973), 1-40.

A bibliographical essay on sources of information about Indian songs in America from 1492-1882. Early chronicles and books are Spanish-language works about Spanish America and the Southwestern part of the U.S. Includes many musical transcriptions, copious footnotes, and a general bibliography.

758. STOCKMANN, Erich. "The Diffusion of Musical Instruments as an Interethnic Process of Communication." In *1971 YIMFC*. Pp. 128-137.

Studies interethnic relations as communication processes that are important in the history and development of musical instruments.

759. STOKOE, John. *Songs and Ballads of Northern England*. Darby, Pa.: Norwood Editions, 1973. 198 pp.

Reissue of a book published in Newcastle-on-Tyne and London: Walter Scott, Ltd., n.d. Presents the words and music of 92 songs and ballads selected from ballad and song collections of Northern England. Contains explanatory notes to the songs.

760. STUART, Wendy Bross. *Gambling Music of the Coast Salish Indians*. Ottawa: National Museums of Canada, 1972. 114 pp. (*Ethnology Division, Paper No. 3.*)

Reports results of a field study of gambling songs sung among the Coast Salish peoples in British Columbia and Washington State. They accompany a bone game called Slahal. Includes many musical transcriptions and analyses, tables, a bibliography, and a brief discography.

761. SUTTON-SMITH, Brian. *The Folkgames of Children*. Austin: University of Texas Press, 1972. xvi, 559 pp. (*Publications of the American Folklore Society Biographical and Special Series, Vol. XXIV.*)

Presents study results and previously published articles, some in collaboration with other scholars. Describes children's games and changes in the games of New Zealand and America, studies the game preferences of children of different ages and cultures, and psychologically analyzes some games. Contains charts and bibliographies.

762. SWETNAM, George. "Folk Songs of Western Pennsylvania." *Western Pennsylvania Historical Magazine* (Pittsburgh), LVI:2 (April, 1973), 171-185.

Surveys many types of folksongs and gives words without music of some examples. Comments in considerable detail on some of them.

763. UITTI, D. Karl. *Story, Myth, and Celebration in Old French Narrative Poetry (1050-1200)*. Princeton, New Jersey: Princeton University Press, 1973. ix, 256 pp.

Offers an excellent and fairly sophisticated introduction to the medieval *Life of Saint Alexis*, the *Song of Roland*, and the works of Chrétien de Troyes. Intended for use by advanced undergraduate and graduate students, the work deals with legendary, mythic, and folkloric aspects of the poems studied.

764. UTLEY, Francis Lee. "The Oral Formula, Its Critics, and Its Extensions." *Studies in Medieval Culture* (Kalamazoo, Michigan), IV/1

(1973), 9-18.

In an excellent expository and critical evaluation the author surveys various studies of formulaic diction as a means of understanding the relationship of such works as the Homeric epic or *Beowulf* to oral tradition. Notes major works in the area and evaluates the implications of each.

765. VAREY, J. E. "La creación deliberada de la confusión: estudio de una diversión de Carnestolendas de 1623." In *Homenaje a William L. Fichter*. Madrid: Castalia, 1971. Pp. 745-754.

Edits a text that depicts a Shrovetide celebration in Madrid. Shows how a dance of masked figures and a burlesque wedding mock certain fundamental values of Spanish life.

766. VINÍCIUS, Marcus. "Algunas notas sobre música no Nordeste." *Revista de Cultura Vozes* (Rio de Janeiro), LXVI:9 (Novembro, 1972), 31-40.

Treats the question of whether the northeastern part of Brazil actually has a regional music and surveys the activities of composers, singers, musical groups, radio and TV stations, etc. during the late 1960's and early 1970's. Deals primarily with non-folkloric music, but some of the polemics between contending groups have revolved around the use or rejection of traditional influences in modern-day music.

767. WADE, Bonnie. "Chīz in Khyāl: The Traditional Composition in the Improvised Performance." *Ethnomusicology*, XVII:3 (September, 1973), 443-459.

Analyzes style of singing, thematic content, poetic characteristics of a contemporary vocal genre of Northern India. Gives numerous musical examples and a brief bibliography. Though the genre is apparently not really folkloric, the manner of improvisation in singing and some texts seem to have their traditional aspects.

768. WADE, Bonnie C. "Songs of Traditional Wedding Ceremonies in North India." In *1972 YIFMC*. Pp. 57-65.

Describes marriage customs in North India and gives words and music of some songs recorded by the author which form part of marriage ceremonies. Analyzes the songs and offers commentary.

769. WALKER, William. *Peter Buchan, and Other Papers on Scottish and English Ballads and Songs*. Norwood, Pa.: Norwood Editions, 1973. ix, 292 pp.

Reissue of the 1915 edition (Aberdeen: William Smith and Sons). Sketches the life and work of ballad collector Peter Buchan, referring to his letters and manuscripts. Presents notes on English and Scottish ballad scholarship and controversy. Contains a bibliography.

770. WALTMAN, Franklin M. "Formulaic Expression and Unity of Authorship in the 'Poema de Mío Cid.'" *Hispania*, LVI:3 (September, 1973), 569-578.

Presents evidence obtained from a computer study of formulaic expressions (as defined by Lord) found in the *Poema de Mío Cid*. The results, along with other stylistic consistencies, suggest a single authorship of the Spanish epic. Contains tables.

771. WARMAN GRYJ, Arturo. *La danza de moros y cristianos*. México: Secretaría de Educación Pública, 1972. 165 pp. illus. (*Sep-Setentas, 46.*)

An excellent historico-cultural treatment of the Moors and Christians dance-drama tradition in Spain and in Mexico. Studies its history in the Old World and the New, problems of its acculturation in Mexico, its development in different places and among different groups, its place in contemporary Mexican life, etc. Includes photographs.

772. WARNER, Anne, and WARNER, Frank. "Frank Noah Proffitt: Good Times and Hard Times on the Beaver Dam Road." *Appalachian Journal* (Boone, North Carolina), I:3 (Autumn, 1973), 162-193.

Recalls in very personal terms the authors' contacts with and friendship for North Carolina folksinger Frank Proffitt (1913-1965) over a span of almost thirty years. Contains reminiscences and excerpts from many personal letters from Proffitt to the Warners. Includes numerous photographs and also words and music of some songs.

773. WHALUM, Wendell Phillips. "James Weldon Johnson's Theories and Performance Practices of Afro-American Folksong." *Phylon* (Atlanta, Georgia), XXXII:4 (December, 1971), 383-395.

Takes note of Johnson's important contribution toward the understanding of Afro-American folksongs as contained in books published during the first quarter of the 20th century. In placing Johnson's work in perspective the author traces quite well the bibliographic history of scholarship in the field.

774. WHITE, John I. "He Put 'Great Grandad' on the Map." *AFFword*, III:2 (July, 1973), 25-32.

Tells the story of the song "Great Grandad" which became immensely popular after Arizona rancher-entertainer Romaine Loudermilk in 1925 concocted music for a poem by California journalist Lowell Otus Reese. Author White made the first recording of the song in 1929. Gives words and music of Loudermilk's version of the song and includes photographs of Loudermilk and Reese.

775. WILGUS, D. K., and HURVITZ, Nathan. "'Little Mary Phagan': Further Notes on a Native American Ballad in Context." *Journal of Country Music* (Nashville, Tennessee), IV:1 (Spring, 1973), 17-30.

Adduces a great deal of additional information by way of supplementing and correcting material contained in an article on the ballad of "Little Mary Phagan" by Saundra Keyes (in *Journal of Country Music* III [1972], 1-16). Includes copious notes. Keyes writes a brief reply that is appended to the Wilgus—Hurvitz article (p. 31).

776. WILKIE, Richard W. *Playing Lead Dulcimer*. Albany, N.Y.: Three City Press, 1972. 44 pp. illus.

Gives instructions for tuning and for various ways of playing the dulcimer. Includes a bibliography, drawings, and a list of dulcimer makers.

777. WIORA, Walter. "Reflections on the Problem: How Old is the Concept of Folksong." In *1971 YIFMC*. Pp. 23-33.

Takes issue with Ernest Klusen who in his *Volkslied, Fund und Erfindung* (1969) declares that Herder created the concept of folksong. Holds that Herder only refined a pre-existing concept.

778. WOLFE, Charles K. "Nashville and Country Music, 1926-1930: Notes on Early Nashville Media and Its Response to Old-Time Music." *Journal of Country Music* (Nashville, Tennessee), IV:1 (Spring, 1973), 2-16.

Seeks to establish a contextual approach in order to explain the success of the Nashville Grand Ole Opry in its early days. Deals with the Opry as an institution and the place of old-time music in the Nashville of the 1920's.

Draws mostly upon the history of radio stations, record reviews, etc.
Includes notes.

779. WRIGHT, William C., and STONE, James H. "New Evidence on
the Authorship of 'All Quiet Along the Potomac Tonight.'" *TFSB*,
XXXIX:4 (December, 1973), 111-112.

Cites evidence obtained from the diary of a Civil War Confederate
soldier which supports the claim that the author of the song "All Quiet
Along the Potomac Tonight" was the hero-soldier from Mississippi, Lamar
Fontaine. Presents the words to the song.

780. YEAGER, Lyn Allison. "A Kaleidoscope of Folk Music Colors,
Part 1." *Pioneer America* (Falls Church, Virginia), V:2 (July, 1973),
48-57.

A simplistic and romanticized discussion of North American folk music
in general (e.g., "the primitive brown of Indian chants," "the cedar tree
green of Eastern mountaineer ballads", etc.) followed by brief sections on
the different types, each containing words and music of some examples.

781. "Your Friend Frank: A Sampling from Frank Proffitt's Letters."
Appalachian Journal (Boone, North Carolina), I:3 (Autumn, 1973),
194-196.

Offers the texts of some letters written by North Carolina folksinger
Frank Proffitt to a friend, Mr. J. C. Brown. They deal with Proffitt
himself, folksongs, banjos, etc. Includes one photograph of Proffitt.

782. ZÁRATE, Dora P. de. *Textos del tamborito panameño*. Panamá:
Dora P. de Zárate, 1971. 355 pp. illus.

Gives words without music of more than five hundred *coplas* collected
in Panama among different ethnic groups. They are sung by women during
the *tamboritos* or dances with drum accompaniment. Discusses the form
and structure, themes, social meanings, and language of the texts. Contains
photographs.

783. ZUG, Charles G., III. "Scott's 'Jock of Hazeldean': The
Recreation of a Traditional Ballad." *JAF*, LXXXVI:340 (April-June,
1973), 152-160.

Treats the re-creation by Sir Walter Scott of the traditional ballad
"John of Hazelgreen" (Child 293) showing that the localization, the plot,
and the romance imagery of his re-creation have parallels in his other
works. Discusses also American versions which show that Scott's treatment
entered oral tradition.

D   DRAMA

[See also numbers 76, 104, 128, 257, 306, 309, 753, 765, 771, 801.]

784. ABRAHAMS, Roger D. "Christmas Mummings on Nevis." *NCFJ*, XXI:3 (September, 1973), 120-131.

Discusses the past tradition and the present performing of Christmas mumming in the circum-Caribbean area. Gives texts of scenes from two plays presented on the island of Nevis: "David and Goliath" and "Shakespeare Lesson."

785. ADEDEJI, Joel. "Folklore and Yoruba Drama: Ọbàtálá as a Case Study." In *African Folklore*. Pp. 321-339.

Examines the significance and function of the Yoruba ritual drama performed at the annual Ọbàtálá festival at Ede. Investigates the validity of myth-ritual theories.

786. BRANDON, James R., comp. *Traditional Asian Plays*. N.Y.: Hill and Wang, 1972. vi, 308 pp.

Provides English translations of five plays and one opera from India, Thailand, Japan, and China. Each is prefaced by a discussion of the history and theatrical techniques of the different dramatic traditions, and in some cases there is attention to folk dramatic tradition.

787. GONZÁLEZ, René Abelardo. "The *Pastorelas* of Rio Grande City and Hebronville, Texas." *FAUFA*, Nos. 4-5 (1972-1973), 10-22.

Describes two popular religious plays (i.e., *pastorelas*) as presented in Rio Grande City in 1893 and Hebronville in 1934 (?) and compares their salient features. Includes portions of the texts along with English translations. There is a brief bibliography.

788. HOY, James F. "On the Relationship of the Corpus Christi Plays to the Corpus Christi Procession at York." *Modern Philology* (Chicago), LXXI:2 (November, 1973), 166-168.

Cites records which show that the exact routes taken by the Corpus Christi plays and Corpus Christi processions at York, England, in the 14th century indicate that the two routes were both distinct and traditional. Thus it is unlikely, as some scholars believed, that the plays developed from the procession.

789. KIRBY, E. T. "Mummers' Plays and the Calendar." *JAF*, LXXXVI:341 (July-September, 1973), 282-285.

Criticizes an article by E. C. Cawte (*JAF*, LXXXV (1972), 375-376) and a book by E. C. Cawte, Alex Helm, and N. Peacock entitled *English Ritual Drama: A Geographical Index* (London, 1967). Claims there is no evidence that mummers' plays are significantly related to specific calendar days, and defends his own theory of shamanic origins.

790. LANDSBERGIS, Algirdas. "Folklore and Drama: An Encounter in Lithuania." *Books Abroad* (Norman, Oklahoma), XLVII:4 (Autumn, 1973), 689-694.

Seeks to show the easy and significant use of folklore in serious Lithuanian drama, even in plays that seem solidly realistic, historico-philosophical, or fashionably modern. Cites numerous examples.

791.   LITVAK, Lily. *El nacimiento del niño Dios*. Austin: Center for Intercultural Studies in Folklore and Oral History, University of Texas, 1973. viii, 67 pp. (*Latin American Folklore Series, No. 3*.)

Gives the text of a *pastorela* (i.e., a play about the birth of Christ that is presented at the Christmas season) collected in the village of Tarimoro, Guanajuato (Mexico). A preliminary study treats the *pastorela* tradition in Spain and Mexico. Includes words and music of some songs and notes.

792.   OTT, Rebeca de. *Danzas folklóricas y días especiales de los ignacianos*. Riberalta, Bolivia: Instituto Lingüístico de Verano en colaboración con el Ministerio de Educación y Cultura, Diciembre, 1971. 47 pp. illus.

Describes fiestas, dancers, customs, masks, etc. studied through field investigation around the old Jesuit mission of San Ignacio de Loyola in the province of Mojos (Bolivia). Treats various festival days. Includes photographs, drawings, and bibliography.

793.   PRESTON, Michael J. "The Oldest British Folk Play." *FForum*, VI:3 (July, 1973), 168-174.

Prints the text of "The Islip Mummers' Play of 1780" from Islip, Oxfordshire, England. This St. George play is considered to be the oldest recorded complete text of the work.

794.   ROBINSON, John W. "On the Evidence for Puppets in Late Medieval England." *Theatre Survey* (Pittsburgh, Pa.), XIV:1 (May, 1973), 112-117.

Adduces some documentary evidence concerning puppets and puppet-players in medieval England.

795.   "Teatro popular tradicional." *Autores, Boletim Mensal da Sociedade Portuguesa de Autores* (Lisboa), Ano XV:71 (Agosto-Outubro, 1973), 8-9.

Sketchy report on the presentation of some popular drama in the Calouste Gulbenkian Park in Lisbon. The plays given, *Auto da Floripes, Os sete infantes de Lara*, and *Ichiloli* are traditional in character. Includes photographs.

796.   YOUNG, Lung-chang. "The Dynamics of Popular Culture: Regional Theatres in Kiangsu." *JPC*, VII:1 (Summer, 1973), 51-67.

A socio-cultural survey of regional theatres in Kiangsu, an eastern province of China, based upon data gathered by cultural workers in the 1950's. Treats such matters as variations in regional theatre due to socio-historical factors, patterns of change and causes of such changes, etc. Much that is said touches on or is related to folk drama.

F   RITUAL–FESTIVAL

[See also numbers 7, 23, 54, 104, 128, 129, 141, 149, 167, 178, 185, 191, 194, 196, 207, 233, 238, 241, 250, 266, 268, 279, 293, 295, 307, 308, 309, 312, 314, 331, 335, 340, 365, 579, 647, 728, 729, 731, 736, 768, 792, 828, 833, 837, 839, 841, 847, 848, 861, 863, 879, 883, 884, 885, 896, 901, 902, 905, 922, 924, 927, 936, 939, 942, 1021, 1040, 1041.]

797. AINSWORTH, Catherine Harris. "Hallowe'en." *NYFQ*, XXIX:3 (September, 1973), 163-193.

Surveys some Hallowe'en customs in the U.S. and Europe. Then gives accounts of Hallowe'en activities as recalled and written down by a group of eighteen and nineteen-year-old informants from the area of Niagara Falls, N.Y. (pp. 174-193).

798. ARMSTRONG, Lucile. "The Verdiales Festival in Málaga (Spain), December 28th, 1971." *Folklore* (London), LXXXIII: Winter, 1972, 329-338.

Describes and interprets a festival that involves mostly competition between musical groups that feature a very large tambourine (i.e., *pandero*) and are called *pandas*. Believes it is an ancient agricultural rite.

799. BELT, Lida M. "Ritual Objects Associated with the Worship of Shango Among the Yoruba." *FForum, Bibliographic and Special Series, No. 11: Studies in Yoruba Folklore* (1973), 17-30.

Describes and discusses the function and significance of ritual objects used in the worship of Shango, the thunder deity of the Yoruba people.

800. BÖHM DE SAURINA, Katty. "Dos contribuciones al folklore de Guancache." *Anales de Arqueología y Etnología* (Mendoza, Argentina), Nos. 24-25 (1969-1970), 197-208.

A first section, "Obtención del agua para cultivos," treats means and procedures for obtaining water for a very dry area and is only marginally about folklore. A second section, "Fiestas patronales en las lagunas del Rosario," describes religious fiestas in the area of Guanacache, Mendoza (Argentina).

801. BRICKER, Victoria Reifler. *Ritual Humor in Highland Chiapas*. Austin and London: University of Texas Press, 1973. xx, 257 pp.

Studies in depth the ritualized humor that is part of fiestas such as Christmas, New Year's, Epiphany, and Carnival in Indian communities of Chiapas. Includes many texts of dialogues, songs, etc., maps, excellent photographs, analyses of jokes, speeches, and language, and extensive bibliography.

802. DALE, Bruce, photographer. "When Gypsies Gather at Appleby Fair." *National Geographic* (Washington, D.C.), CXLI:6 (June, 1972), 848-869.

A photographic essay that refers to Gypsy participation in the traditional fair at Appleby, England. Excellent color photographs with extended but usually not very informative explanatory captions.

803. DRAGOSKI, Graciela, y PÁEZ, Jorge. *Fiestas y ceremonias*

tradicionales. B.A.: Centro Editor de América Latina, 1972. 117 pp. illus.

Discusses some theoretical aspects of studying fiestas and then analyzes a wide range of different types of fiestas and ceremonies. Describes some representative fiestas, mostly religious ones.

804. FARRER, Claire R. "Performances of the Mescalero Apache 'Clowns.'" *FAUFA*, Nos. 4-5 (1972-1973), 135-151

Describes and interprets differing types of clowns and their roles in three Mescalero Apache ceremonies. Includes bibliography.

805. FETROW, Robert S. "The Penitentes of Santo Tomás." *Explorers Journal* (N.Y.), LI:3 (September, 1973), 164-166.

Describes the procession of self-flagellants (i.e., *penitentes*) who do public penance in Santo Tomás (Colombia) on Good Friday. Includes photographs.

806. FISHER, Janice Findley. "The *Quince Años* Celebration". *Katunob* (Greeley, Colorado), VIII:2 (December, 1972 [issued October, 1973]), 85-92.

Describes and comments upon the social and religious aspects of a *Quince Años* (i.e., fifteen years) celebration as observed in an upper middle-class Mexican family in a contemporary Mexican city. Interprets it as a rite-of-passage ceremony for fifteen-year-old girls.

807. FRANCO GRANDE, X. L. "A festa das sete vacas, en Tebra: ¿reminiscencia dun vello culto xermánico." *Grial* (Vigo, España), No. 39 (Xaneiro-Marzo, 1973), 10-34.

Describes a religious festival on September 8 in the town of Tebra, Galicia, where cattle are slaughtered as part of the ritual in honor of Santa María. Offers evidence that this is a Germanic tradition that has survived in Tebra. Includes photographs.

808. FRIEDEMANN, Nina S. de. "Contextos religiosos en una área negra de Barbacoas (Nariño, Colombia)." *RCF*, IV:10 (1966-1969), pp. 61-83.

Describes some ceremonies and practices of popular religion as observed among some black communities in the Department of Nariño (Colombia). Includes a saint's festival, wakes of children (i.e., *angelitos*) and of adults, etc. Includes words without music of some songs and prayers. Also gives a glossary and a brief bibliography.

809. FURST, Peter T., ed. *Flesh of the Gods: The Ritual Use of Hallucinogens*. N.Y.-Washington: Praeger Publishers, 1972. xvi, 304 pp. illus.

Contains ten papers by nine scholars, anthropologists or botanists, with an introduction by the editor. Titles are: "An Overview of Hallucinogens in the Western Hemisphere" by Richard Evans Schultes; "Tobacco and Shamanistic Ecstacy among the Warao Indians of Venezuela" by Johannes Wilbert; "The Cultural Context of an Aboriginal Hallucinogen: *Banisteriopsis Caapi*" by Gerardo Reichel-Dolmatoff; "The San Pedro Cactus in Peruvian Folk Healing" by Douglas Sharon; "To Find Our Life: Peyote among Huichol Indians of Mexico" by Peter T. Furst; "The Divine Mushroom of Immortality" and "What Was the Soma of the Aryans" by R. Gordon Wasson; "Ritual Use of *Cannibis Sativa* L.: A Historical-Ethnographic Survey" by William A. Emboden, Jr.; *"Tabernanthe Iboga*: Narcotic Ecstasis and the Work of the Ancestors" by James W. Fernández; and "Hallucinogens and the Shamanic Origins of Religion" by Weston La Barre. To a greater or lesser degree most of these contributions contain information of interest to folklorists. They have not been listed separately in this bibliography.

810. FURST, Peter. "An Indian Journey to Life's Source." *Natural History* (N.Y.), LXXXII:4 (April, 1973), 34-43.

A non-scholarly but informative description of a peyote hunt by the Huichol Indians of northwestern Mexico. The author participated in the peyote pilgrimage and thus describes first hand many customs, rituals, beliefs, etc. that he observed. Includes excellent color photographs.

811. HOYOS SANCHO, Nieves de. "Algo sobre carnavales en Ibero-américa." *Revista de Indias* (Madrid), Nos. 119-122 (Enero-Diciembre, 1970), 297-314.

A brief country by country survey of Carnival celebrations in Spanish America. Describes the various celebrations noting certain unique qualities of each and then seeks to identify and differentiate between a number of Spanish and American elements. Includes a brief bibliography.

812. LANDÍVAR U., Manual Agustín, and others. "Fiesta del Señor de las Aguas en Girón." *Revista del Instituto Azuayo de Folklore* (Cuenca, Ecuador), No. 4 (Noviembre, 1971), 6-74.

Describes in considerable detail various aspects of two fiestas of the town of Girón in the province of Azuay (Ecuador). Describes practices, foods, drink, fireworks, music, games, dances, organizations, etc. Includes words without music of some songs, dance diagrams, drawings, photographs, and a vocabulary of local terms related to the fiestas.

813. LANGLOIS, Janet. "Yemoja in Bahia." *FForum, Bibliographic and Special Series, No. 11: Studies in Yoruba Folklore* (1973), 43-51.

Discusses the worship of the Yoruba goddess Yemonja in Bahia, Brazil, and other parts of the New World, describes "candomblé" rituals, and considers syncretism with Catholic saints. Contains illustrations.

814. MEIGHAN, Clement W., and RIDDELL, Francis A. *The Maru Cult of the Pomo Indians: A California Ghost Dance Survival*. Los Angeles: Southwest Museum, 1972. 134 pp. (*Southwest Museum Papers, No. 23*.)

A fairly exhaustive anthropological study of the Maru cult of the Pomo Indians who live on the North Coast Range of California. Developed around the 1870's, the cult was studied by the authors from about 1949-1959 in a series of dance ceremonies associated with it. Includes treatment of such things as choreography, dance costumes, banners, forms of ceremonial houses, etc.

815. MEYER, Pamela and MEYER, Alfred. "Life and Death in Tana Toradja." *National Geographic* (Washington, D.C.), CXLI:6 (June, 1972), 792-815.

Describes mostly burial customs and rituals in the highlands of Sulawesi, an Indonesian island. Includes excellent color photographs.

816. NEUMANN, Franke J. "Paper: A Sacred Material in Aztec Ritual." *History of Religions* (Chicago), XIII:2 (November, 1973), 149-159.

Though the author's approach is historical and not folkloric, the data he presents from chronicles and other sources about ancient ritual uses of paper among the Aztecs in ceremonies, fiestas, etc. could well be of value to folklorists.

817. PLASS, Margaret. "The Dance of Sigi." *Expedition* (Philadelphia), XIII:2 (Winter, 1971), 18-21.

Describes preparations among the Dogon people of Mali to celebrate Sigi, the three-months-long festival in honor of tribal ancestors held every sixty years. Includes photographs.

818. POLLAK-ELTZ, Angelina. *Cultos afroamericanos*. Caracas: Universidad Católica "Andrés Bello," Instituto de Investigaciones Históricas, 1972. 258 pp.

Translation of a study published in Dutch with the title: *Afro-americaanse godsdiensten en culten* (Roermond, Holland, 1970). An important comprehensive survey of Afro-American religious cults and practices in Brazil, the Antilles, Venezuela, Surinam, and the U.S. Includes bibliography and indexes.

819. RAMA, Carlos M. "El carnaval de Rio de Janeiro." *Revista de Ciencias Sociales* (Río Piedras, Puerto Rico), XVI:3 (Septiembre, 1972), 365-375.

A sociologist relates the history of Carnival in Rio de Janeiro and describes the Carnival celebrations he observed in 1972. Contains useful information for scholars interested in Carnival customs and practices, though there is little folklore per se in the article.

820. RAY, Benjamin. "'Performance Utterances' in African Rituals." *History of Religions* (Chicago), XIII:1 (August, 1973), 16-35.

Proposes re-examination and application of some existing approaches to the study of "performative utterances" in order to gain insights into what is *done* through the use of words. Applies this approach to the performative aspects of ritual language among the Dinka people of the Southern Sudan and the Dogon of central Mali.

821. RIBEIRO, Margarida. *Cerzedelo e a sua festa das cruces: elementos para o seu estudo*. Lisboa, 1972. 197 pp. illus.

Studies a religious festival in the town of Cerzedelo near the city of Guimarães (Portugal). Gives Cerzedelo's history, describes the region, and gives a detailed description of the festival including attention to the procession, customs surrounding the celebration, popular speech, etc.

822. RIEGELHAUPT, Joyce F. "Festas and Padres: The Organization of Religious Action in a Portuguese Parish." *AA*, LXXV:3 (June, 1973), 835-851.

An anthropological-sociological study of mainly religious festivals in the Portuguese Estremaduran village of São Miguel. The emphasis is on noting the disparity between "folk Catholicism" and the normal Catholic pattern of "Church religion." Includes charts and bibliography.

823. SAAVEDRA S., Hernando. "La fiesta de San Roque." *Boletín de la Academia de Historia del Valle del Cauca* (Cali, Colombia), No. 157 (Julio de 1971). 50-56.

A literary description of the annual fiesta in honor of San Roque as celebrated in the town of Gucarí (Colombia).

824. SANTANDER, Josefa Luisa. *Folklore de la provincia de Jujuy; Fiesta de La Candelaria (Quebrada de Humahuaca y Puna)*. Jujuy, Argentina: Dirección Provincial de Cultura, 1970. 108 pp. illus.

Describes the Puna area in geographical, historical, sociological, and anthropological terms, and then studies in some depth various aspects of the traditional religious life of the region. Treats particularly religious festivals with most attention to the fiesta of La Candelaria and customs, practices, and beliefs associated with it in various communities. Includes charts, notes, a glossary, and an extensive bibliography.

825. SEPÚLVEDA, María Teresa. "Petición de lluvias en Ostolempa." *Boletín INAH* (México), Época segunda, No. 4 (Enero-Marzo, 1973), 9-20.

Studies the ceremonies associated with the traditional petition for rain that takes place annually in April and May at Ostotempa, Guerrero (Mexico). Treats beliefs, oral tradition about the petition, its history, the organization of the pilgrimage to Ostotempa, rituals, sung prayers (some texts are given) etc. Includes photographs and a brief bibliography.

826. VAN ESTERIK, John L. "The Configuration of a Ritual Act and Related Aspects of Thai Culture: A Relational Representation." *Jourral of the Steward Anthropological Society* (Urbana, Illinois), IV:1 (Fall, 1972), 1-38.

Using mathematical techniques the author studies the structure and interrelationships of some ritual acts in Thailand. Many of the practices, beliefs, customs, and ceremonies are folkloric in character, though here they are not studied as folklore. Includes bibliography.

827. VAN ESTERIK, Penny. "Thai Tonsure Ceremonies: A Re-examination of Brahmanic Ritual in Thailand." *Journal of the Steward Anthropological Society* (Urbana, Illinois), IV:2 (Spring, 1973), 79-121.

Studies Thailand rituals of cutting off the topknots of children as observed among city Brahmans and villagers who practice folk-Brahmanism. Includes a chart and bibliography.

H   BELIEF AND PRACTICE

[See also numbers 23, 76, 98, 99, 100, 102, 103, 104, 106, 108, 113, 114, 125, 126, 128, 130, 133, 134, 141, 142, 144, 145, 147, 149, 152, 153, 156, 157, 160, 161, 163, 164, 167, 173, 175, 176, 180, 182, 184, 185, 188, 190, 191, 193, 194, 196, 201, 202, 206, 207, 208, 210, 211, 213, 222, 226, 229, 233, 238, 241, 244, 250, 251, 254, 259, 263, 267, 268, 271, 272, 273, 275, 277, 279, 284, 286, 288, 290, 291, 292, 293, 295, 306, 307, 308, 309, 310, 312, 319, 323, 326, 327, 331, 334, 347, 348, 350, 351, 352, 355, 359, 363, 364, 375, 381, 394, 438, 442, 449, 467, 471, 533, 540, 613, 680, 708, 768, 792, 797, 808, 809, 810, 813, 814, 815, 816, 818, 821, 824, 826, 888, 889, 1009, 1021, 1022, 1028, 1041, 1043, 1058, 1061, 1074, 1085, 1093, 1127, 1202.]

828. ABERNETHY, Francis Edward. "The East Texas Communal Hunt." In *HandH*. Pp. 3-10.

Discusses the traditions, rituals, and beliefs of the communal hunt for game practiced in heavily wooded areas of East Texas.

829. ACKERNECHT, Erwin Heinz. *Medicine and Ethnology; Selected Essays*. Baltimore: Johns Hopkins Press, 1971. 195 pp.

A collection of essays analyzing and discussing methods for studying primitive or folk medicine. Treats medical practices, shamanism, taboos, medicine's social functions, the collecting of data, etc. Includes bibliography.

830. ASHTON, John. *The Devil in Britain and America*. Ann Arbor: Gryphon Books, 1971. x, 363 pp. illus.

Reissue of the 1896 edition (London: Ward and Downey, Limited). Gives an account of demonology and witchcraft in England and America using original sources and thoroughly examining the localized cases of the devil's appearance or influence. Presents many illustrations and a bibliography of the obscure sources consulted.

831. BAÏRACLI-LEVY, Juliette de. *Nature's Children; A Guide to Organic Foods and Herbal Remedies for Children*. N.Y.: Schocken Books, 1971. 146 pp. illus.

Discusses the role of the mother in giving birth and maintaining the health of her children by natural means. Presents herbal remedies for many ailments or diseases and recipes considered natural and healthful. The author is a Gypsy.

832. BARING-GOULD, S. *A Book of Folklore*. Detroit: Singing Tree Press, 1970. 264 pp.

Reissue of the 1913 edition (London: W. Collins and Co. Ltd.). Deals basically with beliefs and superstitions, though the discussion of these usually draws upon folktales, ballads, etc. Chapters are on "The Spirit of Man," "The Body of Man," "Sacrifice," "Pixies and Brownies," and the like. Includes bibliography and an index.

833. BEAN, Lowell John, and SAUBEL, Katherine Siva. *Temalpakh: Cahuilla Indian Knowledge and Usage of Plants*. Banning, California: Malki

Museum Press, 1972. x, 225 pp. illus.

An ethnobotanical study of plants used by the Cahuilla Indians of Southern California. A large part of the book is an annotated list of plants and their uses in rituals, cures, manufacturing (such as basketmaking), etc.

834. BELTING, Natalie Maree. "The Piasa—It Isn't a Bird." *Journal of the Illinois State Historical Society* (Springfield), LXVI:3 (Autumn, 1973), 302-305.

Discusses facts and legends about Indian petroglyphs on some cliffs in Illinois which were described by Father Marquette in the 17th century. The so-called "Piasa bird" is, according to the author, a water monster found in Algonquian and Siouan tradition.

835. BENNETT, Ernest. *Apparitions and Haunted Houses: A Survey of Evidence.* Ann Arbor: Gryphon Books, 1971. xix, 396 pp.

Reissue of the 1939 edition (London: Faber and Faber, Ltd.). Presents 104 accounts of first-hand experiences with apparitions of various kinds selected because they were "well authenticated." Holds that the apparitions were caused by telepathic action.

836. BENNETT, Marj D. "Country Kitchen." *Chronicles of Oklahoma* (Oklahoma City), LI:3 (Fall, 1973), 305-308.

Describes an Oklahoma farm kitchen of the early 20th century. Touches on customs, foods, activities that centered around the kitchen, etc.

837. BENZ, Ernst, and LUCKERT, Karl W. "The Road of Life: Report of a Visit by a Navaho Seer." *Ethnomedizin/Ethnomedicine* (Hamburg), II:3-4 (1973), 405-416.

Relates a visit by the authors, both German historians of religion, to a Navaho diviner and medicine man in order for the latter to divine the cause of a nervous-muscular ailment in the larnyx of one of the visitors. Describes rituals, proposed cures, reaction of the visitors, etc. Includes some bibliography.

838. BIRÓ DE STERN, Ana. "El medio social del habitante del altiplano jujeño." *AI*, XXXIII:3 (Julio-Septiembre, 1973), 771-781.

An ethnographic description of certain aspects of life among the Coya Indians and mestizos who live in the Jujuy highlands of Argentina. Touches on traditional customs, ceremonies and rites, etc.

839. BLACKMAN, Margaret B. "Totems to Tombtones: Culture Change as Viewed through the Haida Mortuary Complex, 1877-1971." *Ethnology*, XII:1 (January, 1973), 47-56.

An ethnographic study of changes that the introduction of Christianity brought about in the Haida mortuary complex at a village in the Queen Charlotte Archipelago off the west coast of Canada. Besides treating traditional beliefs and practices that are of interest per se to folklorists, some of the phenomena of acculturation are broadly pertinent to important concerns of folklorists.

840. BLOSS, Lowell W. "The Buddha and the Nāga: A Study in Buddhist Folk Religiosity." *History of Religions* (Chicago), XIII:1 (August, 1973), 36-53.

Studies of the relationship between the Buddha and the *nāga*, a folk deity possessing the powers of nature, particularly rain, in early Indian folk Buddhism. Draws heavily upon folkloric sources, principally myths and Jātaka tales.

841. BRAIN, Robert. *Bangwa Kinship and Marriage*. N.Y.-London: Cambridge University Press, 1972. ix, 195 pp.

A study of social practices which contains some sections of interest to folklorists (e.g., considerable attention to the rituals of witchcraft and its importance in society, taboos having to do with women and marriage, etc.).

842. BRANDES, Stanley H. "Wedding Ritual and Social Structure in a Castilian Peasant Village." *Anthropological Quarterly* (Washington, D.C.), XLVI:2 (April, 1973), 65-74.

Studies the tenacious retention by the people of a small Castilian town of the traditional wedding custom known as the *ofrecijo* (e.g., an elaborate formal presentation of money to bride and groom by guests at their wedding). Includes bibliography.

843. BRAUNS, Claus-Dieter. "The Peaceful Mrus of Bangladesh." *National Geographic* (Washington, D.C.), CXLIII:2 (February, 1973), 266-286.

A photographic essay with many excellent color photos and brief explanatory commentaries. Deal with dances, ceremonies, customs, etc.

844. BRUNETTI, Michael. "Italian Folklore Collected from Mrs. Stephanie Nappi." *NYFQ*, XXVIII:4 (March, 1973), 257-262.

A high school student reports on some folk beliefs (e.g., evil eye beliefs, etc.) and some tales gathered from his own grandmother.

845. BUDGE, E.A. Wallis. *The Divine Origin of the Craft of the Herbalist*. Ann Arbor, Michigan: Gryphon Books, 1971. xi, 96 pp. illus.

Reissue of the 1928 edition (London: Culpeper House by the Society of Herbalists). Traces the history of herbalists to the Greeks, Egyptians, Sumerians, and other ancient peoples. The author seeks to separate modern herbalists from practitioners of magic, and in so doing he deals with many folkloric subjects. Includes drawings and an index.

846. BUSS, Reinhard J. *The Klabautermann of the Northern Seas: An Analysis of the Protective Spirit of Ships and Sailors in the Context of Popular Belief, Christian Legend, and Indo-European Mythology*. Berkeley, Los Angeles, London: University of California Press, 1973. (*University of California Publications, Folklore Studies: 26*.)

A scholarly study of the Klabautermann, a ship spirit in German legendary folklore who is both loved and feared among sailors of the Northern Seas. The author identifies it as a creature of lower mythology, notes geographical distribution of the term and belief in the spirit, sources of information about it, etc. Establishes a typology of *Klabautermann* lore. Includes copious notes, a long bibliography, and an index.

847. CAMPBELL, John Gregorson. *Witchcraft and Second Sight in the Highlands and Islands of Scotland*. Detroit: Singing Tree Press, 1970. xii, 314 pp.

Reissue of the 1902 edition (Glasgow: James MacLehose and Sons). Presents information from oral sources on witchcraft, death warnings, second sight, and hobgoblins, and describes the ordering, festivals, and observances of the Celtic year in Scotland.

848. CAMPBELL, Joseph. *Myths to Live By*. N.Y.: Viking Press, 1972. x, 276 pp.

Contains twelve lectures on mythological thought and mythologies of the world delivered at the Cooper Union Forum in N.Y. between 1958 and 1971. Among the topics considered are science and myth, the significance of rites, Eastern and Western art and religion, mythologies of love, war, and peace, schizophrenia, and the moon walk.

849. CARLOS, Manuel L. "Fictive Kinship and Modernization in

Mexico: A Comparative Analysis." *Anthropological Quarterly* (Washington, D.C.) XLVI:2 (April, 1973), 75-91.

Analyzes the impact of modernization on the traditional practice of *compadrazgo* or fictive kinship in Mexico. Treats origins of the custom, its existence in rural and urban settings and on different social levels, etc.

850. [CARRUTHERS, Miss]. *Flower Lore*. Detroit: Singing Tree Press, 1972. 233 pp.

Reissue of the 1879 edition (Belfast: McCaw, Stevenson, and Orr Linenhall Works). A miscellany of flower and plant lore that draws mostly on literary sources from many different historical periods.

851. CASCUDO, Luís da Câmara. "Divórcio no talher." *REP*, XVI:2 (Abril, 1971), 1-4 [pagination of a separata; I have not seen the journal].

A humorous discussion of how European table customs have recently all but dispensed with the use of knives. What since the 18th century had been done with knife and fork is now done by the fork alone.

852. CASCUDO, Luís da Câmara. "Uma nota sobre o cachimbo inglês." *REP*, XV:4 (Outubro, 1970), 5-11 [pagination of a separata; I have not seen the journal].

Reflects on the importance of his pipe to a "typical" Englishman and cites lines from various sources, mostly literary ones, that attest to the use of pipes not only by Englishmen but other groups as well.

853. CHASE, Ernest Dudley. *The Romance of Greeting Cards*. Detroit: Tower Books, 1971. xv, 255 pp. illus.

Reissue of the 1926 edition (Cambridge, Mass.: University Press). Discusses the origin and history of Christmas and Valentine cards and greetings for other occasions. Treats the methods used in the industry for designing cards and presents many examples of verse greetings and reproductions of unusual cards.

854. CHOWNING, Ann. "Ceremonies, Shell Money, and Culture among the Kove." *Expedition* (Philadelphia), XV:1 (Fall, 1972), 2-8.

An ethnographic description of the Kove (or Kombe) people on the island of New Britain. Data on customs, rituals, taboos, etc. might be of interest to some folklorists. Includes photographs.

855. CHRISTIAN, William A., Jr. "Holy People in Peasant Europe." *Comparative Studies in Society and History* (N.Y.-London), XV:1 (January, 1973), 106-114.

Treats the question of contemporary cults of folk saints, with particular attention to four little girls in San Sebastián de Garabandel, Santander (Spain), who had a vision of the Archangel Michael in 1961. Also considers two Italian folk saints.

856. CLODD, Edward. *Myths and Dreams*. Ann Arbor: Gryphon Books, 1971. x, 251 pp.

Reissue of the 1891 edition (London: Chatto and Windus). Discusses the evolutionary survival of primitive myths in science, history, philosophy, and theology, and considers the role of dreams in the development of supernatural beliefs.

857. CURRIE, William. *An Historical Account of the Climates and Diseases of the United States of America and of the Remedies and Methods of Treatment, Which Have Been Found Most Useful and Efficacious, Particularly in Those Diseases Which Depend upon Climate and Situation*. N.Y.: Arno Press and The New York Times, 1972. 409. v pp.

Reissue of the 1792 edition (Philadelphia: T. Dobson). Surveys by regions the diseases and cures for diseases found in the various areas of the U.S. The book is written with serious intent, but it is a mine of information about beliefs and traditional cures as they existed late in the 18th century.

858. DALYELL, John Graham. *The Darker Superstitions of Scotland*. Norwood, Pa.: Norwood Editions, 1973. vii, 700 pp.

Reissue of a book published in 1835 (Glasgow: Richard Griffin and Co.). Describes and attempts to explain Scottish superstitions about diseases and their remedies, plants and animals, divination and sorcery, ghosts etc. taken from historical records and other manuscripts. Relates some of them to superstitions of antiquity and beliefs held in other geographical areas.

859. DORADO Y DÍEZ-MONTERO, Alberto. "En torno a la magia." In *PIHS (I)*, 243-262.

Treats magic practices and witchcraft in Spain, basing the discussion mostly on historical and literary sources.

860. "Folk Medicine from Fostoria." *JOFS*, II:2 (August, 1973), 46-48.

Gives some folk cures collected by students in a high school folklore class.

861. GARCÍA BARROS, Manuel. *Aventuras de Alberte Quiñoi*. Vigo: Edicións Castrelos, 1972. 266 pp.

A fictional work in diary form which is replete with folkloric data about life in the Tierra de Tabeirós region of Galicia (Spain). Touches on such things as children's games, festivals, folk medicine, work customs, burial practices, regional cooking, etc.

862. GARRIOTT, Edward B. *Weather Folk-Lore and Local Weather Signs*. Detroit: Grand River Books, 1971. 153 pp.

Reissue of the 1903 edition (Washington: Government Printing Office). A section on "Weather Folklore" (pp. 5-47) deals with various beliefs having to do with weather, storms, winds, seasons, stars, animals, birds, etc. A second section, "Local Weather Signs" (pp. 49-153) reports on weather observations made at 143 cities and towns in the U.S. Includes maps.

863. GIMLETTE, John D. *Malay Poisons and Charm Cures*. Foreword by W. H. Willcox. N.Y. and London: Oxford University Press, 1971 [i.e., 1972]. xiv, 301 pp. illus.

Reissue of the 1929 third edition (London: Oxford University Press). Deals with ritual, medicinal cures, poisons, shamans, spirit dances, exorcism, etc. in the eastern Malay State of Kelantan.

864. GRANDA, Germán de. "Un caso de utilización de datos etnográficos con finalidad lingüística en el área hispanoamericana." *RDTP*, XXIX (1973):1-2, pp. 61-72.

Compares magic beliefs and practices of blacks in San Basilio de Palenque, Departamento de Bolívar (Colombia), with those of a similar group of "congos" in Cuba in order to prove that both are of Bantu origin in Africa. Uses this evidence to support earlier linguistic studies that arrived at similar conclusions.

865. GRANDA, Germán de. "Un caso más de influencia canaria en Hispanoamérica (brujería 'isleña' en Cuba)." *RDTP*, XXIX (1973):1-2, pp 155-162.

Notes that certain beliefs of Cuban blacks about witchcraft are similar to those found in the Canary Islands. Speculates on how this folklore penetrated into Cuba.

866. GUEVARA, Darío. *Un mundo mágico-mítico en la mitad del mundo; folklore ecuatoriano*. Quito: Imprenta Municipal, 1972. 468 pp.

The bulk of the volume (pp. 55-425) is a "Diccionario del folklore mágico-mítico ecuatoriano" which lists alphabetically and defines, often at considerable length, several hundred terms having to do with magic beliefs and practices. An introduction (pp. 11-53) discusses magic, superstitions, witchcraft, and related subjects. Includes a bibliography of 150 items and indexes.

867. HAINING, Peter. *The Anatomy of Witchcraft*. N.Y.: Taplinger Pub. Co., 1972. 212 pp. illus.

Studies the practice of black magic, witchcraft, and voodoo in Modern Britain, the United States, and Europe. Gives examples of rituals and quotes from interviews with practitioners. Contains photographs and a bibliography.

868. HALL, G. D. "Yoruba Numbers." *FForum, Bibliographic and Special Series, No. 11: Studies in Yoruba Folklore* (1973), 1-16.

Surveys the numerical system and the connotations and associations of specific numbers in Yoruba tradition.

869. HAND, Wayland D. "Hangmen, the Gallows, and the Dead Man's Hand in American Folk Medicine." In *MLFS*. Pp. 323-329.

Examines the folk medical practice of using things connected with the dead for curing and preventing illness. Notes modern American instances and European parallels.

870. HENRÍQUEZ, Enrique C. *Crímenes de la brujería; la sugestión criminal en los ignorantes fanáticos*. B.A.: Ediciones Depalma, 1970. xii, 229 pp.

A former prison doctor from Cuba studies crimes committed in the name of witchcraft and beliefs in magic. Stresses particularly practices such as voodoo which have African origins. The approach is medical and psychological, but folklorists interested in magic practices will find much that is of interest.

871. HILLIARD, Addie Suggs. "A Lick o' Lemon." *KFR*, XIX:3 (July-September, 1973), 79-86.

Assembles an interesting body of lemon lore. Includes some beliefs and traditions taken from literature, but mostly the collection revolves around traditional household uses of lemons in cooking, folk cures, preserving freshness of linens, etc. Includes informant data, notes, and bibliography.

872. HILLIARD, Sam Bowers. *Hog Meat and Hoecake: Food Supply in the Old South, 1840-1860*. Carbondale and Edwardsville: Southern Illinois University Press; London and Amsterdam: Feffer and Simons, 1972. xiv, 296 pp.

A historical study of food production in the south. It contains, however, a chapter on southern eating habits that folklorists interested in regional cooking and traditional eating customs may find of value.

873. HITCHCOCK, Ann. "Gods, Graves, and Historical Archaeologists: A Study of a Mormon Cemetery in Tucson." *AFFword*, I:4 (January, 1972), 11-20.

Studies a Mormon cemetery by commentary and a series of photographs, describes types of gravemakers, discusses Mormon burial customs, etc. Includes bibliography.

874. HITCHCOCK, Ann. "Gods, Graves, and Historical Archaeologists: A Study of Two Papago Cemeteries in Southern Arizona."

AFFword, I:2 (July, 1971), 7-17.

Studies two Papago burial grounds and describes many burial customs and beliefs. Includes photographs of graves and grave markers, drawings of graves, etc.

875. HODGE, Robert A. "Some Madstones of Virginia." *Pioneer America* (Falls Church, Virginia), V:1 (January, 1973), 1-8.

Describes some Virginia madstones, provides photographs of a few, and documents various alleged cures of dog and snake bites, insect stings, etc. attributed to them.

876. IBERICO MAS, Luis. *El folklore mágico de Cajamarca*. Trujillo, Perú: Universidad Nacional de Cajamarca, 1971. 213 pp. illus.

Surveys syncretistic magic, witchcraft, and folk cures of Cajamarca, Peru. Includes transcriptions of many legends and beliefs. Presents some photographs and a bibliography.

877. KAAIAKAMANU, D. M., and AKINA, J. K. *Hawaiian Herbs of Medicinal Value Found Among the Mountains and Elsewhere in the Hawaiian Islands, and Known to the Hawaiians to Possess Curative and Palliative Properties Most Effective in Removing Physical Ailments*. Translated by Akaiko Akana. Rutland, Vt.: C. E. Tuttle Co., 1972. 74 pp.

Reissue of the 1922 edition (Board of Health of the Territory of Hawaii). Lists more than 169 plants found in Hawaii which are used as remedies for physical ailments. Describes the plants, notes where they can be found, and discusses their preparation and use as medicine.

878. KARLIN, Alma M. *The Death-Thorn: Magic, Superstitions, and Beliefs of Urban Indians in Panama and Peru*. Detroit: Blaine Ethridge, 1971. 346 pp. illus.

Reissue of the 1934 edition (London: George Allen and Unwin Ltd.). A kind of personal travel book about the author's experiences in Peru and Panama. Though very unscholarly, it does contain information about magic, charms, sorcery, witches, etc. Includes a glossary.

879. KIRK, Malcolm S. "Change Ripples New Guinea's Sepik River." *National Geographic* (Washington, D.C.), CXLIV:3 (September, 1973), 354-381.

Relates experiences on an expedition among peoples of Papua, New Guinea, who live along the Sepik River. Notable for excellent color photographs, the article deals with certain customs, ceremonies, rituals, masks, etc.

880. KOENIG, Edna L. "The Cattle Auction in Central Texas: Analysis of Social Interaction." *FAUFA*, Nos. 4-5 (1972-1973), 60-77.

Describes and analyzes practices observed in several cattle auctions studied in the Austin area of Texas. Treats functional and structural aspects of such auctions, particularly their importance as social institutions. Includes charts and a bibliography.

881. KORS, Alan C., and PETERS, Edward, eds. *Witchcraft in Europe, 1100-1700: A Documentary History*. Philadelphia: University of Pennsylvania Press, 1972. viii, 382 pp. illus.

Offers 44 documents with a general preface and explanatory notes for each subdivision and individual items. Some documents are popular narratives about witches, some are descriptions of witchcraft trials, and others are treatises on witchcraft by intellectuals. Includes reproductions of old woodcuts.

882. LAING, Jeanie M. *Notes on Superstition and Folklore*. Norwood, Pa.: Norwood Editions, 1973. xv, 107 pp.

Reissue of the 1885 edition (Brechin: The Advertiser Office; and
Edinburgh: John Menzies and Co.). Presents Scottish superstitions and
folklore connected with baptism, marriage, death, funerals, and fishing.
Notes legends of ghosts, fairies, brownies, and witches; also superstitions
concerning animals.

883. LAMBERT, Marjorie F. "Christmas Day in a Rio Grande
Pueblo." *El Palacio* (Santa Fe, New Mexico), LXXIX:3 (December, 1973),
6-7.

Describes Christmas customs (e.g., food, ceremonies, dances, singing,
etc.) in a Rio Grande Indian town in northern New Mexico. Brief and
superficial but deals with interesting acculturation that combines Indian
with Spanish-Mexican or North American elements.

884. LARSON, Thomas J. "Ancestor Worship and Group Therapy of
the Hambukushu of Ngamiland." *Virginia Social Science Journal* (Richmond), VIII:2 (July, 1973), 1-8.

An anthropological report on beliefs about spirits of the dead among a
small group of Bantu-speaking people in Ngamiland of Botswana, Africa.
Deals with magic, cures, ceremonies, etc.

885. LEACOCK, Seth, and LEACOCK, Ruth. *Spirits of the Deep:
Drums, Mediums and Trance in a Brazilian City*. Garden City, N.Y.:
Doubleday-Natural History Press, 1972. 416 pp. illus.

Describes and seeks to interpret some Afro-Brazilian cults which the
authors group under the general name *Batuque*. Treats beliefs, mediums,
spirits, possession, curing, ritual, and similar topics, some of them related
to the concerns of folklorists. Includes appendices (one of ceremonial
songs), a glossary, a bibliography, and excellent photographs.

886. LEININGER, Madeleine. "Witchcraft Practices and Psychocultural Therapy with Urban U.S. Families." *Human Organization*
(Boulder, Colorado), XXXII:I (Spring, 1973), 73-83.

Studies witchcraft behavior as a product of the psychocultural struggle
of certain groups to adjust in recent years to rural-urban acculturational
situations. Focuses primarily upon Spanish and Mexican-American
families. Describes therapy employed by the author which allegedly was
successful.

887. LLOMPART, Gabriel. "Penitencias y penitentes en la pintura y
en la piedad catalanas bajomedievales: un estudio de folklore retrospec-
tivo." *RDTP*, XXVIII (1972): Cuadernos 3-4, pp. 229-249.

Studies penitential customs and practices of pilgrims in eastern Spain
over many centuries. Draws upon some tales and popular songs, but
mostly upon medieval paintings, church documents, etc.

888. LONG, Eleanor. "Aphrodisiacs, Charms, and Philtres." *WF*,
XXXII:3 (July, 1973), 153-163.

Surveys various kinds of love-magic as found from ancient times to the
present in many parts of the world. Identifies many motifs, provides
bibliographical data in footnotes, and includes a glossary.

889. LYNAS, Lothian, comp. *Medicinal and Food Plants of the North
American Indians, A Bibliography*. Bronx, N.Y.: Library of the New York
Botanical Garden, 1972. 21 pp.

An unannotated bibliography of close to four hundred items. Some
clearly deal with cures, Indian foods and their preparation, peyotism, etc.

890. MACKLIN, Barbara June, and CRUMRINE, N. Ross. "Three
North Mexican Saint Movements." *Comparative Studies in Society and
History* (London-N.Y.), XV:1 (January, 1973), 89-105.

Studies three internationally known folk saints-curers from Mexico: 'Santa' Teresa of Sonora, who achieved fame in the 1880's; the "Niño Santo" Fidencio of Nuevo León acclaimed in the 1920's; and "San" Damián, a Mayo Indian of Sonora, who received recognition in 1958. Traces and analyzes their careers.

891. MADARIAGA, Benito. "Algunas supersticiones modernas marineras de Cantabria." In *PIHS (I)*, 87-95.

Mentions some superstitions of sailors in Santander and elsewhere concerning priests, animals and fish, people, objects, etc.

892. MANRIQUE CASTAÑEDA, Leonardo. "El sistema de salud en Agua Puerca, San Luis Potosí." *Anales del Instituto Nacional de Antropolgía e Historia* (México), II, 7ª época (1969 [i.e., 1971]), 301-308.

An anthropological survey of certain aspects of life among a small Pame Indian group. Includes some brief sections on illnesses, beliefs about illness, traditional curing practices, witches, etc.

893. MÁRQUEZ YÁÑEZ, Francisco. "Apuntes sobre folclor del café colombiano." *RCF*, Segunda época, IV:10 (1966-1969), 23-45.

Deals with the history of coffee and coffee lore throughout the world and then focuses on Colombia. Discusses customs and practices, popular sayings, songs, beliefs about coffee's curative properties, etc. Gives words without music of a few songs and a short bibliography.

894. MAYORCA, Juan Manuel. *Delincuencia y folklore*. Caracas: Talleres de la Tipografía Vargas, 1972. 186 pp. illus.

Studies three aspects of the folklore of Venezuelan delinquents: their beliefs (i.e., superstitions, religious beliefs, attitudes toward such things as the law of vengeance, etc.), their speech (includes a long list of lexicographical items found in criminal slang), and tatooing (with many illustrations). Includes a copious bibliography.

895. MELLINGER, Marie B. "Land of the Purple People Eaters." *Appalachian Journal* (Boone, North Carolina), I:3 (Autumn, 1973), 222-225.

Notes some Cherokee beliefs about witches, the most powerful of these being Purple Eaters. Focuses particularly upon trees and plants of the Southern Appalachians that were involved in such beliefs. Includes photographs.

896. MÉTRAUX, Alfred. *Voodoo in Haiti*. Translated by Hugo Charteris. N.Y.: Schocken, 1972. 426 pp. illus.

A wide-ranging treatment of voodoo in Haiti. Deals with its origins, voodoo practices as observed mostly in urban settings, the productive role that it plays in such things as artistic expression, attitudes of the "haute bourgeoisie" toward voodoo, etc. Includes illustrations, a glossary, numerous footnotes, and a comprehensive bibliography.

897. MEW, James. *Traditional Aspects of Hell: (Ancient and Modern)*. Ann Arbor, Mich.: Gryphon Books, 1971. xv, 448 pp. illus.

Reissue of the 1903 edition (London: S. Sonnenschein and Company). Examines and describes the conceptions and the figures of hell believed in by Ancient Egyptians, Assyrians, Hindus, Buddhists of India, Japan and China, Zoroastrians, Greeks and Romans, Scandinavians, Jews, Christians, Muslims, and "barbarian" peoples. Contains 79 illustrations taken from original sources.

898. MIDELFORT, H. C. Erik. *Witch Hunting in Southwestern Germany, 1562-1684: The Social and Intellectual Foundations*. Stanford,

California: Stanford University Press, 1972. viii, 306 pp. illus.

Studies large witch-hunts in southwestern Germany (i.e., those resulting in twenty or more executions a year). Considers beliefs about witches, pacts with the devil, demonic power, etc. Draws mostly on legal and archival sources.

899. MINUCHIN DE ITZIGSOHN, Sara, MORENO, Inés T., and PIÑA DE LÓPEZ, Nelly C. "Grupo familiar y matrimonio en una área rural." *AI*, XXXIII:3 (Julio-Septiembre, 1973), 783-800.

An anthropologist reports on beliefs, customs, and practices related to childbearing as observed in three different kinds of hospitals in the Buenos Aires area. Many of the subjects treated are folkloric in character. Includes bibliography.

900. MOOSE, Ruth. "Superstition in Doris Betts's New Novel." *NCFJ*, XXI:2 (May, 1973), 61-62.

Notes the use of North Carolina superstitions and other folklore in *The River to Pickle Beach* (1972).

901. MORGAN, Harry T. *Chinese Symbols and Superstitions*. Detroit: Gale Research Co., 1972. 192 pp. illus.

Reissue of the 1942 edition (South Pasadena, Calif.: P. D. and Ione Perkins). Summarizes or describes myths, legends, ancient beliefs, symbols, feasts and festivals, philosophies, and gods and idols of Chinese culture. Contains numerous illustrations and a bibliography.

902. MULLER, Kal. "Taboos and Magic Rule Namba Lives." *National Geographic* (Washington, D.C.), CXLI:1 (January, 1972), 56-83.

Describes some ethnographic aspects of the life of a Namba group in the New Hebrides. Of possible interest to folklorists are certain taboos, rituals, funeral customs, etc. There are excellent color photographs.

903. NEWTON, Milton, Jr. "The Annual Round in the Upland South: The Synchronization of Man and Nature through Culture." *Pioneer America* (Falls Church, Virginia), III:2 (July, 1971), 63-73.

Describes the annual cycle of events (i.e., the order of planting, cultivation, leisurely activities, harvesting, winter activities) on farms of the Upland South. The traditional round of activities has changed very little in the last two hundred years.

904. NOLAN, Mary Lee. "The Mexican Pilgrimage Tradition." *Pioneer America* (Falls Church, Virginia), V:2 (July, 1973), 13-27.

Gives some basic information about popular religion and religious customs in Mexico (i.e., *santos*, shrines of various images, types of pilgrimages, etc.). Contains maps (one which locates 33 of the principal shrines is quite useful), photographs, and notes.

905. OHNUKI-TIERNEY, Emiko. "The Shamanism of the Ainu of the Northwest Coast of Southern Sakhalin." *Ethnology*, XII:1 (January, 1973), 15-29.

Surveys shamanistic beliefs, practices, and rites of a group now relocated in Hokkaido from the coast of southern Sakhalin. Based mostly on information obtained from an informant who is herself a shaman.

906. OLMSTEAD, Judith. "Ethiopia's Artful Weavers." *National Geographic* (Washington, D.C.), CXLIII:1 (January, 1973), 124-141.

An anthropologist relates for the non-specialist some of her experiences working in the field with the Dorze people of southwestern Ethiopia. Touches on many customs, rituals, crafts (particularly weaving), taboos, etc. Includes excellent color photographs by James A. Sugar.

907. OMOYAJOWO, Joseph Akinyele. "Human Destiny, Personal

Rites and Sacrifices in African Traditional Religion (a means of ultimate transformation)." *Journal of Religious Thought* (Washington, D.C.), XXX:1 (Spring-Summer, 1973), 5-15.

Dealing in global terms with many African religions, the author describes and interprets many beliefs, taboos, charms, sacrifices, etc. that characterize an individual's practice of traditional religion.

908. ORTIZ, Sergio Elías. "Consejas y creencias de tipo folclórico de la región de Pasto (suroeste de Colombia)." *RCF*, IV:10 (1966-1969), 107-114.

Describes five ghosts or supernatural beings who are part of the folklore of the town of Pasto (Colombia). They are La Turumama, El Duende, El Padre Descabezado, La Viuda, and La Mula Herrada.

909. OSORIO GÓMEZ, Oscar. "La institución del compadrazgo entre los indios guambianos." *RCF*, IV:10 (1966-1969), 135-151.

Studies the four types of *compadrazgo* (i.e., ritual kinship) found among the Guambiano Indians in the Department of Cauca (Colombia). Includes photographs and a short bibliography.

910. PANEK, Le Roy L. "Asparagus and Brome's *The Sparagus Garden.*" *Modern Philology* (Chicago), LXVIII:4 (May, 1971), 362-363.

Finds that Richard Brome does not regard asparagus as an aphrodisiac in his play (1635). Considers beliefs of the time which consider asparagus to be a cure for urinary disorders and toothache.

911. PENNINGTON, Campbell W. "Plantas medicinales utilizadas por el pima montañés de Chihuahua." *AI*, XXXIII:1 (Enero-Marzo, 1973), 213-232.

Deals with sickness and its treatment among a small group of about seven hundred Pima Indians who live in the state of Chihuahua (Mexico). Lists medicinal plants used by the Pimas and the illnesses they are supposed to cure.

912. POLLACK, Herman. *Jewish Folkways in Germanic Lands (1648-1806): Studies in Aspects of Daily Life.* Cambridge, Mass.: The M. I. T. Press, 1971. xvii, 410 pp.

Describes in a painstaking way the daily life of Jews in the German-speaking regions of central Europe. There are chapters on Neighborhood and Home, Birth, Marriage and Burial, Education, Clothing, Diet and Table Customs, Folk Medicine, and finally Synagogue, Sabbath, and Festivals. There is much that should interest certain folklorists.

913. POUSHINSKY, J. M., and POUSHINSKY, N. W. "Superstition and Technological Change: An Illustration." *JAF*, LXXXVI:341 (July-September, 1973), 289-293.

Examines from the perspective of societal self-regulation the superstition held by lobster fishermen on the Southwestern Shore of Nova Scotia that wearing white woolen mittens brings good luck during the cold months of the lobster season. Hypothesizes that the superstition has regulated and preserved the forgotten technological advantage of using non-dyed and hence more water repellent wool.

914. PRESS, Irwin. "Bureaucracy Versus Folk Medicine: Implications from Seville, Spain." *Urban Anthropology* (Brockport, N.Y.), II:2 (Fall, 1973), 232-247.

An anthropological investigation into the relationship between modern medical practices in a city that has a very up-to-date system and folk medicine, beliefs in curers, etc. Finds that folk medicine is relatively weak. Includes notes and bibliography.

915. RATIER, Hugo. *La medicina popular*. B.A.: Centro Editor de América Latina, 1972. 109 pp. plates

Deals with Argentine "popular" medicine and cures as observed on various levels (i.e., from the practices of rural *curanderos*, bone-setters, and the like through grandmother's remedies to patent medicines and well known city "curers" who have had mass followers among all social classes). Includes many photographs.

916. REARDEN, Jim, and O'REAR, Charles, photographer. "Nikolaevsk, A Bit of Old Russia Takes Root in Alaska." *National Geographic* (Washington, D.C.), CXLII:3 (September, 1972), 400-425.

Describes the life of a small group of Russian dissenters from the Russian Orthodox Church who live in Nikolaevsk, a village on the Kenai Peninsula of Alaska. Touches on many customs (e.g., Easter customs), costumes, crafts, etc. Notable for excellent color photos.

917. RIBEIRO, Maria de Lourdes Borges. *Inquérito sôbre práticas e superstições agrícolas de Minas Gerais*. Rio de Janeiro: Ministério da Educação e Cultura, Departamento de Assuntos Culturais, 1971. 147 pp. illus. (*Coleção "Folclore Brasileiro," Vol. 6*.)

From fieldwork based on questionnaires the author surveys replies of farmers in Minas Gerais to queries about their agricultural practices in growing corn, cotton, tobacco, coffee, and many other crops. Includes questions about superstitions, proverbs and sayings, music and songs, magic practices, traditional cures, prayers, regional food and drink, etc.

918. RICH, George W., and JACOBS, David F. "Saltpeter: A Folkloric Adjustment to Acculturation Stress." *WF*, XXXII:3 (July, 1973), 164-179.

Notes and analyzes lore about saltpeter as an anaphrodisiac, particularly military lore. Studies it as a manifestation of acculturation stress among soldiers and seeks to show how it serves certain psychological needs.

919. RISCO, Vicente. "Presencia del mito en la vida gallega." *Grial* (Vigo), No. 40 (Abril-Xunio, 1973), 231-234.

Discusses briefly the place of myths in Galician folklore. Deals with spirits, supernatural beings, mythical animals, and the mythology of death.

920. RISSMAN, E. J. "Hog Killing and Soap Making." In *HandH*. Pp. 103-108.

Describes methods of killing hogs and making soap in Texas in the early 1900's.

921. ROBBINS, Walter L. "Christmas Shooting Rounds in America and Their Background." *JAF*, LXXXVI:339 (January-March, 1973), 48-52.

Cites the practice described in 19th-century accounts from Indiana, Missouri, and South Carolina of groups of young men going from house to house on Christmas and firing guns in requesting food and drink. Gives evidence of a German origin for the practice.

922. [ROSNEK, Carl E.] "A Blending of Mysteries." *El Palacio* (Santa Fe, New Mexico), LXXIX:3 (December, 1973), 8-11.

Comments upon Christmas observances in Rio Grande Indian towns of New Mexico. Shows how Indian and Christian traditions have been fused in rituals, dances, pageantry, etc. Includes photographs. Also appends a calendar of Christmas events prepared by Bertha P. Dutton.

923. RUSSELL, Jeffrey Burton. *Witchcraft in the Middle Ages*. Ithaca, N.Y., and London: Cornell University Press, 1972. ix, 394 pp.

A historical study of medieval witchcraft which defines it partially in terms of folklore (other elements being sorcery, heresy, and theology). In pursuing his investigation the author draws upon the work of folklorists.

924. SAWYER, Marileta. "The Navajo Hand Trembling Ceremony." *AFFword*, III:2 (July, 1973), 33-41.

Describes and analyzes the hand-trembling system of magic divination found among Navajo Indians of Arizona. It is used for discovering the cause or cure of an illness, locating lost articles or people, predicting the future, etc. Includes a short bibliography.

925. SÉGUIN, Robert-Lionel. "Le présage dans la litterature orale d'une famille québécoise." *Les Cahiers des Dix* (Montreal), XXXVI (1971), 162-177.

926. SIMEON, George. "The Evil Eye in a Guatemalan Village." *Ethnomedizin/Ethnomedicine* (Hamburg), II:3-4 (1973), 437-441.

Deals with certain salient features of the evil eye as an illness-causing mechanism in the village of Chinautla.

927. SIMPSON, George Eaton. *Religious Cults of the Caribbean: Trinidad, Jamaica, and Haiti*. Rio Piedras: University of Puerto Rico, Institute of Caribbean Studies, 1970. 308 pp. illus.

Republishes the author's *The Shango Cult in Trinidad* and adds eleven papers describing the ceremonies, rituals, and belief systems of other Afro-American religious cults in the Caribbean. Includes studies of the Vodun in Haiti, Revival Zion and Ras Tafari in Jamaica, and the Shouters in Trinidad. Contains photographs, charts, and a bibliography.

928. SMITH, Hope. "A Description of a Black Party." *JOFS*, II:1 (April, 1973), 30-37.

A paper for a college class in folklore. Describes what is purported to be a "typical" party of black college students. Notes different "types" of party-goers, activities, the ways in which white stereotypes of blacks are converted into positive traits, etc.

929. SNOW, Loudell F. "'I Was Born Just Exactly with the Gift': An Interview with a Voodoo Practitioner." *JAF*, LXXXVI:341 (July-September, 1973), 272-281.

Discusses the work of a black folk healer of Tucson, Arizona. Includes an excerpt of an interview and considers the classification of illnesses by neighborhood residents.

930. SPOEHR, Luther W. "Sambo and the Heathen Chinee: Californians' Racial Stereotypes in the late 1870's." *Pacific Historical Review* (Berkeley, California), XLII:2 (May, 1973), 185-204.

A historian using a purely historical approach sheds considerable light on whites' racial stereotypes of blacks and Chinese in California. Though not treated here as folklore, the subject seems to me to fall within the purview of folklorists.

931. STANNARD, David E. "Death and Dying in Puritan New England." *American Historical Review* (Richmond, Virginia), LXXVIII:5 (December, 1973), 1305-1330.

A historian looks at Puritan ideas about death and the tensions which stem from such beliefs. There is little attention to folklore per se, but certain traditional attitudes and concepts touch on the concerns of folklorists. Also, a few photographs of old gravestones contain some interesting traditional death motifs.

932. STEWART, Kenneth M. "The Amatpathenya—Mohave Leprechauns?" *AFFword*, III:1 (April, 1973), 40-41.

Gives five accounts from Mohave Indian informants concerning the *amatpathenya* (i.e., "little people") whom the author suggests are similar to the *leprechauns* of Ireland or the elves of other folk traditions.

933. STEWART, Kenneth M. "The Owl in Mohave Indian Culture." *AFFword*, II:3 (October, 1972), 17-23.

Treats owl and other bird lore among the Mohave Indians of the Colorado River Reservation. Emphasis is upon beliefs concerning owls, which are associated with witchcraft, and five orally collected "accounts" about bewitched people are given along with commentary. Includes bibliography.

934. STEWART, Kenneth M. "Witchcraft among the Mohave Indians." *Ethnology*, XII:3 (July, 1973), 315-324.

Surveys Mohave beliefs and practices related to witchcraft. Includes a brief bibliography.

935. STRÖMBACK, Dag. "Some Notes on the Nix in Older Nordic Tradition." In *MLFS*. Pp. 245-256.

Examines the nix figure as a water-horse and as an anthropomorphic being in various Nordic traditions (e.g., those of Scandinavia, the Orkney Islands, the Shetland Islands, etc.). Uses a philological and historical approach and considers the nix's appearance in ballads from these areas.

936. TANTAQUIDGEON, Gladys. *Folk Medicine of the Delaware and Related Algonkian Indians*. Harrisburg, Pennsylvania: Pennsylvania Historical and Museum Commission, 1972. vi, 145 pp.

Surveys the folk medicine of the Delawares and the Mohegans in separate sections and treats several other groups in appendices. Concerned primarily with current practices, but also includes material on the origins of Indian medical traditions. Deals with herbal remedies, rituals, witchcraft, dreams, etc. Includes a bibliography and an index.

937. THOMPSON, Lawrence S. "The Moon in Kentucky and Elsewhere." *KFR*, XIX:1 (January-March, 1973), 7-10.

Presents beliefs from the United States (primarily Kentucky) and Germany about the moon's influence on human, animal, and plant life.

938. TOWNSEND, Mary Ann. "Hog Killing on Queenfield Farm, Manquin, Virginia." *NCFJ*, XXI:1 (April, 1973), 32-34.

Describes the entire process of acquiring, fattening, killing, and curing hogs on the farm of the author's father in Virginia.

939. *Treasured Polish Christmas Customs and Traditions: Carols, Decorations, and a Christmas Play*. Minneapolis, Minnesota: Polanie Publishing Co., 1972. xii, 197 pp. illus.

Describes Polish Christmas customs. A large part of the book is given over to words and music of songs, descriptions and illustrations of decorations, the text of a play entitled *Jaselka*, and some recipes. Includes photographs and drawings.

940. TWINING, Mary Arnold. "Shared Images in Yoruba and Afro-American Folklore: An Open Question for Further Research." *FForum*, *Bibliographic and Special Series, No. 11: Studies in Yoruba Folklore* (1973), 53-62.

Points out comparable aspects of Afro-American and Yoruba folklore.

941. URBINA TERRAZAS, Adolfo. "La acupunctura, milenaria y actual." *Abside* (México), XXXVI (1972):2, pp. 209-215.

Explains the theories that underlie the practice of acupuncture which originated in China almost five thousand years ago.

942. URLIN, Ethel L. *Festivals, Holy Days, and Saints' Days: A Study in Origins and Survivals in Church Ceremonies and Secular Customs*. Ann

Arbor: Gryphon Books, 1971. xvi, 272 pp.

Reissue of the 1915 edition (London: Simpkin, Marshall, Hamilton, Kent and Co.). Discusses English customs and traces their connections to rituals and observances of the Middle Ages and the pre-Christian era. Contains illustrations.

943. VANDERVELDE, Marjorie. "Moon-Children of San Blas Islands." *Expedition* (Philadelphia), XV:4 (Summer, 1973), 15-24.

Discusses the life of albinos among the Cuna Indians who live on the San Blas Islands off the Atlantic coast of Panama. Information is scanty, but the article does touch on beliefs, customs, attitudes, cures, etc. that are folkloric in character. Includes some good photographs.

944. VESSURI, Hebe. "Brujos y aprendices de brujos en una comunidad rural de Santiago del Estero." *Revista Latino-americana de Sociología* (B.A.), VI:3 (Septiembre-Diciembre, 1970), 443-458.

Studies witches and students of magic in Santiago del Estero (Argentina). Notes their differing roles in society and attributes to changing social conditions the alterations that have been taking place recently in attitudes toward these practitioners of magic.

945. VESTAL, Paul K., Jr. "Herb Workers in Scotland and Robeson Counties." *NCFJ*, XXI:4 (November, 1973), 166-170.

Gives some information about herb doctors and their treatment of ailments as obtained from interviews with three North Carolina herb doctors. Lists herbs and combinations of herbs used by the different doctors and notes the illnesses they are designed to cure.

946. VIDAL, Teodoro. "Aportación al estudio del folklore médico en Puerto Rico." *Revista del Instituto de Cultura Puertorriqueña* (San Juan), Año XIII:50 (Enero-Marzo, 1971), 53-64.

Describes popular cures of rural Puerto Rico, quoting texts of prayers and incantations used. Lists the scientific names of curative plants.

947. VIGIL, Priscilla. "Christmas in Tesuque." *El Palacio* (Santa Fe, New Mexico), LXXIX:3 (December, 1973), 3-5.

A Headstart teacher describes some Christmas customs, dances, etc. in the Río Grande Indian town of Tesuque, New Mexico. Includes photographs.

948. VIVANTE, Armando, and PALMA, Néstor Homero. *Magia y daño por imágenes en la sociedad argentina (antecedentes y actualidad)*. Prólogo de Augusto Raúl Cortázar. Buenos Aires: Ediciones Cabargon, 1971 [i.e., 1972]. 187 pp. illus.

An exhaustive and carefully documented study of magic means for harming intended victims, mostly through piercing or otherwise doing harm to figures which represent them. Argentine practices are the authors' main concern, but their focus is world wide and includes the history of such practices from the earliest times to the present. Includes many photographs, drawings, and a copious bibliography.

949. WALKER, Warren S., and UYSAL, Ahmet E. "An Ancient God in Modern Turkey: Some Aspects of the Cult of Hizir." *JAF*, LXXXVI: 341 (July-September, 1973), 286-289.

Considers the ongoing belief in Hizir, a Moslem saint and an ancient fertility god associated with water, found in current oral as well as written tradition in Turkey.

950. WALSH, James J. *Cures, The Story of Cures That Fail*. Ann Arbor, Michigan: Gryphon Books, 1971. xi, 291 pp.

Reissue of the 1923 edition (N.Y.—London: D. Appleton and Co.).

Debunks various kinds of "cures" that have often been widely acclaimed (e.g., personal healers, drug cures, magnets, Mesmerism, hypnotism, mystical cures, psychoanalysis, etc.). Includes a great deal of folklore having to do with cures.

951. Weaver, Jerry L. "Mexican American Health Care Behavior: A Critical Review of the Literature." *Social Science Quarterly* (Austin, Texas), LIV:1 (June, 1973), 85-102.

A useful survey of literature in the field. Touches on folk medicine, folk psychiatry, and the like.

952. WEBB, Bernice Larson. "A Study of Voodoo Mail-Order Advertising in Louisiana." *Revue de Louisiane/Louisiana Review* (Lafayette, Louisiana), II:1 (Été-Summer, 1973), 65-71.

From a survey of mail-order sources the author describes the kinds of objects which are available (e.g., candles and incense, books, cat skulls, human skulls, herbs such as "Adam and Eve root," "Blessed Spray," "Seven African Powers Soap," etc., etc.).

953. WEIST, Katherine M. "Giving Away: The Ceremonial Distribution of Goods among the Northern Cheyenne of Southeastern Montana." *Plains Anthropologist* (Topeka, Kansas), XVIII:60 (May, 1973), 97-103.

Studies a modern-day custom of the Northern Cheyenne Indians, the give-aways where public distributions of goods take place as a way of honoring individuals.

954. WHITAKER, Dulce Consuelo Andreatta. "Folclore e mudança social." *Boletim [da] Faculdade de Filosofia, Ciências e Letras de Presidente Prudente* (Presidente Prudente, Brasil), 1970, pp. 19-32.

Reports results of some sociological research carried out by the use of questionnaires concerning beliefs about folk cures. The study relates these to changing social conditions in Presidente Prudente.

955. WILDE, Lady. *Ancient Cures, Charms, and Usages of Ireland: Contributions to Irish Lore*. Detroit: Singing Tree Press, 1970. xi, 256 pp.

Reissue of the 1890 edition (London: Ward and Downey Ltd.). Contains explanations of ancient cures and charms taken from Irish manuscripts of the 1400's. Also contains *sagen*, historical legends, proverbs, information concerning festivals and wake games still observed, and some survivalist historical commentary by the author.

956. WINKLER, Louis, and WINKLER, Carol. "A Reappraisal of the Vampire." *NYFQ*, XXIX:3 (September, 1973), 194-205.

Summarizes some vampire lore and gives something of the history of such beliefs. Includes notes.

957. WOOD, James O. "Lost Lore in Macbeth." *Shakespeare Quarterly* (Washington, D.C.), XXIV:2 (Spring, 1973), 223-226.

Looks to certain folk beliefs (e.g., that only a pig can see the wind) in order to interpret six lines from a Restoration manuscript of William Davenant's operatic adaptation of Shakespeare's *Macbeth*.

958. WRIGHT, Thomas. *Narratives of Sorcery and Magic from the Most Authentic Sources*. 2 vols. Detroit: Grand River Books, 1971.

Reissue of the second edition of 1851 (London: Richard Bentley). Draws together information about witchcraft and sorcery and relates accounts of witches, magicians, and sorcerers of many European countries and the U.S. from the medieval period to the 17th century.

959. YEAGER, Lyn Allison. "The Flowers of Christmas." *TFSB*, XXXIX:4 (December, 1973), 113-118.

Discusses the legends and the uses of flowers and trees connected in some way with Christmas throughout the Western World. Includes holly, mistletoe, the Glastonbury Thorn, the bayberry shrub, the poinsettia, and others.

960. YOUNG, Egerton Ryerson. *Stories from Indian Wigwams and Northern Camp-Fires*. Ann Arbor, Michigan: Gryphon Books, 1971. 293 pp. illus.

Reissue of the 1893 edition (London: Charles H. Kelly). A protestant missionary relates his experiences living among Indians in the Lake Winnipeg area of northern Canada. Touches on certain beliefs, ceremonies, magic practices, and charms, etc.

...various editions... Vols. ... are from the library of the Hispanic Society of America; and Vol. VI is from the ...

Canción musical. Bogotá: Impreso por Tercer Mundo, 1971. 256 pp.

... music practices ... This collection of ... has comparatively ... material has to do with folkloric songs, though ...

731. RICH, Kirby. "Our Own Music." *Mountain Life and Work* (Clintwood, Virginia), XLVIII-11 (December 1972), 8-14.

Deals with mountain music from the time of Cecil Sharp's collecting of folk songs until the present day. Includes interviews with some folk musicians and a representative of the Southern Folk Festival.

732. RICHMOND, W. Edson. "Paris og Helen i Trejeborg: A Reduction To Essentials." In *MLFS*. Pp. 229-243.

Examines Scandinavian broadside texts of a ballad about Helen of Troy and shows that they contain two very popular medieval narratives in localized form.

733. RIMBAULT, Edward F. *Musical Illustrations of Bishop Percy's Reliques of Ancient English Poetry: A Collection of Old Ballad Tunes*, etc. Norwood Editions: Norwood, Pa., 1973. xii, 119 pp.

Reissue of the 1850 edition (London: Cramer, Beale, and Co.). A collection of tunes for some of Percy's ballads as taken from old books and manuscripts. Gives 74 tunes with a brief commentary on each.

734. RODNITZKY, J. L. "The Mythology of Woody Guthrie." *Popular Music and Society* (Bowling Green, Ohio), II-3 (Spring 1973), 227-242.

Seeks to assay different interpretations of Woody Guthrie as a "protest" folksinger, predecessor of counter culturists, etc. Includes notes.

735. ROGERS, Edith. "Sena nua en el contexto europeo." *RDTP*, XXVIII (1972), Cuadernos 3-4, pp. 275-281.

Notes the existence in New Mexico of a *romance Sena nua*, that seems to be related to various ballads of northern European tradition (e.g., *Lord Lovel* and *Fair Annie*, a ballad) for which no counterparts have been discovered in Spanish peninsular tradition.

736. ROSS-JONES, Margaret. "Devil Dancers of Yare." *Américas*, XXV, 6-7 (June-July 1973), 12-15.

Describes superficially the performance of the Devil Dancers who are a feature of the Corpus Christi celebration in the town of Yare, Venezuela. Includes photographs.

737. RUEDA, Manuel. *Conocimiento y poesía en el folklore*. Santo Domingo: Instituto de Investigaciones Folklóricas de la Universidad Nacional Pedro Henríquez Ureña, 1971. 63 pp.

An essay which treats some of the basic problems of folklore theory and then analyzes stylistic and thematic aspects of some Dominican songs, ballads, prayers, and verbal conjurations.

738. SCHAFER, William J. "Indian Intermezzi (Play It One More Time, Chief!)." *JAF*, LXXXVI-342 (October-December 1973), 382-387.

Discusses the Indian-song fad that characterized popular music in the U.S. in the first decade or two of the 20th century. Seeks to analyze

M   MATERIAL CULTURE

[See also numbers 47, 76, 90, 98, 114, 119, 126, 128, 134, 137, 154, 155, 160, 163, 174, 176, 180, 193, 202, 207, 208, 222, 238, 241, 244, 251, 254, 259, 263, 277, 281, 291, 296, 308, 312, 317, 327, 336, 347, 350, 359, 453, 638, 792, 812, 814, 833, 853, 872, 873, 874, 879, 894, 906, 916, 920, 931, 939, 948, 952.]

961. ADAMS, Marie Jeanne. "Structural Aspects of a Village Art." *AA*, LXXV:1 (February, 1973), 265-279.

Applies structural analysis to the designs used in cotton mantles produced by craftswomen on Sumba, a small island east of Bali. Finds that dyadic-triadic sets are found in designs and also in many other aspects of Sumbanese life. Includes photographs, drawings, notes, and bibliography.

962. ALLEN, Elsie. *Pomo Basketmaking, A Supreme Art for the Weaver*. Healdsburg, California: Naturegraph Publishers, 1972. 67 pp. illus.

Through text and illustrations the process of making a basket is shown from the gathering and preparing of the materials to the finished work of art.

963. ARROTT, Margaret. "A Unique Method of Making Pottery—Santa Apolonia, Guatemala" *Expedition* (Philadelphia), XIV:4 (Summer, 1972), 17-26.

Describes through detailed text and numerous photographs the step-by-step process of making unglazed earthenware that is used in Santa Apolonia, Guatemala.

964. *Arte popular em Pernambuco*. Recife, Brasil: Departamento de Extensão Cultural da Universidade Federal de Pernambuco, 1971. no pagination.

A series of ten loose cards in a folder. Each card is printed on both sides and each side contains a brief statement of a few paragraphs about one type of popular art (*ceramica, ex-voto, objetos de cuor*, etc.) by a single author. Some of the authors are recognized scholars in the field.

965. *Artesanía folclórica en el Ecuador*. Guayaquil, Ecuador: Directorio y el Rectorado del Colegio Alemán Humboldt, 1972. no pagination. illus.

A collection of excellent photographs, many in color, along with a page of commentary on each of nine sections, devoted respectively to nine different kinds of crafts (e.g., ceramics, flutes, textiles, wood-carving, marimbas, etc.) Includes maps. This book was created as a collective project of one class at the Colegio Alemán Humboldt during the 1971-1972 school year.

966. BARBER, Edwin Atlee. *Pottery and Porcelain of the United States: An Historical Review of American Ceramic Art with a New Introduction and Bibliography*. Watkins Glen/N.Y.: Century House Americana, 1971. 450 pp. illus.

A new edition of Barber's work published earlier in 1893, 1901, and 1909 and said to be still one of the standard single-volume authorities in the field. Treats both craft and industrialized ceramics (i.e., pottery, ornamental tiles, etc.). Revision of the work is limited to a new introduction and an up-dated bibligiography. Includes many drawings and photographs; also an index.

967. BARBERÁN, Cecilio. "La artesanía española como obra nacional." *Mundo Hispánico* (Madrid), XXVII:305 (Agosto, 1973), 36-39.

Calls attention to a new market-exposition established by the Empresa Nacional de Artesanía of the Ministry of Industry. It has been created in Madrid in order to display and sell authentic examples of Spain's regional folk arts (e.g., ceramics, metal work, weaving, etc.). Includes excellent color photographs.

968. BECKER-DONNER, Etta. "Arte popular latinoamericano." *Humboldt* (Munich), Año XIV (1973): 51, pp. 42-61.

In connection with an exposition of Latin American popular art at the Museum für Völkerkunde in Vienna, the author surveys the field. Treats such things as ceramics, masks, weaving, carved figures, lacework, etc. Particularly notable for some superb photographs, a few in color.

969. BENNETT, Mary, and LAUSTEN, Jean, eds. *Help One Another Cookbook, Vol. 2*. Aberdeen, North Dakota: The Dakota Farmer and North Plains Press, 1973 [?]. 191 pp.

A selection of Dakota recipes taken from *The Dakota Farmer*'s "Help One Another" column, which began appearing in 1881. Contains Czechoslovakian, German, American Indian, Scandinavian, and other types of dishes.

970. "Bibliografía en torno a la temática del arte popular latinoamericana." *Humboldt* (Munich), Año XIV (1973):52, p. 92.

Gives 73 titles of books and articles dealing with Latin American popular art. There is no annotation.

971. BIVINS, John, Jr., and RAUSCHENBERG, Bradford L., photographer. *The Moravian Potters in North Carolina*. Chapel Hill: Published for Old Salem, Inc., Winston-Salem, N.C., by the University of North Carolina Press, 1972. xiv, 300 pp. illus.

A historical study of the Moravians who settled in Salem, North Carolina, in the late 18th century and established a diversified craft program as their economic base. Treats types of ceramics produced, techniques used, etc. in making stone tiles, water pipes, figures of animals, dolls, toys, etc. Also includes much social history. There are over two hundred illustrations.

972. BOWEN, Thomas. "Seri Basketry: A Comparative View." *The Kiva* (Tucson, Arizona), XXXVIII:3-4 (Summer, 1973), 141-172.

Compares basket technology of the Seri Indians of Sonora (Mexico) with that of several nearby tribes of California, Arizona, and Baja California. Uses archaeological and ethnographic data. Includes charts, a map, and bibliography.

973. BOYD, E. "Domestic Architecture in New Mexico." *El Palacio* (Santa Fe, New Mexico), LXXIX:3 (December, 1973), 12-29.

A historical study of building design, materials, techniques, etc. used in constructing houses and other buildings over a period of about 200 years. Treats also such things as traditional fireplaces, ovens, doors, etc. Of great value to students of folk architecture since many of the things discussed are still current. Includes photographs.

974. BOYD, E. *The New Mexico Santero*. Santa Fe: Museum of New Mexico Press, 1972. 24 pp. illus.

Traces the history of the making of reproductions of saints by "santeros" in New Mexico from the 18th century to 1900. Shows how craftsmen adapted techniques to the materials available in their isolated environment and how with commercialization the tradition has declined. Presents photographs.

975. BRANDT, Lawrence R., and BRAATZ, Ned E. "Log Buildings in Portage County, Wisconsin: Some Cultural Implications." *Pioneer America* (Falls Church, Virginia), IV:1 (January, 1972), 29-39.

Studies construction details of 28 log buildings in Portage County, Wisconsin, in order to ascertain building methods and relate practices used in such construction to the background of the builders.

976. BRUNVAND, Jan Harold. "The Merry Cemetery of Transylvania." *NCFJ*, XXI:3 (September, 1973), 83-88.

Describes the folk art tradition carried on by Stan Ion Pătraş in the Romanian village of Săpînţa of carving merry or biographical scenes and rhymes on the headboards of graves. Contains sketches.

977. BURGER, Albert. "On Building a Birch-Bark Canoe." *The Beaver* (Winnipeg, Canada), Outfit CCCIV:1 (Summer, 1973), 50-53.

Describes the process of building a birch-bark canoe as performed by an elderly practitioner of the art who learned how to do it from the Cree Indians in northern Alberta (Canada). Includes drawings and photographs.

978. CAMPEN, Richard N. *Architecture of the Western Reserve, 1800-1900.* Cleveland: Press of Case Western Reserve University, 1971. xii, 260 pp. illus.

Surveys photographically the buildings of "architectural interest" in Ohio's Western Reserve counties from pioneer days to the beginning of the 20th century and provides brief notes about each building. Also briefly sketches the history of the Western Reserve and discusses the place of its architecture in national context. Provides a glossary of architectural terms with illustrations and a bibliography.

979. CANDEE, Richard M. "The Old Schwamb Picture Frame Mill: The Preservation of a Small 19th Century Local Industry." *Pioneer America* (Falls Church, Virginia), IV:1 (January, 1972), 1-7.

Surveys briefly the history of the Schwamb factory in Arlington, Massachusetts, now occupied by the Millbrook Art Center. Here traditional and contemporary crafts are today combined and picture frames are still manufactured on 19th-century machinery.

980. "Ceremonial Breads and Cookies: They Look as Good as They Taste." *Lithopinion* (N.Y.), VIII:4, Issue 32 (Winter, 1973), 48-63.

Discusses pastry-forming traditions from ancient antiquity to the present and focuses particularly on the Swiss tradition of molding sweet bread. Gives photographs of some old carved or ceramic Swiss molds that are in the Musée National Swisse in Zurich.

981. CHANG, S. "Kimono, from Its 12th-Century Origins, Is Recognized as a Lasting Sartorial Triumph." *Smithsonian* (Washington, D.C.), IV:8 (November, 1973), 60-69.

Gives something of the kimono's long history in Japan and discusses current attitudes toward it as traditional dress. Includes excellent color photographs.

982. CHARLES, Barbara Fahs. "Mix Antique Charm and Artistry, Add Children and Spin." *Smithsonian* (Washington, D.C.), III:4 (July, 1972), 40-47.

Touches on the history of merry-go-rounds in the U.S. and Europe and identifies makers of merry-go-rounds and the carved horses and other animals that are used on them. Calls attention to the figures on display at the Smithsonian Institution's exhibits of American folk art. Includes superb color photographs.

983. CHASE, Judith Wragg. *Afro-American Art and Craft.* N.Y.: Van Nostrand Reinhold Co., 1971. 142 pp. illus.

Traces the history of Afro-American art discussing artistic works and the role of the artist in West Africa, the craftsman-slave and his artistic work, Negro artists and craftsmen in the U.S. from pioneer days to the present, etc. Includes many photographs, bibliography, and a map.

984. COCHRAN, Martha, and COCHRAN, Bob. "An Interview with Brice Tyler—Bird Carver." *NYFQ*, XXIX:1 (March, 1973), 21-37.

An interview with a Maryland carver of wooden duck decoys. This is a traditional craft on the eastern shore of Maryland. Discusses something of its history, types of decoys, materials and techniques used, etc. Includes photographs.

985. CORTAZAR, Augusto Raúl. "Exposición representativa de artesanías argentinas del Fondo Nacional de las Artes." *Anales de la Sociedad Rural Argentina* (B.A.), CVI:6 (Junio, 1972), 16-19.

Tells about the organization of the 3ª Exposición Representativa de Artesanías Argentinas in 1971 and notes problems encountered and resolved. Explains the criteria used in selecting folkloric objects to be displayed. Includes photographs.

986. COUSINS, Peter H. *Hog Plow and Sith: Cultural Aspects of Early Agricultural Technology* Dearborn, Michigan: Greenfield Village and Henry Ford Museum, 1973. 21 pp. illus.

Discusses the form, function, and derivation of a hog plow and a sith, two Dutch farming instruments used in 18th and early 19th-century New York, and considers the lack of their being transmitted to neighboring but different cultural areas of New York. Contains maps and illustrations.

987. CROWNOVER, David, and KOHLER, William, photographer. "Gold Beads from the Gold Coast." *Expedition* (Philadelphia), XV:3 (Spring, 1973), 25-29.

Brief commentary about gold beads amulets, etc. from the Republic of Ghana. Describes the traditional methods used by the craftsmen who make them. Includes some good photographs.

988. CUNNINGHAM, Keith. "Ethno Cuisine: Goat Roast." *AFFword*, II:4 (January, 1973), 44-46.

Describes a traditional method of roasting goat and preparing the trimmings (biscuits and potatoes). Includes photographs.

989. D'AMATO, Janet, and D'AMATO, Alex. *African Animals Through African Eyes.* N.Y.: Julian Messner, 1971. 63 pp. illus.

Surveys sculpted, carved, and painted representations of animals, birds, and reptiles created by African artists and craftsmen of Sub-Saharan Africa from ancient to more recent times. Alludes to fables, myths, proverbs, etc. in noting the cultural significance of the figures. Contains many illustrations and some maps.

990. DAVIDSON, Marshall B. "The WPA's Amazing Record of American Design." *American Heritage* (N.Y.) XXIII:2 (February, 1972), 65-80.

Calls attention to the Index of American Design, now at the National Gallery in Washington, which was compiled by the WPA (Works Progress Administration) from 1935-1942. It is a record of American artifacts.

Included here are many illustrations in color.

991. *Devoción y sugestión de las imágenes de vestir*. B.A.: Museo Municipal de Arte Hispanoamericano "Isaac Fernández Blanco," Noviembre, 1970. no pagination. illus.

A catalogue of an exhibition of religious figures dating from the 16th to the 19th century which represent the ancient tradition, cultivated particularly in Spain, of dressing such images. Eighty images from Spain and various South American countries (with two from the Philippine Islands) are listed. There are twenty excellent photographs.

992. ESPEJEL, Carlos. *Las artesanías tradicionales en México*. México: Secretaría de Educación Pública, 1972. 158 pp. illus. (*Sep-Setentas 45*.)

Surveys traditional arts and crafts noting the types that are produced and the places that produce them. There are sixteen sections on as many crafts (e.g., ceramics, textiles, wood, glass, leather, toys, etc.). Includes numerous photographs.

993. FALKNER, Ann. "The Canadian Inventory of Historic Building." *Canadian Geographical Journal* (Ottawa, Ontario), LXXXVI:2 (February, 1973), 44-53.

An excellent description of the comprehensive methods developed by the Canadian Government to classify the architectural elements and building techniques found in Canadian buildings from the earliest surviving ones to those of the early 1900's. The system, which uses computer data processing, is called Canadian Inventory of Historic Building (C.I.H.B.). The article describes all this and offers many photographs.

994. FERRARA, Armand B. "Old Circus Wagons are Restored to Glory in Baraboo." *Smithsonian* (Washington, D.C.), III:12 (March, 1973), 64-71.

Tells about the Circus World Museum at Baraboo, Wisconsin. Treats particularly the restored wagons that are preserved there. Includes superb color photographs.

995. FOX, Lilla Margaret. *Folk Costume of Southern Europe*. Boston: Plays, Inc., 1973. 64 pp. illus.

Surveys the regional dress of peoples in Italy, Switzerland, the Mediterranean Islands, Spain, and Portugal. Notes historical influences on the typical dress and the continued wearing of some costumes for special occasions. Contains maps and many illustrations.

996. FRASER, B. Kay. "Techniques with Tole." *Relics* (Austin, Texas), V:6 (April, 1972), 18-20, 24.

Gives instructions for painting and glazing designs on tinware and furniture.

997. GARDNER, Gail I. "Ethno Cuisine: Cooking in a Dutch Oven." *AFFword*, I:2 (July, 1971), 21-22.

Tells the cattleman's way of cooking biscuits and "sorefinger" bread in a Dutch oven.

998. GERSTELL, Vivian S. *Silversmiths of Lancaster, Pennsylvania, 1730-1850*. Lancaster, Pa.: Lancaster County Historical Society, 1972. ix, 145 pp. illus.

Studies the history of silversmithing in Lancaster County with main attention to the men who pursued the craft (42 in Lancaster County with five more in outlying areas and seventeen silver platers).

999. GLASSIE, Henry. "The Nature of the New World Artifact: The Instance of the Dugout Canoe." In *Festscrift für Robert Wildhaber*, ed. by

Walter Escher, Theo Gantner, and Hans Trümpy. Basel: Schweizerische Gesellschaft für Volkskunde, 1973. Pp. 153-170.

An analytical history of the dugout canoe as a traditional artifact in America.

1000. GONZÁLEZ ECHEGARAY, Joaquín. "Yugos y arados en la provincia de Santander." In *PIHS(III)*, 123-168.

An ethnographic study of various different kinds of yokes for oxen used in the Santander region of Spain. Describes them, gives their history, and tells how they are made. Includes many drawings and photographs.

1001. GONZÁLEZ-HONTORIA DE ÁLVAREZ ROMERO, Guadalupe. "Aztec Featherwork." *Américas*, XXV:1 (January, 1973), 13-18.

A popularized discussion of pre-conquest Aztec featherwork as represented by museum pieces in various parts of the world. Also treats subsequent cultivation of featherwork as a popular art down to the present time in both Spain and Mexico. Includes illustrations.

1002. GOULD, Mary Earle. "The Curious History of Our Tin Graters." *Antiques Journal* (Dubuque, Iowa), XXVII:9 (September, 1972), 18-19.

Describes early tin graters used to grate potatoes, carrots, and cheese. Includes illustrations.

1003. GREENBERG, Andrea. "American Quilting." *IF*, V:2 (1972), 264-279.

Discusses quilting as a North American craft. Treats types of quilts, methods of quilting, something of the craft's history, names used to identify quilts, quilting as a social activity, etc. Includes drawings of some patterns and notes.

1004. GRITZNER, Charles F. "Log Housing in New Mexico." *Pioneer America* (Falls Church, Virginia), III:2 (July, 1971), 54-62.

Studies the main features of the Spanish American log housing tradition with special reference to the log structure covered with adobe that is found in northern New Mexico. Includes illustrations.

1005. GUEYMARD, Ernest. "Louisiana's Creole-Acadian Cuisine." *Revue de Louisiane/Louisiana Review* (Lafayette Louisiana), II:1 (Été-Summer, 1973), 8-19.

Tells something of the history of Creole and Cajun cooking and notes differences between the two cuisines. Describes many regional dishes.

1006. GUILLAND, Harold F. *Early American Folk Pottery*. Philadelphia: Chilton Book Co., 1971. xii, 322 pp. illus.

Presents plates and detailed descriptions of American earthenware and stoneware selected from the Index of American Design. Discusses the adaptation of European methods and design to the new environment and the history and distribution of folk pottery in America. Includes a bibliography.

1007. HAGERMAN, Robert L. *Covered Bridges of Lamoille County*. Essex Junction, Vermont: Essex Publishing Co., 1972. 32 pp.

Photographs of fifteen covered bridges in Lamoille County (Vermont) with pertinent information about their name or names, age, length, construction details, and present physical condition. Also gives historical facts and legends about each bridge.

1008. HAMILTON, T. M., and BAGBY, Nancy, eds. *Native American Bows*. York, Pennsylvania: George Shumway Publishers, 1972. xiv, 148 pp. illus.

An ethnographic and archaeological study of American Indian and

Eskimo bows. Deals with the history of bows, types of bows, methods of construction, etc. Includes appendices, a glossary of archery terms, illustrations, bibliography, and an index.

1009. HAYBALL, Gwen. "Historic Lobsticks and Others." *Canadian Geographical Journal* (Ottawa, Ontario), LXXXVI:2 (February, 1973), 62-66.

Deals with the "lobsticks" of northern and northwestern Canada. A lobstick is "a tall, conspicuous spruce or pine denuded of all but its topmost branches to serve as a mark of honor for a friend, as a monument, or often as a living talisman of the man for whom it was made." Notes famous and not-so-famous lobsticks from the 18th century to the present. Includes photographs.

1010. HOLM, Bill. *Crooked Beak of Heaven: Masks and Other Ceremonial Art of the Northwest Coast*. Seattle: University of Washington Press for the Thomas Burke Memorial Washington State Museum and the Henry Art Gallery, 1972. 96 pp. illus.

Catalogues 124 items (84 photographs) collected by Mr. and Mrs. Sidney Gerber and recently presented to the Thomas Burke Memorial Washington State Museum in Seattle. Included are artefacts of the Kwakiutl, Nootka, and other tribes of the Northwest Coast. Holm provides a brief introduction.

1011. HOSTETTLER, Agnes Freudenberg. "The Art of Christmas Baking in Southern Germany and Switzerland." *NCFJ*, XXI:4 (November, 1973), 160-165.

Comments briefly on the history of baking molds from ancient Mesopotamia to present-day Germany and Switzerland. Notes kinds of molded Christmas cookies made today in various German cities and in Pennsylvania. Includes photographs.

1012. HOWARD, James H. "John F. Lenger: Music Man among the Santee." *Nebraska History* (Lincoln), LIII:2 (Summer, 1972), 195-216.

Looks at a Bohemian bandmaster who organized a brass band of Sioux Indians in 1884. Presents a detailed study of the band costumes as examples of the syncretism of Native American dress and European band uniforms.

1013. HURAS DE HOLLSTEIN, Elsa. "Traveling in the Land of Folk Arts." *Américas*, XXV:4 (April, 1973), 31-38.

Discusses the relationship between the folk arts and tourism. Calls for greater development of folk arts intended for tourists, particularly in Latin America. Includes many photographs of Latin American folk arts.

1014. HUTSLAR, Donald, and HUTSLAR, Jean L. "The Log Architecture of Ohio." *Ohio History* (Columbus, Ohio), LXXX:3-4 (Summer-Autumn, 1971), 172-271.

A superb historical monograph on Ohio log buildings. Treats their introduction into Ohio, techniques of construction, problems of dating, tools and materials used, the design of log buildings, etc. Includes many photographs and drawings and a long bibliography.

1015. *Image and Identity: The Role of the Mask in Various Cultures*. Los Angeles: University of California Museum of Cultural History, 1972. 36 pp. illus.

Presents a guide to masks from around the world exhibited at the UCLA Museum of Cultural History, April 11-June 3, 1972. Discusses geographic distribution, production materials, and functions of masks. Contains photographs of some.

1016. JONES, Michael Owen. "Violations of Standards of Excellence and Preference in Utilitarian Art." *WF*, XXXII:1 (January, 1973), 19-32.

Shows by interviews with Appalachian chairmakers that inferior products of folk art are not necessarily due to "absence of creative vision" or "lack of technical mastery," but to such things as customer demands and time limitations. Contains photographs.

1017. JORDAN, Robert Paul. "Easter Greetings from the 'Ukrainians.'" *National Geographic* (Washington, D.C.), CXLI:4 (April, 1972), 556-563.

Reports on the preservation around Minneapolis and St. Paul, Minnesota, of the traditional Ukrainian custom of decorating Easter eggs (i.e., *pysanky*) with exquisitely intricate designs. Includes superb color photographs by James A. Sugar.

1018. JORDAN, Terry G. "Evolution of the American Windmill: A Study in Diffusion and Modification." *Pioneer America* (Falls Church, Virginia), V:2 (July, 1973), 3-12.

A brief historico-cultural article on the use of windmills in Europe and their evolution in the eastern part of the U.S. from colonial times to the 20th century. Includes maps, drawings, photographs, and notes.

1019. KAHLENBERG, Mary Hunt, and BERLANT, Anthony. *The Navajo Blanket*. Los Angeles: Praeger Publishers in association with the Los Angeles County Museum of Art, 1972. 111 pp.

Gives historical, artistic, and technical information about the Navajo blanket as an American art form. Includes almost one hundred photographs, sixteen of them in color, and a bibliography.

1020. KELLER, Irish. "Apple Art." *Relics* (Austin, Texas), V:6 (April, 1972), 16-17, 30.

Berta Shier of British Columbia explains to the author how she carves faces on apples, an old Indian art.

1021. KELLY, Roger E., LANG, R. W., and WALTERS, Harry. *Navaho Figurines Called Dolls*. Santa Fe, New Mexico: Museum of Navaho Ceremonial Art, 1972. 75 pp. illus.

Kelly in a study entitled "Navaho Ritual Human Figurines: Form and Function" discusses wooden hand-carved figurines. Lang and Walters in "The Remaking Rite of the Navaho: Causal Factors of Illness and Its Nature" deal in depth with the Navaho concept of illness and the curative rites in which dolls are used. Contains a bibliography, charts, and many illustrations.

1022. KING, Dick. "Funeral Notices." *Relics* (Austin, Texas), V:6 (April, 1972), 14-15, 29-30.

Studies the disappearing custom of printing funeral notices in Stephenville, Texas. Reproduces notices dating from 1883 to 1947.

1023. KISSELL, Mary Lois. *Basketry of the Papago and Pima Indians*. Glorieta, New Mexico: The Rio Grande Press, Inc., 1972. 147 pp. illus.

Reprints Vol. XVII, Part IV, of *Anthropological Papers of the American Museum of Natural History* published in 1916. Presents the results of a study of basketry among the Pima-speaking tribes of southern Arizona carried out in the winter of 1910-1911. Examines functions, designs, and productions methods, and provides pictures and diagrams.

1024. LAMME, Ary J., III, and MCDONALD, Douglas B. "Folk Housing Micro-Studies: A Central New York Example." *NYFQ*, XXIX:2 (June, 1973), 111-120.

By studying in Cazenovia, New York, over 160 houses known as the Federal Gable-front type, the author seeks to demonstrate how folk architecture investigations can contribute to understanding of cultural patterns at specific locations. Includes a drawing, maps, and notes.

1025. LASTRA VILLA, Alfonso de la. "Artesanía del hierro en las rejas de nuestra arquitectura civil." In *PIHS(III)*, 169-178.

Discusses the use of iron in Santander in various tools and implements and then treats different kinds and designs of iron grillwork used on windows. Includes drawings.

1026. LE BON, J. W., Jr. "The Catahoula Hog Dog: A Folk Breed." *Pioneer America* (Falls Church, Virginia), III:2 (July, 1971), 35-45.

Treats a spotted, white-eyed breed of dog that has been used traditionally in east-central Louisiana to gather feral hogs. It may be descended from the Boar Dog of Germany.

1027. LIGHTFOOT, William E. "'I Hardly Ever Miss a Meal Without Eating Just a Little': Traditional Sorghum-Making in Western Kentucky." *MSF*, I:1 (Spring, 1973), 7-17.

Studies the way in which sorghum is manufactured by traditional methods in western Kentucky. Includes interviews with a sorghum-maker, Ben Woodburn of Sacramento, Kentucky. There are notes and a drawing.

1028. LONG, Amos, Jr. *The Pennsylvania German Family Farm*. Breiningville, Pa.: Pennsylvania German Society, 1972. xvi, 518 pp. illus.

Thirty-one chapters which deal with virtually every type of building found on Pennsylvania German farms in the 18th and 19th centuries (e.g., the house, the barn, the smokehouse, the pigpen, the sheepfold, etc.). A final portion of each chapter is labeled "Folklore" and deals with such things as barn symbols, beliefs, etc. Includes many photographs.

1029. LOWENSTEIN, Eleanor. *Bibliography of American Cookery Books, 1742-1860*. Worcester, Mass.: American Antiquarian Society, 1972. xii, 132 pp.

Lists something over eight hundred cookbooks, about thirty of them from the 18th century and the rest from the 19th century. Many are regional books, others are about specific kinds of cookery or food preparation (e.g., breadmaking, cider-making, etc.). A few are foreign language cookbooks.

1030. LYLE, Royster, Jr. "Corner Chimneys in Lexington, Virginia." *Pioneer America* (Falls Church, Virginia), IV:1 (January, 1972), 9-19.

Describes in some detail the corner chimneys found in certain 18th-century houses and other buildings in Lexington, Virginia. Posits that the methods of construction, designs, etc. may be derived from Swedish tradition.

1031. MACSWIGGAN, Amelia E. "Symbolic Marks on Oriental Porcelain." *Antiques Journal* (Dubuque, Iowa), XXVII:9 (September, 1972), 21-23, 48-49.

Explains 26 emblems and motifs found on pieces of early Chinese porcelain.

1032. MALO DE RAMÍREZ, Gloria, and others. "Pan, panaderías y sistoplástica en la ciudad de Cuenca." *Revista del Instituto Azuayo de Folklore* (Cuenca, Ecuador), No. 4 (Noviembre, 1971), 75-100.

An ethnographic description of breadmaking practices in Cuenca. Treats bakers, bakeries, hours and working conditions of the bakers, ingredients used, manufacturing processes, kinds of ovens used, utensils employed, and different kinds of bread produced. There is a brief section on specialty breads made in the shape of animals, angels, etc. Includes photographs.

1033. MARSHALL, Howard Wight. "The 'Thousand Acres' Log House, Monroe County, Indiana." *Pioneer America* (Falls Church, Virginia), III:1 (January, 1971), 48-56.

Close description of an early Indiana log house located near Harrodsburg, Indiana, and built in the Southern Mountain tradition. Shows elements of traditional folk architecture and influences from British folk housing. Includes photographs and drawings.

1034. MARTÍNEZ PEÑALOZA, Porfirio. "Arte popular en México." *Anuario Indigenista* (México), XXXI (1971), 49-63.

Concerns the pioneering study of Mexican folk art by Gerardo Murillo, *Las artes populares en México* (1921). Describes the book's contents and discusses Murillo's importance in attempting definitions in the field of folk art. Also considers his proposals for protecting popular arts and crafts.

1035. MICHAEL, Ronald L., and JACK, Phil R. "The Stoneware Potteries of New Geneva and Greensboro, Pennsylvania." *Western Pennsylvania Historical Magazine* (Pittsburgh), LVI:4 (October, 1973), 365-382.

Studies the history of stoneware pottery in New Geneva and Greensboro. Although produced mostly in factories on a commercial basis, it is clear from lists of potters' names that the production of such pottery was a kind of community or family tradition for many people. Includes charts, graphs, maps, etc.

1036. MOFFETT, Lee. *Water Powered Mills of Fauquier County, Virginia*. Warrenton, Virginia: Mrs. Meredith J. Moffett, 1972. viii, 189 pp.

Lists mills which are or were located on streams in Fauquier County, traces the ownership of each mill, provides photographs and drawings of extant mills or ruins, gives anecdotal accounts of mills, etc. Of possible interest to students of Virginia folklife.

1037. MONTAGUE, Richard W. "More Native Art." *Alaska Journal* (Anchorage, Alaska), I:4 (Autumn, 1971), 31-34.

Reports on the Alaska Festival of Native Arts held each June. Native artists and craftsmen display their work at the Anchorage Historical and Fine Arts Museum. Includes photographs of the 1969 exhibition.

1038. MORA DE JARAMILLO, Yolanda. "Artes y artesanías populares." *RCF*, Segunda época, IV:10 (1966-1969), 7-22.

Discusses folkloric and popular arts in Colombia and problems related thereto (e.g., transculturation, definition of types of popular arts, preservation of arts and crafts, etc.). Includes a short bibliography and photographs.

1039. MORA DE JARAMILLO, Yolanda. "Viaje de observación a algunos centros de educación indígena, artística y artesanal del suroeste americano." *RCF*, IV:10 (1966-1969), 125-133.

The author, an anthropologist, reports on her trip to Vanderbilt University in Nashville, Tennessee, and to various places in Arizona and New Mexico to study arts and crafts. She was concerned mainly with programs of education in arts and crafts among Indian groups of the Southwest.

1040. MOREL, Tomás. "Las caretas de los lechones del Carnaval de Santiago." *Cuadernos populares del "Museo Folklorico" de Tomás Morel*

(Santiago, República Dominicana), No. 1 (Marzo, 1973), no pagination (9 pp.)

Treats Carnival masks used in Santiago (Dominican Republic). Includes photographs.

1041. MOSER, Edward. "Seri Basketry." *The Kiva* (Tucson, Arizona), XXXVIII:3-4 (Summer, 1973), 105-140.

Describes Seri baskets and the techniques of their manufacture both as a traditional craft and also as a modern activity. Discusses the functional role of baskets in traditional Seri culture with emphasis on beliefs and ritual activities. The Seris reside along the coast of Sonora (Mexico). Includes photographs and bibliography.

1042. MYERS, Olevia E. "Implements of Bread Making." *Relics* (Austin, Texas), V:6 (April, 1972), 15, 28-29.

Describes wooden bread trays and bowls used in Arkansas in the middle of the 19th century. Includes illustrations and a recipe.

1043. NEWALL, Venetia. *An Egg At Easter: A Folklore Study*. Bloomington: Indiana University Press, 1971. 448 pp. illus.

Examines the usages, the decorations, the decorative techniques, and the cultural significance of eggs. The geographical scope is worldwide and includes the study of the egg in myths and tales both ancient and modern. Contains an extensive bibliography and many illustrations.

1044. NEWTON, Ada L. K. "The Anglo-Irish House of the Rio Grande." *Pioneer America* (Falls Church, Virginia), V:1 (January, 1973), 33-38.

Studies the physical and structural characteristics of a type of house found in the northeastern area of Mexico which shows tangible evidence of Irish influence. There were many Irish settlers in the area in the 19th century. Includes photographs, drawings, a map, and notes.

1045. OLDHAM, Evelyn. "Renaissance of Coast Indian Art." *Canadian Geographical Journal* (Ottawa, Ontario), LXXXVII:5 (November, 1973), 32-37.

Describes 'Ksan Historic Indian Village near Hazelton, British Columbia, where the traditional arts and crafts of the Gitksan Indians, all but extinct twenty years ago, are being revived and preserved. Songs, legends, and dances are also being recorded or performed. Includes photographs.

1046. OLDS, Elizabeth Fogg. "Cowboy Ghosts Feel at Home at Texas Museum." *Smithsonian* (Washington, D.C.), III:8 (November, 1972), 82-89.

Describes the Ranch Headquarters being developed as an outdoor living museum on a twelve-acre site at Texas Tech University in Lubbock, Texas. It will contain authentic old buildings rebuilt at the museum and things that go with them (furniture, tools, buggies, etc.). Includes excellent color photographs.

1047. OLSON, Sandi. "Ethno Cuisine: Lefse, Lutefish and Rommegrøt." *AFFword*, III:1 (April, 1973), 44-45.

Gives recipes for three dishes that are the main components of a Norwegian Christmas Eve dinner as traditionally prepared by the author's family.

1048. ORTIZ, Elizabeth Lambert. *The Complete Book of Caribbean Cooking*. N.Y.: M. Evans, 1973. 450 pp. illus.

Over 450 recipes represent the Caribbean kitchen.

1049. OSGOOD, Cornelius. *The Jug and Related Stoneware of Bennington*. Rutland, Vermont: Charles E. Tuttle Co., 1971. 222 pp.

Concerns the activities of the Norton family of Bennington, Vermont, potters through most of the 19th century. Deals mostly with stoneware pottery (i.e., shapes, designs, clays, glazes, etc.) and offers 38 plates, some in color.

1050. PALOWSKI, Marie, ZALUCKI, Kathy, and NOGORKA, Suzanne. "Traditional Polish Cooking." *NYFQ*, XXVIII:4 (March, 1973), 271-285.

Three high school students collaborate in gathering and publishing recipes for some Polish recipes as prepared by informants from the N.Y. area. Gives data about informants.

1051. PARSONS, Charles Sidney. *The Dunlaps and Their Furniture*. Manchester, New Hampshire: The Currier Gallery of Arts, 1970. 310 pp. illus.

An exhibition catalogue which discusses and pictures the work of a family of country cabinetmakers in 18th century New Hampshire. Deals with the lives, the work, the tools, etc. of these craftsmen. Contains a full transcript of Major John Dunlap's account book, many illustrations and charts, and a bibliography.

1052. PATTERSON, Bob. "A House History: 2955 Rosendale Road, Schenectady, New York." *NYFQ* XXVIII:4 (March, 1973), 305-313.

Describes the construction details of an old house. Includes photographs, drawings, floor plans, and information gained by tracing deeds back to 1871.

1053. PÉREZ VIDAL, José. "Del codonate a la mermelada." *RDTP*, XXIX (1973):1-2, pp. 3-21.

A scholarly historical study of the introduction of the quince (i.e., *membrillo*) from the Orient into Europe in ancient times and its subsequent use in Spain for making sweets such as *codonate* and marmelade. Draws on folkloric sources for allusions to such products.

1054. PESÁNTEZ DE MOSCOSO, Gloria. "Tejas, ladrillos y adobes en la parroquia de Sinicay, cantón Cuenca." *Revista del Instituto Azuayo de Folklore* (Cuenca, Ecuador), No. 4 (Noviembre, 1971), 181-201.

An ethnographic description of tile-making and brick-making practices. Treats materials used, manufacturing processes, ovens, etc. Includes drawings and photographs.

1055. PLATH, Oreste, and others. *Folklore y arte popular de Pica y Matilla*. [Santiago]: Imprenta del Departamento de Extensión Universitaria y Acción Social, Universidad de Chile, n. d. [1971]. 98 pp. drawings.

Reports on fieldwork done by a folklore class under the direction of Professor Plath. Deals mostly with material culture (e.g., pottery, basketry, embroidery, textiles, food, religious images, etc.) and to a lesser degree with songs (words but no music) of the Pica y Matilla region near Iquique. Includes many drawings.

1056. PLUMAR, Cheryl. *African Textiles: An Outline of Hand Crafted Sub-Saharan Fabrics*. East Lansing, Michigan: African Studies Center, Michigan State University, 1971. 146 pp.

Summarizes in outline form and by geographical regions the textiles made in various parts of Africa. Treats such things as the history of weaving, yarns used, looms, weavers, etc.

1057. POESE, Bill. "Farming Antiques Can Be Rescued." *Antiques Journal* (Dubuque, Iowa), XXVII:9 (September, 1972), 30-32.

Discusses the use of several old tools and gives advice on building up a collection of farm tools.

1058. POULSEN, Richard C. "Polynesians in the Desert: A Look at the Graves of Iosepa." *AFFword*, III:1 (April, 1973), 2-15.

Describes a graveyard in the now abandoned town of Iosepa, Utah, until 1915 a settlement of Hawaiian Mormons. Notes certain aspects of the graves and gravestones with attention to details that may have been traditional. Includes photographs, notes, and a bibliography.

1059. QUEREILHAC DE KUSSROW, Alicia Cora. "Artesanías folklóricas argentinas." *Productos Roche* (B.A.), Año I:1 (Junio, 1972), [8 pp.].

Characterizes folk crafts, distinguishing them from other types of production (e.g., folk art, manufactured articles, etc.) and reviewing the state of such crafts in Argentina at the present time.

1060. REABURN, Ronald, and REABURN, Tauline. "Lime Kilns—Remnants of Pioneer Technology." *Canadian Geographical Journal* (Ottawa, Ontario), LXXXVI:1 (January, 1973), 14-17.

Describes processes used by pioneers for extracting lime from limestone and takes note of many different kinds of old kilns from the 19th century that are still found in southern Ontario. Includes nine photographs.

1061. REED, Ethel. *Pioneer Kitchen, A Frontier Cookbook*. San Diego, California: Frontier Heritage Press, 1971. 182 pp. illus.

A large collection of recipes from the West gathered from many sources (i.e., orally collected, taken from manuscripts, lifted from old cookbooks). Also contains a section on frontier home remedies. Includes some drawings.

1062. RENDÓN, Silva. "Las alfarerías vidriadas en México: varias consideraciones." *Anuario Indigenista* (México), XXXI (1971), 65-76.

Describes the process of glazing clay vessels in Mexico and discusses its aesthetic and practical functions.

1063. RICHMOND, Stephen. "The Indian Way." *Directions: A Guide to the Southern Highlands* (Asheville, North Carolina), I:2 (Fall-Winter, 1972), 40-45.

Interviews Cherokee craftsmen in order to ascertain how they learned their craft. Includes a crafts calendar.

1064. ROBBINS, Warren. "How to Approach the Traditional African Sculpture." *Smithsonian* (Washington, D.C.), III:6 (September, 1972), 44-51.

An informative article for the general reader that seeks to clarify some of the basic concepts underlying African art. Seeks to show that much that has been considered "primitive" and of interest only to ethnographers is actually quite sophisticated.

1065. RODGERS, Ava D. *The Housing of Oglethorpe County, Georgia, 1790-1860*. Tallahassee: Florida State University Press, 1971. xi, 79 pp. illus.

Describes and reproduces pictures of extant ante-bellum houses found in rural northeast Georgia ranging from log cabins to various kinds of "plain style" and Greek Revival homes. The author obtained information about builders, owners, and construction dates from oral interviews and county records. Also provides some floor plans and a bibliography.

1066. ROSELLÓ, Guillém, BONET, Biai, and BARCELÓ, Miguel. *Cerámica popular mallorquina*. Palma de Mallorca: Exposición en la Sala Pelaires, Junio de 1972. 9 pp. illus.

A catalogue to an exhibition of Mallorcan popular ceramics held in the Sala Pelaires in the city of Palma, Mallorca. Includes 25 illustrations and brief commentaries.

1067. RUTSTRUM, Calvin. "Sourdough." *The Beaver* (Winnipeg, Canada), Outfit CCCIV:2 (Autumn, 1973), 40-43.

An informative article about the history of sourdough bread, methods of making it, its therapeutic qualities, etc. Includes photographs.

1068. SAFFORD, Carleton L., and BISHOP, Robert. *America's Quilts and Coverlets*. N.Y.: E. P. Dutton, 1972. 313 pp. illus.

A non-scholarly but handsome and expensive picture book that provides sketchy information allegedly gathered from some three hundred institutions, historical societies, museums, etc. The excellent photographs are, of course, of interest.

1069. SANSBURY, Roy. "The Whooey Stick." *NCFJ*, XXI:1 (April, 1973), 23-24.

Describes the use and means of construction of a wooden folk toy called a "whooey stick" or a "whimmey-diddle" made by the author's father orginally of Timmonsville, South Carolina.

1070. SCHADEN, Egon, and MUSSOLINI, Gioconda. *Povos e trajes da America Latina*. São Paulo: Universidade de São Paulo, Escola de Comunicações e Artes, 1972. 69 pp.

Surveys certain cultural or ethnic types from various Latin American countries (e.g., the gauchos of Brazil and Argentine, the Araucanians of Chile, the Incas of Peru, groups from certain countries such as Mexico, Guatemala, and Panama who are considered to have unusually interesting costumes, etc.) and describes the traditional dress of such types.

1071. SEXTON, Lena Anken. "The Best Cook Is a Basque Cook." *Lifestyle* (Hendersonville, North Carolina), No. 7 (October, 1973), 50-51.

Gives eight recipes of Basque dishes as prepared by the Basques of Idaho.

1072. "Ship Figureheads." *Lithopinion* (N.Y.), VIII:3, Issue 31 (Fall, 1973), 24-40.

A brief commentary on the custom of decorating the prows of vessels with carved figureheads is followed by superb color photographs of examples of this type of folk art from the U.S. and from Europe.

1073. SIMON, Mrs. Billy. "Ethno Cuisine: Cactus Jelly." *AFFword*, II:3 (October, 1972), 36-37.

Tells how to gather and cook cactus fruit in order to make juice and ultimately jelly.

1074. SISMEY, Eric D. "'Saunas' of the Okanagan Indians." *Canadian Geographical Journal* (Ottawa, Ontario), LXXXVII:3 (September, 1973), 26-27.

Describes the traditional Quil'-sten of the Okanagan Indians, a sweat-lodge that plays a prominent role in legends and also in modern Okanagan life. Includes photographs.

1075. SMITH, Charles R., and STOFFLE, Richard W. "The Skimmer: An Analysis of Continuations and Modifications of a Traditional American Activity." *Ethnohistory* (Tempe, Arizona), XIX:1 (Winter, 1972), 37-52.

Describes the making of sorghum molasses on a farm in Briar Ridge, Kentucky. Includes photographs.

1076. SPOONER, Brian. "Afghan Carpets: Weavers and Dealers." *Expedition* (Philadephia), XV:2 (Winter, 1973), 9-16.

Gives basic facts about the production and sale of Oriental carpets.

Tells something of their history, weaving techniques, types of dyes, etc. Much of the production comes from individual folk craftsmen. Includes many photographs.

1077. STEPHENS, David E. "Coopers and Hoopers." *Relics* (Austin, Texas), V:6 (April, 1972), 6-7.

Describes how barrels are made by hand and by machine. There are drawings of the hand tools used.

1078. SWART, Margaret. "Educational Eskimo Toys." *Alaska Journal* (Anchorage, Alaska), I:4 (Autumn, 1971), 55-56.

Discusses the importance of toys in teaching children the Eskimo way of life and gives illustrations of toys in the collection of the University of Alaska Museum at College, Alaska.

1079. TOOR, Frances. *Mexican Popular Arts [Being a Fond Glance at the Craftsmen and Their Handiwork in Ceramics, Textiles, Metals, Glass, Paint, Fibres, and Other Materials]*. Illustrated by L. Alice Wilson. Detroit: Blaine Ethridge, 1973. 107 pp. illus.

Reissue (with slight changes and additional plates) of the 1939 edition (Mexico City: Frances Toor Studios). An introduction to the subject which under 22 headings deals in a preliminary way with almost all of the popular arts and crafts of Mexico.

1080. TURNER, Ruth M., and TURNER, Ralph E. "Athabascan Art." *Alaska Journal* (Anchorage, Alaska), I:4 (Autumn, 1971), 25-30.

Deals with art forms of the Indians from the interior of Alaska. Most Athabascan art was utilitarian and few old things have survived because an individual's possessions were usually destroyed when he died. Some traditional things like sheep horn spoons, wooden spoons, bowls, etc. are still used.

1081. VAN STONE, James W. "The First Peary Collection of Polar Eskimo Material Culture." *Fieldiana Anthropology* (Chicago), LXIII:2 (December 27, 1972), 31-80.

Tells the story of Robert E. Peary's expedition to northwest Greenland in 1891 in order to assemble a collection of ethnographic materials for the Columbian Exposition in 1893. Surveys the items he brought back and provides photographs of many of them. Of possible value to folklorists interested in material culture.

1082. VASALLO, Jesús. "Los hórreos de Asturias y Galicia, bajo la protección del estado." *Mundo Hispánico* (Madrid), XXVII:305 (Agosto, 1973), 27-31.

Describes the traditional *hórreos* (i.e., silos) of northern areas of Spain whose origins some scholars trace to pre-Roman times. Discusses their importance and reports on recent laws that protect them from destruction on the grounds that they are part of the region's artistic patrimony. Includes photographs.

1083. VLACH, John M. "The Fabrication of a Traditional Fire Tool." *JAF*, LXXXVI:339 (January-March, 1973), 54-57.

Describes the traditional process employed by a blacksmith in Charleston, South Carolina, to make a fire poker. Contains diagrams.

1084. WACKER, Peter O. "Folk Architecture as an Indicator of Culture Areas and Culture Diffusion: Dutch Barns and Barracks in New Jersey." *Pioneer America* (Falls Church, Virginia), V:2 (July, 1973), 37-47.

A historical study which uses 18th-century newspaper advertisements and revolutionary war claims for damages in order to plot cultural influences manifested by two types of Dutch folk architecture: barns and barracks (a device for storing hay, straw, or grain). Includes maps, photographs of barns and barracks still extant, and notes.

1085. WADE, Edwin, and EVANS, David. "The Kachina Sash: A Native Model of the Hopi World." *WF*, XXXII:1 (January, 1973), 1-18.

Publishes the results of field investigations begun in 1968 in northeast Arizona among the Hopi Indians to determine through interviews with weavers the Hopi interpretation of the symbolism on the ceremonial "kachina sash." Contains photographs. Summaries of seven interviews are given in an appendix.

1086. "Weathervanes: Native American Sculpture." *Lithopinion* (N.Y.), VIII:2, Issue 30 (Summer, 1973), 32-47.

Brief commentary about the history of weathervanes in the U.S. followed by some superb photographs, mostly in color, by Bill Joli.

1087. WELLS, Kenneth. "Ethno Cuisine: Pit-Barbecue and Beans." *AFFword*, I:3 (October, 1971), 22-23.

Describes a method of cooking in a pit barbecue as practiced in Williams, Arizona.

1088. WILHELM, Hubert G. H. "German Settlement and Folk Building Practices in the Hill Country of Texas." *Pioneer America* (Falls Church, Virginia), III:2 (July, 1971), 15-24.

Studies the adaptation of German building types and traditional methods of construction to the conditions and materials found in Texas. Includes illustrations.

1089. WILSON, Eugene M. "Some Similarities between American and European Folk Houses." *Pioneer America* (Falls Church, Virginia), III:2 (July, 197), 8-14.

Compares the central passage house (i.e., dogtrot) which evolved in the southeastern U.S. with similar houses in England and other parts of Europe.

1090. WILSON, Raymond E. "Twenty Different Ways to Build a Covered Bridge." *Technology Review* (Cambridge, Massachusetts), LXXIII:8 (June, 1971), 49-56.

Studies nineteen different structural types of covered bridges and discusses their distribution. Notes that almost one thousand bridges remain of over ten thousand constructed in the U.S. between 1805-1885.

1091. WOLFER, Maria Georgina. *Noções de arte popular*. Rio de Janeiro: Ministério da Educação e Cultura, Campanha de Defesa do Folclore Brasileiro, 1971. 8 pp. (*Cadernos de Folclore, 13*.)

Discusses the nature of folkloric art and considers some Brazilian examples such as sculpture, ex-votos, ceramics, etc.

1092. ZIMILES, Martha, and ZIMILES, Murray. *Early American Mills*. N.Y.: Clarkson N. Potter, 1973. xii, 290 pp. illus.

A non-scholarly but frequently informative treatment of mills and factories, mostly in New England. Some of the material about pre-industrial mills and buildings may be of interest to students of material folklore and folk architecture. Includes many illustrations, maps, a glossary, and selected bibliography.

S SPEECH

[See also numbers 11, 23, 55, 60, 76, 100, 108, 118, 133, 134, 137, 139, 142, 149, 153, 164, 173, 179, 180, 181, 189, 198, 201, 205, 207, 211, 213, 222, 224, 229, 246, 249, 250, 275, 286, 296, 304, 327, 330, 332, 333, 334, 344, 348, 359, 422, 446, 480, 533, 534, 578, 649, 665, 737, 801, 820, 821, 824, 866, 894, 1008, 1217, 1221, 1222, 1223, 1226, 1227, 1230, 1240.]

1093. ÁLVAREZ NAZARIO, Manuel. *La herencia lingüística de Canarias en Puerto Rico: estudio histórico-dialectal.* Prólogo de Manuel Alvar. San Juan de Puerto Rico: Instituto de Cultura Puertorriqueña, 1972. 352 pp.

Studies immigration to Puerto Rico from the Canary Islands and then analyzes some of the effects of Canarian linguistic influence upon the Spanish spoken in Puerto Rico. Much of this deals with folk speech, and there are sections on folkloric matters such as customs, superstitions, songs, dances, food, traditions, etc. Includes a long bibliography and indexes.

1094. ASHLEY, Leonard R. N. "You Pays Yer Money and You Takes Yer Choice: British Slang for Pounds and Pennies, Old and New." *Names,* XXI:1 (March, 1973), 1-21.

Surveys British slang having to do with money over a period of several hundred years. Includes many words and expressions in word lists and in running commentary.

1095. BARDSLEY, Charles Wareing. *Curiosities of Puritan Nomenclature.* Detroit: Gale Research Company, 1970. ix, 252 pp.

Reissue of the 1897 edition (London: Chatto and Windus). Traces English naming practices from the post-1300 pet-name epoch, through the use of scripture names before and during the Reformation, and later to Puritan eccentricities in naming.

1096. BEN-AMOS, Dan. "The 'Myth' of Jewish Humor." *WF,* XXXII:2 (April, 1973), 112-131.

Opposes the widely accepted assumption of Freud that self-degradation is the unique quality of Jewish jokes. Consideration of the joke-telling situation and the narrator's social class or role shows that verbal aggression and social differentiation are the functions of such joking. Gives as examples the texts of several jokes collected in the United States.

1097. BERSHAS, Henry N. "The Use of *Cras* in Golden Age Texts." *Hispanic Review* (Philadelphia), XL:2 (Spring, 1972), 206-209.

Concerns the use of the archaic word *cras* meaning "tomorrow" or "caw" in Spanish literature and proverbs of the 16th and 17th centuries.

1098. BIRNEY, Adrian. "Collectanea: Crack Puns: Text and Context in an Item of Latrinalia." *WF,* XXXII:2 (April, 1973), 137-140.

Examines the structure, meaning, and context of puns written in the cracks between tiles on university restroom walls in San Diego, California, and Jacksonville, Florida.

1099. *Boletín de la Academia Porteña del Lunfardo* (B.A.), II:5 (Octubre-Diciembre, 1971), 1-90; III:6 (Enero-Abril, 1972), 1-68; III:7 (Mayo-Agosto, 1972), 1-81.

These numbers of this journal have crossed my desk in the last year. The journal deals with the *lunfardo* speech of Buenos Aires and articles in it sometimes touch on matters related to folk speech. I have not, however, listed them separately in this bibliography except to call attention to Enrique del Valle's "Bibliografía fundamental del lunfardo" (see item no. 1208 below).

1100. BRUNVAND, Jan Harold. "'Don't Shoot, Comrades': A Survey of the Submerged Folklore of Eastern Europe." *NCFJ*, XXI:4 (November, 1973), 181-188.

Comments upon the nature of political jokes which the author collected in various countries in the Russian sphere of influence. Gives some examples under four headings: Defects in the System, Propaganda and Managed News, Repression of Freedom and of Opinion, and Dislike for the Russians.

1101. BULL, Elias B. "The Islands of the Littoral (Part III)." *NSC*, XVIII (Winter, 1971), 24-28.

Gives names of 55 islands and explains their origins. For earlier installments of this series see item no. 1086 of my "Folklore Bibliography for 1972."

1102. CALLARY, Robert E. "Indications of Regular Sound Shifting in an Appalachian Dialect." *Appalachian Journal* (Boone, North Carolina), I:3 (Autumn, 1973), 238-240.

Shows that certain phonemes that differentiate the dialect of Western North Carolina from "Standard" English occur systematically when certain phonological environments are present.

1103. CANTERA, Jesús. "Notas sobre el judeoespañol de oriente." *Filología Moderna* (Madrid), XIII:46-47 (Noviembre-Febrero, 1973), 105-115.

Tells something of the history of the Spanish used by Sephardic Jews in various parts of Europe and the Near East. Ponders reasons why this language, which has survived since the Jews were expelled from Spain in 1492, is doomed to disappear very soon.

1104. CASCUDO, Luís da Câmara. "Tres notas brasileiras." *Boletim da Junta Distrital de Lisboa* (Lisboa), LXXIII-LXXIV, III Série (1970), 3-14 [pagination of a separata; I have not seen the journal].

Three brief chapters: the first on the use of the nautical verb "navegar" meaning to travel by land; the second on the custom of writing letters to heaven (i.e., *cartas do Ceu*); and the third on oral phrases or gestures used to extend greetings or to say good-bye.

1105. CASSANO, Paul Vincent. "La [b] del español del Paraguay, en posición inicial." *Revue Romane* (Copenhague, Danemark), VII (1972):2, pp. 186-188.

Deals with the pronunciation of an initial *b* in Paraguayan Spanish and considers alleged Guaraní influence on the pronunciation of this consonant.

1106. CASSIDY, Frederic G. "The Names of Green Bay, Wisconsin." *Names*, XXI:3 (September, 1973), 168-178.

Traces the history of the names used for the bay now called Green Bay, Wisconsin, noting the confusion which surrounded its various names in English, French, and Indian languages. Notes the role played at times by oral tradition.

1107. CHANDLER, William H. "Some Historic Churches in Williamsburg County." *NSC*, XVIII (Winter, 1971), 28-32.

Gives mostly historical data about some old churches in Williamsburg County, South Carolina.

1108. CHENEY, Roberta C. *Names on the Face of Montana: The Story of Montana's Place Names*. Missoula: University of Montana Publications in History, 1971. xix, 275 pp.

Lists place names alphabetically and tries to fix the time and circumstances of each town's origin, with secondary attention to sources of names. Draws upon anecdotal material. Includes an informative preface and introduction along with maps and a good bibliography.

1109. CHUKS-ORJI, Ogonna. *Names from Africa, Their Origin, Meaning, and Pronunciation*. Chicago: Johnson Publishing Co., 1972. vi, 91 pp.

Lists female and male African names in alphabetical order, gives aid to pronunciation, and explains meanings. Besides some commentary by the author there is also an important essay by Keith E. Baird who discusses ceremonies associated with naming babies in Africa, how names are formed, beliefs about names, etc.

1110. COMENDADOR, Napoleão [pseud.]. *Humor negro em 3 dimensões*. São Paulo, Brasil: n. p., 1972?. 269 pp.

A curious collection of jokes, nonsense, cartoon drawings, etc. Little of it is folklore, but students of Brazilian folk speech will probably find a "Dicionário de palavrinhas" (pp. 205-236) of interest. It is made up of several hundred items from Brazilian obscene speech.

1111. DAGGETT, Rowan K. "The Place-Names of Chester Township, Wabash County, Indiana." *Indiana Names* (Terre Haute, Indiana), IV:1 (Spring, 1973), 4-30.

Lists place names, gives locations, and explains origins whenever possible. Includes an introduction, notes, bibliography, and a list of informants.

1112. DE VORSEY, Louis, Jr. "Names from Cherokee Boundary Lines." *NSC*, XVIII (Winter, 1971), 13-15.

Discusses ten South Carolina place names related to land cessions and negotiated boundaries before 1776.

1113. DÍAZ GÓMEZ, Alberto. "Vocabulario de términos montañeses de la región de Carmona." In *PIHS (III)*, 109-122.

A word-list that defines 217 items of folk speech collected in the Carmona region of Santander (Spain).

1114. DILLARD, J. L. "Creole Studies and American Dialectology." *Caribbean Studies* (Río Piedras, Puerto Rico), XII:4 (January, 1973), 76-91.

A review of a recent book on American dialects, this long review-article criticizes most work done on Negro dialects in the U.S. for ignoring the creolization process that students of popular speech in the Caribbean area and elsewhere have investigated in some depth. Includes good bibliography.

1115. DOLAN, J. R. *English Ancestral Names: The Evolution of the Surname from Medieval Occupations*. N.Y.: C. N. Potter, 1972. xvi, 381 pp.

Treats the origin and proliferation of English surnames derived from medieval occupations. Focuses particularly on methods and materials used by artisans. Contains charts and a bibliography.

1116. DOYLE, Charles Clay. "Title-Author Jokes, Now and Long Ago." *JAF*, LXXXVI:339 (January-March, 1973), 52-54.

Opposes the structural definition of title-author jokes proposed by Dundes and Georges. Also refutes their belief that such jokes were non-existent before 1928. Cites 17th-century English mock booklists that used obscene puns to insult Puritans and other anti-royalist groups.

1117. DUCKERT, Audrey R. "Place Nicknames." *Names*, XXI:3 (September, 1973), 153-160.

Surveys various types of nicknames that are applied to places, sometimes with affection, sometimes in jest, and sometimes with disgust. Gives examples of the various kinds.

1118. DUNCAN, Alderman. "Feminine Place Names". *NSC*, XVIII (Winter, 1971), 32-36.

Discusses feminine names of South Carolina towns, post offices, geographical features, etc.

1119. EASTMAN, Jean. "Colloquial Names of South Carolina Plants." *NSC*, XVIII (Winter, 1971), 19-24.

Gives folk names and Latin names of plants collected from the *South Carolina Market Bulletin*.

1120. ELEAZAR, J. M. "Name Origins of Some Places in the Dutch Fork Area." *NSC*, XVIII (Winter, 1971), 10-13.

Gives origins of 23 names from an area northwest of Columbia, South Carolina, which was settled by Germans between 1730 and 1770.

1121. "Evangelização e linguistica"—"Referencias e incidentes pastorais." *Portugal em Africa, Revista de Cultura Missionária* (Braga, Portugal), Nos. 175-178 (Janeiro-Agosto, 1973), 5-256.

An entire issue of *Portugal em Africa* is devoted to the speech of various areas of Portuguese Africa. There are articles by many writers divided under the two general headings given above. I have listed none of these studies separately in this bibliography, but students of African folk speech might find some of them of interest.

1122. FARMER, John S. *Americanisms-Old and New. A Dictionary of Words, Phrases, and Colloquialisms Peculiar to the United States, British America, the West Indies, etc., etc.* Ann Arbor, Michigan: Gryphon Books, 1971. xx, 564 pp.

Reissue of the 1889 edition (London: Thomas Poulter and Sons). A list of Americanisms in alphabetical order. Includes many colloquialisms and items of popular speech and cites examples of usage.

1123. FERNÁNDEZ, César Aníbal. "Nuevos aportes para el estudio de los topónimos indígenas." *RDTP*, XXVIII (1972):Cuadernos 3-4, pp. 283-289.

Discusses problems of place-name research on Araucanian names of Chile and then gives explanations with notes and bibliography of four such names: Alicura, Caleufu, Mallín, and Malo.

1124. FIELD, John. *English Field-Names: A Dictionary*. Detroit: Gale Research Co., 1973. xxx, 219 pp. illus.

Lists the names of open fields, furlongs, and enclosed lands of 19th and 20th-century England. Interprets, explains, and gives the linguistic derivation of the names listed. A brief introduction discusses name analysis, history, classification and collecting. Includes appendices, a photograph, a map, and a bibliography.

1125. FONTANELLA DE WEINBERG, María Beatriz. "Comporta-

miento ante -*s* de hablantes femeninos y masculinos del español bonae-
rense." *Romance Philology* (Berkeley, California), XXVII:1 (August,
1973), 50-58.

A technical study of the regional pronunciation of final -*s* in the city of
Bahía Blanca, Argentina. Finds that there are extralinguistic variables that
exert an influence, the sex of the speaker being the most important one.

1126. FROST, Thomas. *Circus Life and Circus Celebrities*. Detroit:
Singing Tree Press, 1970. xvi, 328 pp.

Reissue of the 1875 edition (London: Tinsely Brothers). A history of
circuses, a description of circus life, and a survey of outstanding circus
performers in England, with passing mention also of the U.S. Deals with
certain traditions and the slang of circus people. Includes an index.

1127. FRY, Donald K. "Wulf and Eadwacer: a Wen Charm." *Chaucer
Review* (University Park, Pennsylvania), V (1971):4, pp. 247-263.

Suggests that this poem, which has generally been interpreted as an
elegiac monologue involving a woman, her lover, and her husband, is
actually a charm against wens.

1128. GALVÁN, Roberto A. "Chicano, vocablo controvertido."
Thesaurus, XXVIII:1 (Enero-Abril, 1973), 111-117.

Discusses the rise of the word *chicano* to refer to Mexican-Americans in
the United States, examines its usage, suggests possible etymologies, and
speculates on its possible fate in the future.

1129. GARCÍA GUAL, Carlos. "Sobre πιϑηκίζω «Hacer el mono»."
Emerita, Revista de Lingüística y Filología Clásica (Madrid), XL (1972):
Fasc. 2º, pp. 453-460.

Traces to Greek fables and other literary sources the use of the term
"monkey" as an insult.

1130. GLANZ, Rudolf. *The Jew in Early American Wit and Graphic
Humor*. N.Y.: KTAV Publishing House, 1973. 269 pp. illus.

A compilation of jokes, puns, stories, and graphic art which come
mostly from magazines and other publications of the late 19th century.
Provides insights into public attitudes toward Jews, particularly the Jewish
stereotype, that prevailed until the 20th century.

1131. GLENN, Emily Smith. "Some Names around Eutaville." *NSC*,
XVIII (Winter, 1971), 39-41.

Discusses the origins of some names of South Carolina towns, plantations, roads, etc.

1132. GNERRE, Maurizio. "Sources of Spanish *Jívaro*." *Romance
Philology* (Berkeley, California), XXVII:2 (November, 1973), 203-204.

Traces the origin of the word *jívaro* back to a Spanish chronicle of
1550. Then notes the different meanings that the word has acquired in
different areas of América.

1133. GOLDIE, Alain. "Reflexiones sobre la toponimia de la Montaña." In *PIHS (I)*, 147-165.

Analyzes the origins of many place names in the Montaña region of
Spain (e.g., names based on geography, vegetation, animals, pagan cults,
historical happenings, etc.)

1134. GOLDIN, Harry. *The Golden Book of Jewish Humor*. N.Y.: G.
P. Putnam's Sons, 1972. 252 pp.

A large collection of Jewish jokes and stories taken from printed
sources. Sources of specific jokes are seldom indicated. The work is for the
entertainment of the general reader, but it contains a lot of ethnic humor
of possible interest to folklorists.

1135. GONZÁLEZ DEL VALLE, Máximo. "Geografía e idioma en el valle de Lamasón." In *PIHS (I)*, 167-173.

Comments upon the regional speech of an informant from the Lamasón valley of the Santander area of Spain. Lists 38 items of popular speech with definitions.

1136. GRANDA, Germán de. "Notas sobre el léxico de los marihuaneros en Bogotá." *RDTP*, XXVIII (1972): Cuadernos 3-4, pp. 269-273.

Notes some sociological factors that enter into the use of marihuana in Colombia and then gives some lexicographical items from the argot of marihuana users.

1137. GRANDA, Germán de. "Papiamento en Hispanoamérica (siglos XVII–XIX)." *Thesaurus*, XXVIII:I (Enero-Abril, 1973), 1-13.

Studies in a historical way the spread of *papiamento* (i.e., the "Creole" language used by black slaves in Curazao, Aruba, and Bonaire) to Puerto Rico, Venezuela, Cuba, and other places in Spanish America.

1138. GREEN, Bennett Wood. *Word-Book of Virginia Folk-Speech*. N.Y.: Benjamin Blom, Inc., 1971. 435 pp.

Reissue of the 1899 edition (Richmond, Va.). Lists the dialect words of "Lower Peninsula" Virginia speech describing or giving examples of their usage. Also presents some folk sayings and discusses the pronunciation of names of the area.

1139. GREGORIO DE MAC, María Isabel de. "Diferencias generacionales en el empleo de eufemismos." *Thesaurus*, XXVIII:I (Enero-Abril, 1973), 14-28.

Studies the use of certain euphemisms in the Spanish of Rosario (Argentina). Compares those employed by informants between 20 and 35 years of age with those used by people over 55.

1140. HALL, Virginius Cornick, Jr. "Virginia Post Offices, 1798-1859." *Virginia Magazine of History and Biography* (Richmond), LXXXI:I (January, 1973), 49-97.

Merely a listing without commentary of Virginia and West Virginia post offices. However, the list would be a useful reference source for students of place names.

1141. HAMBURG, James. "Postmasters' Names and South Dakota Place-Names." *Names*, XXI:I (March, 1973), 59-64.

Comments upon the origins of South Dakota place names and calls attention to the fact that more than three hundred post offices were named after their first postmasters. Lists them.

1142. HARPER, Jared, and HUDSON, Charles. "Irish Traveler Cant in Its Social Setting." *SFQ*, XXXVII:2 (June, 1973), 101-114.

Discusses the social function and derivation of the language used by the itinerant Irish in the southern United States. Reconstructs a 1927 mule trading situation between the Travelers and a farmer in South Georgia.

1143. HASKINS, Jim. *Jokes from Black Folks*. Garden City, N.Y.: Doubleday and Co., 1973. 116 pp.

A collection of jokes with an introductory commentary. Some are ethnic jokes but many are not, and sources are not indicated for any of them.

1144. HEDBLOM, Folke. "Place-Names in Immigrant Communities. Concerning the Giving of Swedish Place-Names in America." *Swedish Pioneer Historical Quarterly* (Chicago), XXIII (1972):4, pp. 246-260.

1145. HEDGES, James S. "Two Phrasal Folk Verbs: *To possum off* and *To cabbage on to*." *FForum*, VI:3 (July, 1973), 174-175.

Discusses the semantic variants of *to possum off* and *to cabbage on to*, phrasal verbs found in Indiana agrarian dialects.

1146. HELLER, L. G. "Late Indo-European Water Deity as Spearman: Greek *Triton* and Old English *gārsecg*." *Names*, XXI:2 (June, 1973), 75-77.

An etymological note about the origins of the Old English word *gārsecg*, meaning "spear warrior" and "ocean". Under discussion is a question of possible folk etymology.

1147. HEMPERLEY, M. R. ed. "Indian Place Names in Georgia." *Georgia Historical Quarterly* (Athens, Georgia), LVII:4 (Winter, 1973), 562-579.

Lists some two hundred place names and explains their origins. The editor provides a brief preface that states some basic facts about place names of Indian origin.

1148. HOLMGREN, Eric, and HOLMGREN, Patricia M. *2,000 Place Names of Alberta*. Saskatoon, Saskatchewan: Modern Press, 1973. 210 pp.

An alphabetical listing of Alberta place names with explanations of origins for many of them. There is an introductory essay and end paper maps are provided.

1149. IRWIN, Godfrey, ed. *American Tramp and Underworld Slang: Words and Phrases Used by Hoboes, Tramps, Migratory Workers and Those on the Fringes of Society, with Their Uses and Origins, with a Number of Tramp Songs*. Ann Arbor, Michigan: Gryphon Books, 1971. 264 pp.

Reissue of the 1930 edition (N.Y.: Sears Publishing Co.). A glossary of slang with an introduction appears on pp. 11-198. A section entitled "Songs of Jungles and Drag" (pp. 199-252) contains words without music of thirty songs. A section on "The American Underworld and English Cant" ends the volume (pp. 255-264).

1150. IWUNDU, Mataebere. "Igbo Anthroponyms: Linguistic Evidence for Reviewing the Ibo Culture." *Names*, XXI:1 (March, 1973), 46-49.

Seeks to show how names assigned to people in Igbo, the language of the Ibo group of Nigeria, express attitudes, sentiments, or historical facts. Holds that the study of such anthroponyms has value for understanding social, religions, historical, and political aspects of Ibo culture.

1151. KIRK, F.M. "Mexico, Peru and Ophir." *NSC*, XVIII (Winter, 1971), 49-51.

Discusses the names of some plantations founded by Huguenot settlers in South Carolina. Locates them on a map.

1152. KIRKCONNELL, Watson. "An Introduction to Manitoban Onomastics." In *Onomastica Canadiana 1971*, ed. by I. Gerus-Tarnawecky. Winnipeg: Canadian Institute of Onomastic Sciences and Ukrainian Free Academy of Sciences (UVAN), 1972. Pp. 3-10. (*Onomastica, No. 44.*)

Surveys briefly the history of place names in Manitoba and notes the English, French, Indian, and other sources of the names.

1153. KNAPP, Mary, and KNAPP, Herbert. "Tradition and Change in American Playground Language." *JAF*, LXXXVI:340 (April-June, 1973), 131-141.

Examines the terms "time out," "cooties," and "jinks" used by children in nationally popular playground games and discusses their possible origins. The informants were fifth graders from Monroe County, Indiana, and student and adult Americans living in the Canal Zone.

1154. KUUSI, Anna-Leena. "On Factors Promoting Phrase Formation." *Proverbium*, No. 21 (1973), 776-782.

Studies the generation of folkloric phrases using English, Finnish, German, and French examples.

1155. LAWSON, E. D. "Men's First Names, Nicknames, and Short Names: A Semantic Differential Analysis." *Names*, XXI:1 (March, 1973), 22-27.

Using electronic data-processing equipment, the author reports results of a study designed to determine whether stereotypes of short names and nicknames exist and, if so, how they compare with first names. Includes charts.

1156. LEIGHLY, John. "Gallic Place-Names for Vermont, 1785." *Names*, XXI:2 (June, 1973), 65-74.

Discusses the interest of Michel-Guillaume St. Jean de Crèvecoeur, *alias* Hector St.John, in place names and the suggestions he made in 1785 to Ethan Allen for giving French names to certain places in Vermont.

1157. LLOMPART, Gabriel. "Experiencia religiosa y lengua mallorquina: materiales para el estudio de una interrelación." *RDTP*, XXIX (1973):1-2, pp. 73-129.

Lists 991 expressions from the popular speech of Mallorca that refer to religious subjects (e.g., the Virgin and saints in general, the Church, personal piety, virtues, etc.). They are taken from oral tradition, dictionaries, lists of proverbs, etc. dating from the 18th century to the present. There is an introduction and a bibliography.

1158. LÓPEZ MORALES, Humberto. *Estudios sobre el español de Cuba*. N.Y.: Las Américas Publishing Co., 1971. 188 pp.

A collection of nine previously published articles. Some deal with subjects of interest to students of folk speech (e.g., *indigenismos*, African elements in Cuban Spanish, phonetic characteristics of Cuban speech, place names, etc.).

1159. MCDAVID, Raven I., Jr., and MCDAVID, Virginia. "*Cracker* and *Hoosier*." *Names*, XXI:3 (September, 1973), 161-167.

Offers some observations on the use of the words *cracker* and *Hoosier* to refer to people from certain geographical areas of the U.S. Using methods associated with linguistic atlases, the author studies the geographical distribution of the terms and the differing meanings given to them. Includes a map.

1160. MACDONALD, Judy Smith. "Cursing and Context in a Grenadian Fishing Community." *Anthropologica* (Ottawa, Canada), XV (1973):1, pp. 89-127.

Surveys cursing practices and obscene language among fishing people who live in the town of Gouyave on the west coast of the island of Grenada (West Indies). Emphasis is on the social aspects of cursing, attitudes toward it, etc. Includes bibliography.

1161. MCDOWELL, John H. "Performance and the Folkloric Text: A Rhetorical Approach to 'The Christ of the Bible.'" *FForum*, VI:3 (July, 1973), 139-148.

Examines the metanarrative use of pronouns in the text of a sermon appearing in Bruce Rosenberg's *The Art of the American Folk Preacher*. Shows how the use of pronouns establishes the tone and accomplishes the rhetorical strategy of the performance.

1162. , MCGAHA, Michael D. "Oaths in *Don Quixote*." *Romance Notes* (Chapel Hill, North Carolina), XIV:3 (Spring, 1973), 561-569.

Discusses the place of oaths in Spanish usage and makes a statistical count of selected oaths as used by Don Quixote and Sancho Panza in Cervantes' novel.

1163. MARDON, Ernest G. *The History of Place Names in Southern Alberta*. Lethbridge-Winnipeg: Canadian Institute of Onomastic Sciences and the Ukrainian Free Academy of Sciences, 1972. (*Onomastica, No. 43*).

Surveys the origins of place names in southern Alberta. There are short sections on place names derived from nature, Indian names, surveyors and settlers who gave their names to settlements or towns, etc.

1164. MATTHEWS, C. M. *Place Names of the English-Speaking World*. N.Y.: Charles Scribner's Sons, 1972. xi, 370 pp.

Treats place names in English all over the world. Tells the stories behind many names as the author uses them as subjects for writing popular history.

1165. MILES, Joyce C. *House Names Around the World*. Detroit: Gale Research Co., 1973. 135 pp.

The American edition of a book published in 1972 (London: David and Charles Ltd.). Lists and examines the trends in the names people have given and are giving to their homes. Concentrates on Britain, but also provides examples from former Commonwealth countries and the United States as well as continental Europe. Includes a bibliography.

1166. MILLER, Linda. "'Playing the Dozens' among Black High School Students." *JOFS*, II:1 (April, 1973), 20-29.

A paper for a college course in folklore. Offers a transcription of the dialogue between two black boys as they "played the dozens" in a Columbus, Ohio, high school class.

1167. MORENO DE ALBA, José G. "Frecuencias de la asibilación de /R/ y /RR/ en México." *Nueva Revista de Filologia Hispánica* (México), XXI (1972):2, pp. 363-370.

A follow-up article to one by Giorgio Perissinotto (see item No. 1182 below). Moreno de Alba brings more statistical data on the pronunciation of /r/ and /r/ in México. Includes charts and a map.

1168. MOSS, Bobby G. "Post Offices and Voting Precincts in Cherokee County, 1900." *NSC*, XVIII (Winter, 1971), 36-39.

Explains the origins of twenty South Carolina place names and locates them on a map.

1169. MOYD, Olin P. "Elements in Black Preaching (The Style and Design of Dr. Sandy F. Ray)." *Journal of Religious Thought* (Washington, D.C.), XXX:1 (Spring-Summer, 1973), 52-62.

From seventeen manuscripts and nine tape recordings the author analyzes the preaching of Dr. Sandy Frederick Ray of the Cornerstone Baptist Church in Brooklyn, N.Y. as a "model of admirable, affirmative, wholesome, and valuable Black Preaching." Treats the subject under two general headings: the style and the design of Dr. Ray.

1170. MULLER, H. N., III. "The Name of Vermont: An Afterword." *Vermont History* (Burlington, Vt.), XLI:2 (Spring, 1973), 79-81.

Expresses doubts about the etymology of the name Vermont that Joseph Palermo suggests in item No. 1177 below.

1171. NAGARA, Susumu. *Japanese Pidgin English in Hawaii: A Bilingual Description*. Honolulu: University Press of Hawaii, 1972. 322 pp.

A linguistic study of the pidgin English used by Japanese immigrants in Hawaii. Said to be a pioneering effort.

1172. NALIBOW, Kenneth L. "The Opposition in Polish of Genus and Sexus in Women's Surnames." *Names*, XXI:2 (June, 1973), 78-81.

Discusses recent changes in the traditional gender-marking of women's names in modern Polish. The new system is said to reflect a change in the status of the modern Polish woman.

1173. NEUFFER, Claude Henry. "Notes on Names." *NSC*, XVIII (Winter, 1971), 5-10.

Offers some South Carolina place names that were submitted by correspondents.

1174. O'BANNON, Joyce S. "Disappearing Place Names in Barnwell County." *NSC*, XVIII (Winter, 1971), 41-49.

Ferrets out some South Carolina place names and their origins by studying wills, memoirs, court records, etc.

1175. OGUNDIPE, Ayodele. "Yoruba Tongue Twisters." In *African Folklore*. Pp. 211-220.

Studies the nature, content, and function of Yoruba tongue twisters recently collected in Nigeria. Presents several texts in Yoruba with English translations.

1176. OWEN, Guy. "Playing the Dozens." *NCFJ*, XXI:2 (May, 1973), 53-54.

Presents eight ritualized rhymed insults collected at a day-camp in Raleigh, N.C., in 1972 from black children. Most are welfare insults.

1177. PALERMO, Joseph. "The Mythical Etymology of the Name of Vermont." *Vermont History* (Burlington, Vermont), XLI:2 (Spring, 1973), 78-79.

A translation by Maurice Kohler of "L'etymologie mythique du nom du Vermont" that appeared in *Romance Notes* (Chapel Hill, N.C.), III (1971), 188-189. Finds that the name comes from *vers-mont*, not *verts monts*, as English colonists assumed. See a reply by H. N. Muller, III, in item No. 1170 above.

1178. PALMER, A Smythe. *The Folk and Their Word-Lore: An Essay on Popular Etymologies*. Ann Arbor, Michigan: Gryphon Books, 1971. viii, 194 pp.

Reissue of the 1904 edition (London: George Routledge and Sons; N.Y.: E. P. Dutton and Co.). Tells what folk etymology is and gives many English examples grouped under successive chapter headings such as "Popular Etymologies," "Mistaken Analogies," "Misinterpretations," etc. Includes an index of words studied.

1179. PALMER, A. Smythe. *Some Curios from a Word-Collector's Cabinet*. Ann Arbor, Michigan: Gryphon Books, 1971. vi, 197 pp.

Reissue of the 1907 edition (London: George Routledge and Sons; N.Y.: E. P. Dutton and Co.). A collection of eighty little explanatory essays that deal with as many words, their origin, their meaning, etc. Some tie in with folk speech, popular sayings, beliefs, etc.

1180. PARTIN, Robert. *Lee County Jokes 100 Years Ago: A Case Study in Reconstruction Humor in Alabama*. Loachapoka, Alabama: Lee County (Alabama) Historical Society, March, 1973. 32 pp.

Gathers together jokes and humorous stories gleaned from newspapers published in Opelika (Alabama), the county seat of Lee County, in the 1870's. Some are of possible value to folklorists interested in traditional humor.

1181. PÉREZ SALA, Paulino. *Estudio lingüístico de Humacao*. Madrid: Ediciones Partenón, 1971. 109 pp.

By means of a questionnaire the author analyzes the phonetics, morphology and syntax, and vocabulary of informants who represent different social levels in the municipality of Humacao, Puerto Rico. Includes photographs, maps, tables, and bibliography.

1182. PERISSINOTTO, Giorgio. "Distribución demográfica de la asibilación de vibrantes en el habla de la ciudad de México." *Nueva Revista de Filología Hispánica* (México), XXI (1972):1, pp. 71-79.

Studies statistically by sex, age-group, and socio-economic status the pronunciation of the simple vibrant /r/ and a variant assibilated fricative /r/. The latter is a fairly recent development and some of the findings about its use by certain groups, particularly women, have implications not only for studies of folk speech but perhaps also for folklore in general (e.g., women are *not* conservative bearers of linguistic tradition in this instance).

1183. PHILLIPS, James W. *Alaska-Yukon Place Names*. Seattle and London: University of Washington Press, 1973. xix, 149 pp.

Lists some 600-700 place names and explains their origin. There is an introduction, a selected bibliography, and maps.

1184. POULSEN, Richard C. "Black George, Black Harris, and the Mountain Man Vernacular." *Rendezvous, Journal of Arts and Letters* (Pocatello, Idaho), VIII:1 (Summer, 1973), 15-23.

Treats the literary use of mountain men's speech in some novels of Emerson Bennett where Black George is the protagonist and also in George Ruxton's description of a real mountain man, Black (Moses) Harris, in *Life in the Far West*. Both men wrote around 1850.

1185. PRESTON, Kathleen A., and PRESTON, Michael J. "A Note on Visual Polack Jokes." *JAF*, LXXXVI:340 (April-June, 1973), 175-177.

Describes commercial posters reading "Ski Poland" and reproduces a "fold-in" drawing of the Polish "Computer System '350'" showing that the qualities attributed to Poles in "Polack jokes" are also manifested in these visual forms.

1186. RAMÍREZ, Carlos. "Forma lingüística del habla rural de la provincia de Cautín (Chile)." *Estudios Filológicos* (Valdivia, Chile), No. 7 (1971), 197-250.

A linguistic-ethnographic study of the speech of the Cautín area. Contains an introduction and then four sections on phonetics, morphology, lexicogenesia, and syntax.

1187. RICHARDS, Henry. "Trinidadian Folk Usage and Standard English: A Contrastive Study." *Word* (N.Y.), XXVI:1 (April, 1970 [pub. in 1973]), 79-87.

A brief survey that contrasts the syntactical structures of Trinidadian folk speech with those of Standard English. Has sections on nouns, personal pronouns, demonstratives, interrogatives, reflexive and intensive pronouns, verbs, and other parts of speech.

1188. ROBINSON, Brian S. "Elizabethan Society and Its Named Places." *Geographical Review* (N.Y.), LXIII:3 (July, 1973), 322-333.

A geographer considers some theoretical assumptions that cultural geographers have used in studying place names and takes note of some English places named in the Elizabethan period.

1189. ROMIG, Walter. *Michigan Place Names*. Grosse Point, Michigan: Walter Romig Publisher, n.d. 673 pp.

A collection of over five thousand place names arranged alphabetically with information about their locations and their origins. Includes a bibliography and a long index of personal names.

1190. ROSE, Howard N. *A Thesaurus of Slang*. Detroit: Gale

Research Co., 1972. x, 120 pp.

Reissue of the 1934 edition (N.Y.: The MacMillan Co.). Presents slang words and phrases used in various places (e.g., New England) or by certain groups (e.g., college students, hoboes, lumberjacks, etc.), or in certain activities (e.g., war).

1191. ROSEN, Karl M. D. "Community Names from Personal Names in Kansas: Post Offices." *Names*, XXI:1 (March, 1973), 28-39.

Shows how 368 community names in Kansas were formed in various ways from the names of their first postmaster.

1192. ROWLAND, Robert J., Jr. "Onomastic Remarks on Roman Sardinia." *Names*, XXI:2 (June, 1973), 82-102.

Analyzes Sardinian place names of Roman and of African origin, notes their geographical distribution, percentages, relationships to names in Italy and Africa, etc. Includes many maps.

1193. RUDNYĆKYJ, J. B. *Slavic Geographical Names in Manitoba*. Winnipeg: Canadian Institute of Onomastic Sciences and The Ukrainian Free Academy of Sciences, 1973. 24 pp. (*Onomastica, No. 45.*)

Lists 91 place names of Slavic origin and indicates their origins. There is a brief introduction.

1194. RUNCIE, John F. "Truck Drivers' Jargon." *American Speech* (N.Y.), XLIV:3 (Fall, 1969 [1973]), 200-209.

A glossary of truck drivers' in-group jargon with a brief introductory commentary.

1195. RYDJORD, John. *Kansas Place-Names*. Norman: University of Oklahoma Press, 1972. xii, 613 pp. illus.

Relates the history of nearly three thousand place names categorized in 42 chapters. The author states that much of what he writes is based solely on legend and hearsay.

1196. SALA, Marius. *Phonétique et phonologie du judéo-espagnol de Bucarest*. Paris: Mouton, 1971. 224 pp.

Studies the Judeo-Spanish spoken by the Jews of Bucharest. The first part of the book treats phonetics both historically and descriptively and the second part deals with phonology in a synchronic and comparative way. Includes bibliography and indexes.

1197. SÁNCHEZ, Rosaura. "Nuestra circunstancia lingüística." *El Grito* (Berkeley, California), VI:1 (Fall, 1972), 45-74.

Offers some thoughts and observations about linguistic problems of Chicanos in the U.S. and then describes some of the characteristics of Chicano Spanish that differentiate it from standard Spanish.

1198. SCHULMAN, Steven A. "Logging Terms from the Upper Cumberland River." *TFSB*, XXIX:2 (June, 1973), 35-36.

Lists 27 recently collected terms and definitions used by lumberjacks in the Upper Cumberland River Valley of Kentucky.

1199. SCHWARTZ, Alvin. *Witcracks: Jokes and Jests from American Folklore*. Philadelphia and N.Y.: J. B. Lippincott Co., 1973. 126 pp.

A miscellany of different kinds of jokes (e.g. tall tales, riddles, puns, Little Moron jokes, "hate" jokes, "sick" jokes, shaggy dog stories, etc.). They come from oral tradition, newspapers, journals, and books. Includes notes and a bibliography. There are drawings by Glen Rounds.

1200. SIMMEN, Edward R. "Chicano: Origin and Meaning." *American Speech* (N.Y.), XLIV:3 (Fall, 1969 [1973]), 225-227.

Notes the origins and changing meaning of the word *chicano* as used to refer to Mexican-Americans.

1201. SPEARS, James E. "The Metaphor in American Folk Speech." *NYFQ*, XXIX:1 (March, 1973), 50-57.

Offers commentary and a glossary (112 items) of folk poetic metaphors in the pattern of "as. . . as. . ." (e.g., as bald as an eagle).

1202. STENHOUSE, T. *Lives Enshrined in Language or The Sociological Aspect of Words*. Ann Arbor, Michigan: Gryphon Books, 1971. xv, 290 pp.

Reissue of the 1928 edition (London: Simpkin, Marshall, Hamilton Kent and Co.). A curious collection of information about English words (i.e., nouns, adjectives, and verbs) derived from the names of persons. The author's explanations about origins and meanings often touch on folklore or draw upon folklore (e.g., beliefs, customs, legends, etc.). Includes indexes.

1203. STOELTJE, Beverly. "'Bow-Legged Bastard: A Manner of Speaking' Speech Behavior of a Black Woman." *FAUFA*, Nos. 4-5 (1972-1973), 152-178.

Studies and interprets in linguistic and social terms certain speech behavior among black women in an urban neighborhood. The paper is based on data provided by a single informant. Includes lengthy transcriptions of conversations and a bibliography.

1204. SULLIVAN, David Herbert. "Pre-1850 Laurens County Churches." *NSC*, XVIII (Winter, 1971), 15-19.

Gives names and historical information about 43 churches.

1205. TAMONY, Peter. "Western Words." *WF*, XXXII:1 (January, 1973), 39-48.

Notes the coinage of new words by California businesses for new developments and discusses their influence on and denomination of social change. Focuses on the business and social history of "Levis," "hard hats," "Caterpillars," and "tanks."

1206. UNBEGAUN, B. O. *Russian Surnames*. Oxford: Oxford University Press, 1972. xviii, 529 pp.

A scholarly study of the Russian surname system. Treats the history of surnames, their forms, their origins (i.e., occupational names, local names, nicknames, etc.), names of non-Russian origin, etc. Includes a copious bibliography and an index of more than ten thousand Russian surnames.

1207. UTLEY, Frances Lee. "Hog Crawl Creek Again." *Names*, XXI:3 (September, 1973), 179-195.

A scholarly study of various etymological aspects of the name of Hog Crawl Creek, Georgia, which was earlier studied by John H. Goff in 1958. The main problem is the relationship of *crawl* to Spanish *corral* and Dutch *kraal* meaning a pen or enclosure.

1208. VALLE, Enrique Ricardo. "Bibliografía fundamental del lunfardo." *Boletín de la Academia Porteña del Lunfardo* (B.A.), II:5 (Octubre-Diciembre, 1971), 67-73; III:6 (Enero-Abril, 1972), 44-51; III:7 (Mayo-Agosto, 1972), 61-68.

These installments give items nos. 125-243 of a continuing and still incomplete bibliography on the *lunfardo* speech of Buenos Aires.

1209. VELILLA BARQUERO, Ricardo. *Contribución al estudio del vocabulario alavés*. Alava: Diputación Foral de Alava, Consejo de Cultura, 1971. 54 pp.

Studies the phonetic aspects of the regional speech of Alava in the Basque region of Spain. Includes bibliography.

1210. WALLIS, Ethel E. "The Trimodal Structure of a Folk Poem."

Word (N.Y.), XXVI:2 (August, 1970 [pub. in 1973]), 170-193.

Offers a structural linguistic analysis of a traditional 18-line poem in the Mezquital Otomí language, "The Spider and the Little Spider." Considers three dimensions of the poem: the phonological, the grammatical, and the lexical. Includes many charts.

1211. WESCHE, Marjorie Bingham. "Place Names as a Reflection of Cultural Change: An Example from the Lesser Antilles." *Caribbean Studies* (Río Piedras, Puerto Rico), XII:2 (July, 1972), 74-98.

Studies the process by which place names were given, maintained intact, modified, or replaced on four islands of the Lesser Antilles, Tobago, Grenada, St. Vincent, and Dominica, from 1763 to the present. Includes maps, many charts, and a brief bibliography

1212. WESLAGER, C. A. "Place-Names on St. David's Island in the Bermudas." *Names*, XXI:2 (June, 1973), 126-128.

A note which calls attention to some place names of an island that had no inhabitants until the coming of the first Europeans. Besides mostly English names there are a few which are of American Indian origin.

1213. WILKINSON, Ron. "Labelling the Land: Canada Needs 2,000,000 More Place Names." *Canadian Geographical Journal* (Ottawa, Ontario), LXXXVII:1 (July, 1973), 12-19.

Surveys the seventy-five year history of the Canadian Permanent Committee on Geographical Names and tells what it does. Notes problems that arise in the field of Canadian place names and how some are resolved. Lists some odd, interesting, or amusing names. Includes drawings and photographs.

1214. WILLIAMS, Melvin D. "Food and Animals: Behavioral Metaphors in a Black Pentecostal Church in Pittsburgh." *Urban Anthropology* (Brockport, N.Y.), II:1 (Spring, 1973), 74-79.

Examines the speech used by members of a church in Philadelphia for evidence that black migrants from the south have a unique organization of symbols that reveal them to perceive themselves as being in a strange, alien, urban context. Many have to do with food and animals.

1215. ZAMORA, Juan Clemente. "Lexicología indianorrománica: *chingar* y *singar*." *Romance Notes* (Chapel Hill, North Carolina), XIV:2 (Winter, 1972), 409-413.

Points out difficulties in the usual etymologies given for the popular Spanish Americanism *chingar: fornicar*, with *singar* being a derived form. Suggests that *singar* was the first form and that *chingar* was derived from it.

V   PROVERBS

[See also numbers 11, 65, 76, 99, 102, 142, 161, 164, 181, 189, 210, 229, 235, 250, 275, 288, 306, 314, 331, 333, 334, 917, 955, 1097, 1157.]

1216. ARNER, Robert D. "Proverbs in Edward Taylor's 'God's Determinations.'" *SFQ*, XXXVII:1 (March, 1973), 1-13.

Examines the existence and function of folk expressions and proverbs in Edward Taylor's Calvinistic poem, "God's Determinations Touching His Elect." Views them as adding a colloquial dimension to the work.

1217. BALLARÍN CORNELL, Angel. "Refranes, adivinanzas y dichos benasqueses." *RDTP*, XXVIII (1972): Cuadernos 3-4, pp. 251-267.

Offers some Catalan proverbs, riddles, and sayings that come from the port town of Benasque (Spain). Provides explanations of meaning and usage.

1218. BARRICK, Mac E. "The Dust of the Sheep (Again)." *Proverbium*, No. 21 (1973), 805.

Offers additional comments on a proverb, "The dust of the sheep is a collyrium for the eyes of the wolf," that is of Oriental provenience but is widely used in Spain. Archer Taylor studied the proverb earlier in *Proverbium*, No. 9, p. 214.

1219. BOADI, Lawrence A. "The Language of the Proverb in Akan." In *African Folklore*. Pp. 183-191.

Holds that among Akan-speaking people in Ghana and the Ivory Coast proverbs are used for their aesthetic or poetic rather than their didactic value. Presents the texts of fourteen proverbs.

1220. BOUZA BREY, Fermín. "Un proverbio evangélico popular en boca de San Rosendo." *Cuadernos de Estudios Gallegos* (Santiago de Compostela), XXVI (1971): Fasc. 80, pp. 319-328.

Finds a source for a proverb ("El que a hierro mata a hierro morirá") in two medieval chronicles about the history of Galicia and of San Rosendo.

1221. BROWN, Marshall, ed. *Wit and Humor of Well-Known Quotations*. Ann Arbor, Michigan: Gryphon Books, 1971. xxii, 354 pp.

Reissue of the 1905 edition (Boston: Small, Maynard and Co.). The author gives at the beginning of the book a list-index of about four hundred quotations (i.e., proverbs, popular sayings, etc.). The body of the book consists of humorous comments, mostly from literary sources, upon each of the quotations.

1222. CASCUDO, Luís da Câmara. "Folclore nos autos camoneanos" *REP*, XVI:1 (Janeiro, 1971), 1-13 [pagination of a separata; I have not seen the journal].

Gives what amounts to footnote explanations of certain popular phrases, proverbs, etc. found in three 16th-century plays of Luis de Camões. They are *Auto chamado dos enfatriões, Auto chamado de Filodemo*, and *El rey Seleuco*.

1223. DOYLE, Charles Clay. "The Popular Aspect of Sir Thomas More's Latin Epigrams." *SFQ*, XXXVII:2 (June, 1973), 87-99.

Shows the popular nature of many of Sir Thomas More's Latin epigrams first published in 1518. Identifies Thompson motifs and Aarne-Thompson types for many and notes parallels found in jestbooks.

1224. EASTMAN, Carol M. "The Proverb in Modern Written Swahili Literature: An Aid to Proverb Elicitation." In *African Folklore*. Pp. 193-209.

Examines the function and meaning of seven Swahili proverbs by obtaining informants' responses to proverbs found in four modern Swahili plays and a biography. An appendix contains the Swahili text and English translations for thirteen proverbs.

1225. GLUSKI, Jerzy, comp. and ed. *Proverbs, Proverbes, Sprichwörter...* [etc.]: *A Comparative Book of English, French, German, Italian, Spanish and Russian Proverbs with a Latin Appendix*. Amsterdam/London/N.Y.: Elsevier Publishing Co., 1971. xxxviii, 448 pp.

A collection of several hundred proverbs grouped into topical sections. Each proverb is given in the six languages (equivalencies, of course, not straight translations). Likewise the preface, table of contents, index, and appendix are all given in six languages.

1226. GONZÁLEZ REBOREDO, José M. "Refranes toresanos." *RDTP*, XXIX (1973):1-2, pp. 169-178.

A list of three hundred proverbs and sayings from the city of Toro, Zamora (Spain), and surrounding regions. Includes a brief commentary.

1227. IBÁÑEZ DE SÁMANO, M. Julia, ed. *Mil y un refranes*. México: Imprenta Aldina, 1973, 155 pp.

Lists in alphabetical order a large collection of proverbs with explanations of their meanings. Also mixes a few *coplas* and popular phrases with the proverbial expressions. An appendix (pp. 139-151) contains "Proverbios y refranes charros," but these are not explained. Includes a small bibliography. No sources are given for any texts.

1228. JOHNSTON, Thomas F. "Tsonga Proverbs in Cultural Context." *TFSB*, XXXIX:3 (September, 1973), 69-76.

Shows how proverbs function in social situations by relating personal experiences gained while doing fieldwork among the Tsonga of Africa during the years 1968-1970.

1229. KNOWLTON, Edgar C., Jr. "Chinese Proverbs." *American Notes and Queries* (New Haven, Connecticut), X:5 (January, 1972), 73.

A very brief note that ordinarily I would not list. However, it contains very useful bibliographical leads to books, dictionaries, etc. that would be of value to anyone beginning an investigation of Chinese proverbs.

1230. LOTT, Robert E. "Frases populares y pintorescas empleadas en Córdoba, Colombia." *Hispania*, LV:3 (September, 1972), 506-510.

Lists alphabetically by first key word a hundred proverbs and phrases used in Montería, Colombia.

1231. LUOMALA, Katharine. "The Narrative Source of a Hawaiian Proverb and Related Problems." *Proverbium*, No. 21 (1973), 783-787.

Reinterprets a proverb thought previously to be a wellerism. Finds two variants of a narrative source for the proverb. The discussion leads into the question of whether wellerisms actually exist as a type of Hawaiian proverb and also the relationship between proverb-making and string-figure chants.

1232. MAXWELL, Nicole. "The Dichos of Doña Imelda." *Américas*, XXV:8-9 (August-September, 1972), 48-51.

A literary sketch that deals with the author's Bolivian cook, Doña

Imelda, who has a proverb or saying for any situation. Cites examples, most of them old Spanish sayings.

1233. MIEDER, Wolfgang. "Proverbs in Carl Sandburg's Poem 'The People, Yes.'" *SFQ*, XXXVII:1 (March, 1973), 15-36.

Lists and annotates 322 proverbs from Carl Sandburg's poem, "The People, Yes" (1936), holding that they reflect American common life between the two World Wars.

1234. OINAS, Felix. "In the King's Castle the Entrance Is Wide But the Exit Narrow." In *Festschrift für Robert Wildhaber zum 70. Gerburtstag am 3. August 1972*. Basel: G. Krebs AG, 1973. Pp. 487-491.

Suggests that this proverb, which appears in Irish, Old Icelandic, Swedish, Danish, Estonian, Finnish, and Russian, may have its origin in the East.

1235. SKEMER, D. C. "An Unknown Proverb of the Waning Middle Ages." *Proverbium*, No. 21 (1973), 799-801.

Offers a possible interpretation of an aphoristic exhortation in Latin that the author discovered inside the front cover of a 15th-century Netherlandish manuscript: "Dilige me et in pace te collocabo. Spes probat, ecce leones stant modo pacificati." Speculates on the proverb's origin and significance. Includes notes.

1236. STURM, Harlan, ed. *The "Libro de los buenos proverbios."* Lexington: University of Kentucky Press, 1971. 148 pp. (*Studies in Romance Languages, 5.*)

An edition of a manuscript in the Escorial Library of a Spanish translation of the Arabic *Kitâb âdâb al-falâsifa* by the 9th-century physician, translator, and author, Hunain ibn Ishaq. There is an introduction by the editor which describes the manuscript, explains his editing procedures, gives bibliography of other works translated during the same period, etc.

1237. UTLEY, Francis Lee. "Chaucer's Way with a Proverb: Allas! Allas! That Evere Love Was Synne." *NCFJ*, XXI:3 (September, 1973), 98-104.

Interprets the Wife of Bath's change in the use of the proverb "Lechery is no sin" by noting the way it is employed in other medieval works.

1238. VILLAFUERTE, Carlos. *Refranero de Catamarca*. B.A.: Academia Argentina de Letras, 1972. 335 pp.

Lists alphabetically and defines approximately three thousand proverbs and popular sayings from Catamarca (Argentina). Defines or explains them and in some cases gives bibliographical or comparative notes. Includes a brief bibliography.

1239. VLACH, John M. "The Functions of Proverbs in Yoruba Folktales." *FForum, Bibliographic and Special Series, No. 11: Studies in Yoruba Folklore* (1973), 31-41.

Discusses the narrative and didactic functions of proverbs in a corpus of 107 Yoruba folktales.

1240. ZAMORA MOSQUERA, Federico. *Refráns e ditos populares galegos*. Vigo: Editorial Galaxia, 1972. 283 pp.

Contains more than five thousand Galician proverbs, popular sayings, phrases, etc. arranged alphabetically. Includes a brief introduction.

W RIDDLES

[See also numbers 65, 142, 200, 306, 331, 333, 471, 1217.]

1241. BIGGS, R.D. "Pre-Sargonic Riddles from Lagash." *Journal of Near Eastern Studies* (Chicago), XXXII:1-2 (January-April, 1973), 26-33.

Gives 67 texts of riddles found on a Sumerian tablet excavated at al-Hiba and dating from the 24th century B.C. They deal with the names of towns and these are suggested by different types of clues. Includes drawings and commentaries.

1242. CARPENTER, Inta. "Latvian Mathematical Riddles." *FForum*, VI:2 (April, 1973), 103-106.

Presents transcriptions of four mathematical riddles told by Janis Plavnieks, a Latvian immigrant to the United States, and provides a brief biographical sketch of his life.

1243. CRO, Stelio. "Una adivinanza medieval—el "Indovinello veronese"—en boca de los gauchos." *Romance Notes* (Chapel Hill, North Carolina), XIV:1 (Autumn, 1972), 57-60.

Suggests that an 8th-century riddle that Italian philologists have considered to be of Italian origin was probably of Mozarabic origin from Spain. Cites as tentative proof the fact that the Argentine writer Leopoldo Lugones gives a gaucho form of the riddle eight years before the Italians discovered the 8th-century Mozarabic manuscript wherein the riddle appears.

1244. GUTHRIE, Charles S. *Riddles from the Cumberland Valley*. Introduction by William Hugh Jansen. Bowling Green, Kentucky: Kentucky Folklore Society, 1973. 35 pp.

Contains 124 orally collected riddles from Cumberland County, Kentucky, grouped into two large sections (i.e., True Riddles and Other Riddles) with many subsections. Includes informant data, comparative notes, commentary, an index according to answers, etc.

1245. HULLUM, Jan. "The 'Catch' Riddle: Perspectives from Goffman and Metafolklore." *FAUFA*, Nos. 4-5 (1972-1973), 52-59.

Analyzes the character of two "catch" riddles (sometimes called "pretended obscene" riddles) and discourses on the social interaction that takes place when such riddles are told. Includes bibliography.

1246. LEACH, Maria. *Riddle Me, Riddle Me, Ree*. N.Y.: The Viking Press, 1970. 142 pp.

A collection of riddles from all over the world grouped according to subject matter (e.g., mankind, animals, plants, etc.) or types (e.g., story riddles, elephant riddles, etc.). Sources are indicated in notes and Thompson motif numbers are given. Includes a bibliography. There are drawings by William Wiesner.

1247. MORAIS FILHO, Nascimento. *O que é o que é? (enigmas populares)*. São Luís, Maranhão, Brasil: Sioge, 1972. 291 plus 26 unnumbered pages.

Offers a large collection of riddles apparently orally collected in the Maranhão region of Brazil. Riddle texts having a given answer are all grouped together, but no informant data are proved.

1248. SWINSON, Ward. "Riddles in Finnigan's Wake." *Twentieth Century Literature* (Los Angeles, California), XIX:3 (July, 1973), 165-180.

Considers briefly the nature of riddles in folk tradition and then examines James Joyce's use of riddles in his novel, *Finnigan's Wake*.

INDEX